James Morrison CMG is a former British diplomat. James has spent his professional career in senior roles in London and Brussels working on some of the thorniest foreign policy issues facing the UK and the EU. Throughout, he always relied on two things: a good knowledge of history—helpful in understanding the underlying motivations and drivers behind most foreign policy issues—and good written and oral communication skills, enabling him to influence the course of policy. Cars, by contrast, have always remained a private passion.

For Helen, Josephine, Beatrice and Sophia who kindly edited this dedication…

James Morrison

Twenty Cars that Defined the 20th Century

The Automobile as a Vehicle for History

AUSTIN MACAULEY PUBLISHERS™

LONDON • CAMBRIDGE • NEW YORK • SHARJAH

A CIP catalogue record for this title is available from the British Library.

ISBN 9781035803859 (Paperback)
ISBN 9781035803866 (Hardback)
ISBN 9781035803873 (ePub e-book)

www.austinmacauley.co.uk

First Published 2024
Austin Macauley Publishers Ltd®
1 Canada Square
Canary Wharf
London
E14 5AA

Aside from my long-suffering family, I would also like to thank my father for feeding both my love of history and of cars and my mother for putting up with a hobby that still sees piles of obscure car parts cluttering up her hallway.

Thanks also to my history teachers, the late Nicholas Henshall and Stephen Cross who never quite managed to make a 'historian' of me but did leave me with an abiding interest in their subject.

Particular thanks to Chris Spennewyn without whose friendship and classic mini restoration skills, I would never have been able to feed my passion.

Special thanks also to Peter Kellner and Cathy Ashton for their endless encouragement, without which I would never have embarked on writing this, much less ever finished it…

Table of Contents

Introduction

When I was a boy growing up in the Northwest of England in the late 1970s and early 1980s, I had two overriding passions: history—my favourite subject at school—and cars. From an early age I realised that while my friends were interested in footballers, I was much more interested in the automotive exotica they drove.

My passion for history eventually came in useful in my professional career in the diplomatic service, where knowing the back story to current events is key to understanding the underlying motivations and drivers of those who shape them. Cars, by contrast, remained a private passion largely exercised through my love of Issigonis's Mini and all of its many variants and through a weakness for hopelessly uneconomic and long-running restoration projects.

The inspiration for this book came to me by chance one day when I was reading something on the origins of the First World War. There amongst the text was a photograph of Archduke Franz Ferdinand and his wife in Sarajevo in the back of a large Graf and Stift Double Phaeton. I wondered what happened to the car, how did the Archduke and his wife come to be in it and what happened to the company of Graf and Stift?

I did a little research and discovered that the story of the car—which still exists—was fascinating in its own right. The thought struck me that the defining and unifying feature of the twentieth century was the automobile and that, when I came to think about it, the photos and accounts of pretty much every major political event during that century featured a car of some description playing a supporting role.

Although the history of the individuals was usually well recorded, that of the cars involved, by contrast, was generally less well known—indeed if at all. These cars not only had their own stories in terms of design, ownership, the role they played in the particular event and what happened to them subsequently, but they were also a way of telling the story of the events themselves—literally a vehicle for history.

So, this book contains twenty cars that were intimately linked to the history of the twentieth century. I could easily have chosen more but I decided to limit it to twenty. I also deliberately chose real cars and real figures—so anyone hoping to find James Bond's Aston Martin DB5 in the following pages is likely to be bitterly disappointed. And I chose cars linked to events that interested me—either because I had dealt with them in my professional career or because I'd always wondered about them.

James Morrison
2022

Chapter 1
1899 Daimler 12hp

The year is 1899. The photo is taken in front of Highcliffe Castle in Dorset, built for the diplomat Lord Stuart de Rothesay between 1831 and 1836 using architectural salvage form a French medieval abbey and the home of the Honourable Edward Montagu-Stuart-Wortley a senior British Army officer. The car is a green 12hp Daimler. At its wheel is its owner, the Honourable John Douglas-Scott-Montagu MP, a relation of Edward.

The occupant of the passenger seat dressed in a natty matching light tweed suit and cap is Albert Edward of Saxe-Coburg and Gotha, the Prince of Wales. Montagu-Stuart-Wortley would soon earn promotion to the rank of Lieutenant Colonel for his part in commanding the King's Rifles in the Relief of Ladysmith during the Second Boer War.

He would go on to rise to the rank of Major General in the First World War where his glittering military career would come to an ignominious end when he was partly blamed for the failure of the Somme Offensive in 1916 after the troops under his command failed to regroup and to protect the flank of another Division. Douglas—Scott-Montagu, the MP for New Forest and a talented engineer, would go on, in 1905, to succeed his father to become the second Lord Montagu of Beaulieu.

A keen motorist he would found and edit "The Car Illustrated" magazine and serve on the Road Board. The Prince of Wales would succeed his late mother in January 1901 and become Edward VII, King of the United Kingdom and the British Dominions and Emperor of India, until his death nine years later. An equally keen motorist as his friend Lord Montagu, Edward would buy the first Royal Car the same year as the photo was taken—also a Daimler—would appoint a "Master of the Motors" in the royal household to oversee the royal cars and would grant the Royal Automobile Club its charter in 1907.

The Daimler 12hp had been bought new by Montagu in May 1899 and he regularly drove it from his home and constituency in the New Forest to London. Indeed, it was the first petrol-engined vehicle to enter the Palace Yard of the House of Commons. However, Montagu was not content with this pioneering, yet comparatively sedate, commute.

Keen to test the car's limits, he entered it in the August 1899 Paris—Ostend road race making him one of the first two British drivers to compete in a European motor race—the other was C S Rolls (see Chapter 4) Finishing third in the Touring Class, Montagu's appetite for long distance motoring had been whetted and the following year he entered the car in the Thousand Mile Trial organised by the Automobile Club of Great Britain and Ireland in April and May of 1900.

The car was eventually registered AA16 following the passing of The Motor Car Act 1903, which meant that from 1 January 1904 it was compulsory for every motorcar to be registered with a number plate (an idea that originated in the Netherlands five years earlier) The first registration mark to be issued in London was A1 registered to Earl Russell who camped out all night to secure it. AA16 survives to this day in the National Motor Museum in Beaulieu.

The Prince of Wales's ride in Montagu's Daimler was not his first encounter with the marque, nor would it be his last. He was famously photographed again in April 1902 at Beaulieu in a 24hp Daimler belonging to Montagu. The—by then—King had taken a short trip on the Royal Yacht Alberta and disembarked at Buckler's Hard where he was met by Montagu in the Daimler. Montagu had driven the King to Beaulieu and had then taken the King for a drive before the latter took tea at 5 PM. He had then driven the King back to Buckler's Hard and the Royal Yacht.

The King's decision to purchase his own Daimler 6hp Mail Phaeton in March 1900 (subsequently registered A7) was certainly therefore influenced by Montagu's choice of the 12hp but according to the Sandringham Museum, where the first Royal Daimler is on permanent display, it was Mr Oliver Stanton, the Prince's cycling tutor, who was instrumental in persuading him to buy the marque.

The Prince first test drove the model in January 1900 and A7 was delivered in June the same year which necessitated the recruitment of a new position in the Royal household—"the Prince of Wales's Mechanician" (the French term chauffeur had yet to be adopted). By 1905, the King had a small collection of motor cars and had engaged the services of Charles Stamper as his motor engineer. Stamper was a coachbuilder by profession and was tasked with maintaining the King's two 40hp Mercedes, the Daimler and the Renault Landaurette (for London use).

All of the cars were painted the same claret colour and all featured a small painted Royal Coat of Arms on the coachwork. Stamper's duties also included planning the routes and itineraries for the King's drives. Stamper would sit next to the chauffeur in the front seat of the car on each journey while the King (amply filling the back seat of the vehicle) used to time the journey using a stopwatch.

That the King was interested in cars and indeed ready to embrace the new invention, was a testament to his parentage and education. His father Prince Albert, a keen sponsor and early adopter of technological innovation, had sought to ensure that his eldest son continued in his footsteps. Albert had died long before Edward's first forays into motoring but would doubtless have approved.

Edward was born in Buckingham Palace on the morning of 9 November 1841 and christened Albert ("Bertie") Edward on 25 January in St George's Chapel, Windsor Castle. The eldest son of Queen Victoria and Prince Albert, it is fair to say that the weight of expectation was piled heavily on his shoulders from the outset.

Automatically becoming Duke of Cornwall and of Rothesay upon birth, by December 1841 he was also Prince of Wales. His father's desire to create a well-rounded constitutional monarch from him succeeded in a certain sense—that of his waistline—but not as a result of the comprehensive and rigorous education that he was subjected to from the age of seven. Constantly in the shadow of Victoria his elder sister, Bertie was neither as clever nor as disciplined as his sibling, indeed it was not until university when he was eighteen that he actually began to enjoy studying at all.

Where Edward scored highest was on likeability. His good humour and wide-ranging interests coupled with his flamboyant love of socialising made him a considerable diplomatic asset for the Royal family. His 1860 tour of North America—the first by a Prince of Wales was a huge success, strengthening relations with both Canada and the US. But his mother, the Queen, viewed him as fundamentally not serious—an impression that his penchant for womanising did little to dispel.

In 1861, his parents sent him to Germany on the pretext of watching some military exercises. However, the primary purpose of the trip was to introduce him to his Princess Alexandra of Denmark whom his parents, in the interests both of dynastic expansion but also in the hope of taming his behaviour, had decided he would marry. The couple were engaged the following autumn in Laeken in Belgium and married at St George's Chapel the following spring.

However, despite being married, Edward's playboy tendencies continued along with a string of mistresses including the actresses Lillie Langtree and Sarah Bernhardt, the Countess of Warwick and the singer Hortense Schnieder. The first of a number of public scandals broke in 1870 when he was required to attend court as a witness in the divorce case of Sir Charles Mordaunt, having narrowly escaped being named as a co-respondent.

The negative publicity came at a particularly dangerous time for the Monarchy with the defeat of Napoleon III of France in the Franco-Prussian War and the establishment of the Third Republic. However, Edward's popularity was saved by his nearly dying of typhoid fever the following winter. Such was the outpouring of public concern followed by relief at his recovery, that all was forgiven in terms of his prior personal conduct.

Edward, however, would find himself back in the newspapers and in court, the following year when he became embroiled in the Royal Baccarat scandal where a fellow player at an illegal card game who had been accused of cheating decided to sue the other players.

The scandal did not have the same impact as the Mordaunt divorce perhaps because by then the public had largely priced in the Prince of Wales's wayward tendencies. The death of his eldest son in 1892 once again evoked national sympathy and affection as did his survival of an assassination attempt by a fifteen-year-old named Jean Baptiste Sipido in Belgium on 4 April 1900.

It was something of a relief therefore that he lived to become King following his mother's death on 22 January 1901. Interestingly, he chose the name Edward rather than Albert as a mark of respect to his late father.

His interest in foreign affairs and the Army and Navy made him exactly the right King at the right time. Thanks to his parent's foresight in marrying his siblings to the Royal families of Europe, Edward had a ready-made network which, coupled with his command of French and German, made him a potent diplomatic asset.

The German Kaiser, the Tsar of Russia and the King of Norway were his nephews while the Queen of Spain, the Crown Princesses of Sweden, Romania and Greece as well as the Empress of Russia were his nieces. The Kings of Denmark and Greece were his brothers-in-law while those of Belgium, Bulgaria and Portugal were his second cousins. Aside from his large extended family, Edward was particularly fond of France where he paid an official visit in 1903 as a guest of the President Emile Loubert.

The historical enmity between Britain and France stretched back centuries. Yet, the combination of Edward's love of all things French, the need to agree a territorial division of North Africa and his dislike of his awkward and inept nephew Kaiser Wilhelm II of Germany resulted in one of his greatest diplomatic triumphs: the Entente Cordiale of 1904.

This was a remarkable volte-face given that Prussia had been part of the alliance that had helped defeat Napoleon at Waterloo and that Edward himself was of German descent, with Hanoverians having acceded to the British throne in 1714 and his father being a Coburg Prince. The natural alliance should therefore have been between Germany and the UK. The problem was Wilhelm.

Here again is a link with the photograph. Despite loathing him, Edward suggested that, in 1907 following a bout of illness, the Kaiser should stay at Highcliffe Castle for three weeks to recover his health. This visit was widely publicised. Whilst at Highcliffe, the Kaiser complained to Stuart Wortley about being 'misjudged' over the Boer War, saying he had worked behind the scenes to help Britain.

Feeling sympathetic, Stuart Wortley, rashly, arranged an interview with the Daily Telegraph, which, predictably, went badly with the Kaiser raging about 'humiliating England to dust'. The Kaiser's tendency to make the wrong judgement calls resulted in the formation of the Triple Entente alliance between Britain France and Russia against his own with Austria-Hungary.

Arguably, this just made the Kaiser's paranoia worse and Edward should have avoided cornering his nephew however much he disliked him. Just how disastrous this was to prove is covered in Chapter 2.

1899 Daimler 12hp

The 1899 12hp Daimler was a direct development of the 1897 model. Unlike Daimler's first successful car built the year before which had followed the "horseless carriage" principle, adopted by Benz, where the engine was mounted at the rear of what was essentially a traditional carriage, the 1897 Daimler re-wrote the rule book and in many ways therefore can be viewed as the first true motor car in the modern sense.

Daimler's adoption of the Levassor principle with an engine at the front and a gearbox featuring sliding spur gears, a cross shaft and differential and final drive via external chains made the 1897 Daimler markedly different from its competitors. However, this technological revolution came about accidentally. Levassor had been employed to build engines by a friend of Daimler's named Sarazin who had the rights to the Daimler patents for France.

When Sarazin died suddenly in 1887, Levassor married his widow who inherited the rights. These were commercial gold dust and Levassor decided to exploit them by manufacturing cars himself. This in turn led him to arrive at the novel (for the time) innovation of putting the engine at the front of the car— something Daimler was quick to adopt in 1897 but his competitor Benz would take a further five years to incorporate into his design. This also meant the abandonment of tiller steering and its replacement by a steering rack, column and wheel.

Montagu's 12hp featured a larger 3053cc, four-cylinder engine with automatic inlet valves and ignition by the terrifying "hot tube" system whereby the tubes were heated with naked flames. The transmission featured a cone clutch and a four-speed gearbox using sliding gears mated to a chain-driven final drive. Braking was via a contracting and spoon system (on the outside of the solid tyre) at the rear only.

The wheels where of a larger diameter at the rear compared to the front and were made of wood with solid rubber tyres. The car was capable of a modest—though doubtless terrifying given the lack of braking capacity—30mph. The price was a huge £775—the equivalent of £100,000 today.

Daimler

The Daimler Motor Company was founded in 1896 by H J Lawson and was based in Coventry having bought the right to use the Daimler name from the Daimler Motoren Gesellschaft (DMG) of Cannstatt near Stuttgart, Germany. DMG also manufactured cars, but from 1901 these tended to be badged as Mercedes (see Chapter 9).

The UK company soon ran into financial difficulties and was taken over by the Birmingham Small Arms Company (BSA) in 1904 who continued to control the company until 1960 when the company was sold to Jaguar (see Chapter 19). Daimler cemented its niche in the status market when it was awarded the Royal Warrant in 1902—something it held for the next fifty years until the exploits of Lady Docker, the wife of BSA's chairman and some clever manoeuvring by Rolls Royce resulted in it being withdrawn.

The UK company came about as a result an Anglo German engineer—Frederick Richard Simms—who befriended Gottlieb Daimler while working on a rail car featuring Daimler's engine for the 1889 Bremen exhibition. Simms subsequently obtained the British and Empire rights to Daimler's engine design in February 1891. Simms designed a motorboat using Daimler's engine and set up an office as a consulting engineer at 49 Leadenhall Street in London. Trading as Simms and Co, he demonstrated the motorboat on the Thames and the orders rolled in.

However, a financial scandal involving the company's solicitor forced Simms to found a new company: the Daimler Motor Syndicate Limited in 1893. Seeing the growing interest in and market for motor cars, in June 1895, Simms decided to branch out. This he did by acquiring the Daimler patents. This immediately gave the company a 10% commission on any Daimler-engined car sold in the UK.

Simms also acquired the first license to operate a Daimler patented car—in this case a 3.5hp Panhard and Levassor. The car had been ordered by one of Simms best customers—the Honourable Evelyn Ellis—who had bought no fewer than three of his Daimler-engined motorboats and who had a house at

Datchet. Thus, when the vehicle arrived at Southampton docks it was driven by Ellis to Datchet, picking up Simms en route. This was the first long distance motorcar journey in the UK and it was completed in a Daimler.

Buoyed by this success, Simms founded the Daimler Motor Company Limited in 1895 with Gottlieb Daimler as consulting engineer. Simms purchased premises on Eel Pie Island in the Thames and drew up plans for a new factory with a workforce of 400 to build Daimler cars.

However, the same year Simms was approached by Harry Lawson of the British Motor Syndicate Limited who persuaded him to float the new company so that Lawson could buy a majority shareholding. Doing this meant transferring the licenses from Simms to the new company which meant that Daimler Motoren Gesellschaft would need to agree. This they did in return for £17,500 and a re-merger of Daimler with DMG and Maybach.

Lawson then incorporated the Daimler Motor Company Limited in January 1896 and issued a prospectus. The shares were oversubscribed within 24 hours of being floated. Simms once again became consulting engineer of the new company while remaining a Director of the parent DMG company in Cannstatt. Simms was tasked with identifying a site for the new company's factory. He chose the, recently bankrupt, Trusty Oil Engine Works in Cheltenham on the basis that the site already had a foundry and a skilled engineering labour force.

However, in the first sign of the mismanagement that was to result in the firm's early demise. Lawson took advantage of Simms's absence overseas to persuade the Board to buy a disused cotton mill in Coventry owned by one of his friends instead.

The net result was that Daimler wasted the rest of 1896 waiting for machinery and building facilities that it could have bought ready installed at the Cheltenham site. The first Daimler produced in January 1897 had a Panhard engine—something which was superseded in March with the introduction of the Coventy-built Daimler engine. Production had reached a total of 20 cars by July. The basic design was the same as the Montagu—owned Daimler 12hp in the photograph.

Unfortunately, Lawson was again engaging in sharp practice—his Great Horseless Carriage Company was behind in its payments to DMG. In an attempt at leverage, Lawson forbade the sharing of drawings for the new 4hp model with the parent company in Cannstatt. Simms resigned as Consulting Engineer. The motorboat works on Eel Pie Island was sold at a huge loss of £700 and Lawson was forced to resign in October 1897. Gottlieb Daimler followed in July of the following year by which time the company by then headed by Henry Sturmey was under investigation. Sturmey was forced to resign in May 1899.

However, in a final twist, while Simms had resigned as Consulting Engineer of the ailing UK company he had remained on the Board of Directors of the parent company in Germany. With Lawson and Sturmey gone and the UK company re-structured, he proposed a merger between the two companies. This was—foolishly—rejected by the UK side, which limped on until a further financial collapse in 1904 meant that the company was wound down and a new one formed to pay off its debts under the control of BSA.

A final postscript—not only did a Daimler complete the first long distance motor car journey in the UK and become the first Royal car but the marque also earned the dubious honour of having been involved in the first fatal motor car accident in the UK in 1899. The passenger of a 6hp Daimler was killed when the wooden rear wheel of the car collapsed while simultaneously cornering and braking hard on an incline in Harrow on the Hill. The occupants of the car were thrown clear but once landed on his head, fracturing his skull and resulting in his death in hospital three days later.

Chapter 2
1910 Graf & Stift 28/32 PS Double Phaeton

Vor dem Attentat in Sarajewo: Erzherzog Franz Ferdinand und Gemahlin bei der Abfahrt zum Rathause   Phot. Gebr. Hädel.

The story is a familiar one and one that was to define much of the twentieth century. It begins on a bright Sunday morning in Sarajevo in 1914 when Archduke Franz Ferdinand, heir to the Austro-Hungarian throne and his wife Sophie Duchess of Hohenberg, stepped off the Ilidža Spa to Sarajevo train to the strains of a small military band and were met by Governor Oskar Potiorek.

The Archduke was in good spirits—he liked travelling because it was one of the few occasions he was able to be seen in public with his beloved wife who—for protocol reasons and as a pre-condition of securing the Emperor Franz Josef's permission to marry—was not normally allowed to sit beside him. Together they emerged from the large doorway of Sarajevo station at 09:30 into the Bosnian early morning sunshine.

In fact, the couple had already paid an impromptu visit to the city the previous Thursday evening when, at Sophie's request, they had motored into town to visit the stall in the bazaar that had supplied the furnishings for the hotel they were they were staying in Ilidža. They had been spotted and crowds had formed and amongst them was a young man with a pistol hidden in his pocket named Gavrillo Princip who, perhaps because of the police, had made no attempt to harm the couple—an act of restraint he would not repeat 72 hours later.

As a result, the couple returned to Ilidža unscathed and Sophie felt confident enough to visit the city again in the following two days. But Sunday's arrival by train was more formal. Before them was the motorcade—a row of six smart black cars. The cars were borrowed locally or provided by their wealthy, aristocratic owners. The budgetary constraints facing the increasingly inefficient and as a result cash-strapped, Austro-Hungarian Empire made this the normal modus operandi for visits outside of Vienna.

The first car carried the Archduke's chief special security officer and three local policemen. The second car carried the Mayor Fehim Curcic and the Chief of Police of Sarajevo Dr Gerde. The Archduke's car was the third—driven by Leopold Lojka—a 1910 Graf and Stift 28/32 PS Double Phaeton belong to Count Franz von Harrach—a friend of the Archduke's who was also travelling in the vehicle along with Governor Potiorek and Gustav Schneiberg one of the Archduke's hunting staff.

Car four was driven by the famous racing driver Otto Merz and was owned by Count Alexander von Boos-Waldeck who was accompanied in it by Baron Rumerskirch; Sophie's lady-in-waiting, Countess Lanjus von Wallenburg and Potiorek's adjutant, Colonel Erich von Merizzi. The last two cars carried other members of the Archduke's entourage: Colonel Karl Bardolff the head of the Archduke's military chancery and various local officials. The last car was a back-up vehicle and was empty.

Although the original plan had been to travel with the canvas hood of the Phaeton up, the good weather meant there was a last-minute change of plan and the convoy's departure was delayed while the hood was lowered and stowed neatly in its tonneau cover. After all, the purpose of the visit was to be seen to be in the capital of Bosnia Herzegovina—a territory captured by the Austro-Hungarian Empire from the Ottoman Empire only six years earlier in 1908.

What better way to be seen than by travelling in an open topped car for the crowds to admire the finery of the Archduke's military tunic and plumed hat and to appreciate the beauty of Sophie's pale pink silk dress? But the decision was to prove fateful, as a similar decision nearly 50 years later involving a switch of vehicles to a convertible was for President John F Kennedy.

For the visibility afforded by an open-topped car is not only a benefit to be enjoyed by admiring crowds of well-wishers. It is a gift for any would-be assassin, offering as it does a clear shot at the target. And Sarajevo that day was host to a number of young men with murder on their minds.

Despite the risk of attack by Serb nationalists being known, the logistics and planning of the visit suggested at best a cavalier attitude to security and at worst a naivety bordering on amateurism. The date chosen for the visit was 28 June— St Vitus' Day—the day the Ottoman Empire had defeated the Serbs in 1389 at the Battle of Kosovo Field heralding more than 500 years of Ottoman rule in the Western Balkans. For Serb nationalists this was a day of huge significance in their struggle for Serbian independence.

A visit to a disputed territory by the heir-apparent of Serbia's mortal enemy—the Austro-Hungarian Empire—was already provocation enough. But to do it on St Vitus' day was to rub salt into an already festering wound. This unhappy coincidence of location and date had not escaped the notice of the Black Hand organisation of Serb nationalists operating in the region and the decision was taken that this should be the Archduke's last ever public engagement.

Added to this diplomatic ineptitude, the route of the motorcade had been made public as early as March that year and published in the local newspapers to allow the crowds to select the best vantage points. The Archduke's motorcade would follow narrow streets, bounded by the Miljacka river where U turns were impossible.

No contingency planning had been done in the event of a breakdown, let alone an attack. Security arrangements in Sarajevo were limited and the local military commander, General Michael von Appel, had proposed that troops line the intended route only to be rebuffed and told that this would offend the loyal citizenry. Protection for the visiting party was therefore left to the Sarajevo police, of whom only 60 were on duty on the day of the visit.

In short, there was no Plan B. And Plan A looked pretty shambolic. In fact the only people happy with the arrangements were Gavrillo Princip and his fellow Serb nationalist assassins of the Black Hand. They couldn't believe their luck that the plan of the route was public. Bombs and pistols were tricky things to use at all but the closest of ranges. But luckily the progress of the slow-moving motorcade would afford them some unmissable—in all senses of the word—opportunities to get very close indeed to their target.

The Black Hand was a secret network of Serb nationalists headed by Dragutin Dimitrijevic—a Colonel in the Serbian army—committed to the re-creation of the "greater Serbia" that had existed before the Ottoman invasion in the fourteenth century.

In early 1914, Dimitrijevic had ordered seven of its members including Gavrilo Princip, Nedeljko Cabrinovic and Muhamed Mehmedbasic to assassinate Archduke Franz Ferdinand giving each a pistol and two grenades. Princip and Cabrinovic were well chosen. Both had incurable tuberculosis and so had nothing to lose given that they were already effectively under sentence of death.

The motorcade's first stop was to inspect the Sarajevo military barracks. At 10:00 am, the motorcade left the barracks en route to the town hall following the Appel Quay of the river. Having examined the published route, the seven members of the Black Hand had chosen this location as the point where the motorcade would be closest to the crowd. They had arranged themselves amongst the cheering crowd at strategic points.

First in line was Mehmedbasic who was standing by the Austro-Hungarian bank on the corner of the Quay. For whatever reason—perhaps he lost his nerve—Mehmedbasic let the convoy pass claiming later that there was a Policeman standing behind him which made a successful attack impossible. Next in line was Nedeljko Cabrinovic who saw his chance and threw a hand grenade at the Archduke's car.

Fortunately, the Archduke's driver Lojka saw the bomb coming and accelerated causing it to bounce off the bodywork with a dull thud into the path of the following car where it exploded wounding the occupants and some of the crowd. In the ensuing chaos, Nedeljko swallowed a cyanide capsule and threw himself into the river only to discover that the poison was past its sell by date and therefore ineffective.

For the Black Hand assassins, the failure of the attack and ensuing pandemonium effectively ruled out a second attempt. The Archduke's car sped on to the City Hall to an official reception where he delivered a speech splattered with the blood of his friend Count von Boos-Waldeck.

Back at the Governor's residence, the Archduke was furious with Potiorek shouting angrily, "So this is how you welcome your guests—with bombs?"

Potiorek was apologetic and, mindful of his position as the person responsible for maintaining law and order in Bosnia Herzegovina, sought to play down the gravity of the incident. After several heated exchanges, the Archduke regained his composure and, concerned for the wellbeing of his friends, insisted that the programme be changed to allow him and Sophie to visit the wounded in the local hospital.

At this point, a member of his staff questioned whether this might be dangerous. Potiorek was dismissive and scoffed, "Do you think Sarajevo is full of assassins? I will take responsibility." The afternoon's engagements were therefore modified to include the hospital visit.

Unfortunately, nobody communicated this to the drivers. The royal party exited the residence and got back into the remaining five cars. The convoy drew away following the original published route. This meant the first car took a right turn on the narrow Latin Bridge. The others followed before the mistake was spotted leading the convoy to grind to a halt.

By unlucky chance another member of the Black Hand was consoling himself about the failed assassination attempt at a café on the corner by the bridge. Gavrillo Princip was nursing a coffee at a table on the pavement in front of Schiller's Delicatessen when the convoy drove past and suddenly halted. There was much confusion with the need to reverse several vehicles coupled with the difficulty of selecting reverse in those cars that had it and pushing those that didn't meant that the convoy was motionless and its occupants exposed for several minutes.

Princip saw his moment. He got up and casually walked across the street pulled out the FN Model 1910 pistol modified to accept a .380 cartridge which Colonel Dimtrijevic had given him. He fired twice from close range hitting Sophie in the abdomen and then Franz Ferdinand in the neck. Princip was wrestled to the ground by the police as the car reversed away to return to Potiorek's residence. Harrach was uninjured and jumped out of the car onto the running board to protect the royal couple from any further fire.

At this stage nobody fully realised the seriousness of the injuries. A thin trickle of blood began to drip from the side of the Archduke's mouth onto Harrach's cheek. On seeing this Sophie collapsed in her seat falling forward. Harrach assumed she had fainted at the sight of her injured husband. But the Archduke sensed something more serious was wrong. Despite the bright red blood soaking through the Archduke's tunic from a wound in his neck, he bent down and spoke to his wife, "Dear Sophie! Don't die! Stay alive for our children."

He then slumped forward himself, his plumed hat falling off onto the floor of the car. Harrach tried to sit him up again asking, "Is your Imperial Highness suffering very badly?"

Franz Ferdinand replied, "Es is nichts (it is nothing)." The Archduke's staff tried to undo his tunic to stem the bleeding. But he had been sewn into it to give a more flattering, slimmer, line and as a result he bled to death on the way to the hospital. Sophie too was dead on arrival.

The events that followed fuelled by the complex series of alliances and ententes that maintained the Edwardian balance of power and aided by diplomatic misjudgements led directly to the First World War.

The driver, Leopold Lojka, was given the unenviable task of telegraphing Emperor Franz Joseph I and Kaiser Wilhelm II to inform them of the assassinations, as well as the Archduke's children to tell them of the murder of their parents. He was paid off by the Emperor Karl, bought an inn in Brno, Czechoslovakia and died peacefully in 1926.

The car—a bit part player but a hugely significant one in the events that day—was never driven again and now resides in the military museum in Vienna. And of course by a bizarre coincidence its registration number—11 11 18— would be the eventual date of the Armistice marking the end of an unprecedented four year period of industrial scale, mechanised slaughter of an entire European generation.

Graf & Stift

The 1910 Graf and Stift Double Phaeton was a luxury hand-built motorcar made by an Austrian manufacturer founded in 1902 by three brothers Franz, Heinrich and Karl Graf and an investor named Willhelm Stift. The Graf brothers, who had begun by repairing bicycles before eventually moving onto manufacturing them, were quick to see the potential of the motor car.

The first Graf car was designed and built in 1900 by Josef Kainz and arguably pioneered front wheel drive since it used a single cylinder, water-cooled, De Dion-Bouton engine at the front of the vehicle. Despite patenting this powered front axle, Graf and Stift never used the technology again preferring traditional rear wheel drive instead. The *voiturette* car was therefore a one off and still remains in existence.

Investor and car importer Willhelm Stift's involvement with the company from 1901 resulted in the establishment of a joint company in 1904. The first Graf and Stift cars were made for the famous Vienna motor dealer Arnold Spitz who sold De Dion, Mercedes and Benz cars. These cars were badged as "Spitz" and designed by racing driver Otto Hieronymus. It was not until 1907—three years before Count Harrach's Phaeton—that Graf and Stift started producing cars under their own brand.

The standard fayre at the time, as with many other manufacturers and coachbuilders across Europe, was to build big, bespoke, luxury cars. Graf and Stift found a ready market amongst the Austrian nobility and even the Royal family itself. A Graf and Stift was the vehicle of choice for the Austro-Hungarian Emperor Franz-Joseph, who was no fan of motorised vehicles having once witnessed one running out of control at a military display, until his death in 1916.

Fittingly, his successor, the last Austro-Hungarian Emperor Karl, was driven into exile in Switzerland in a Graf and Stift in 1919 when the Empire finally collapsed.

Ironically, given the central role a Graf and Stift had played in triggering the conflict, the First World War was kind to Graf and Stift who switched to making trucks and special vehicles for the Austro-Hungarian army. These lucrative government contracts put the company on a sound financial footing allowing it to resume car making in 1920 with the Typ VK—a two litre saloon.

By 1921, the luxury coach-built car market was well and truly back and Graf and Stift were ready to exploit the rising demand with big six cylinder limousines including the Typ SR4 which featured an advanced overhead valve six cylinder 7.75 litre, 110hp, engine capable of propelling its sleek modern coachwork to a dizzying 85mph. 1930 saw the company's first eight cylinder—the Typ Sp8—nicknamed the "Rolls-Royce of Austria" an alloy and cast iron 6 litre, straight eight developing 125 bhp with a top speed of almost 100mph.

To ensure sufficient scale and market share in an increasingly crowded and competitive segment, Graf and Stift also launched smaller cars—the G35 and G36 of its own with four-cylinder side valve engines and also went into partnership, first with Citroen to assemble a 2.65 litre six-cylinder model—the MF6—and, later with Ford who allowed some of their V8 powered cars to be assembled and badged as Graf-Ford V8.

By the late 1930s demand in the luxury automobile market was saturated and Graf and Stift decided they could no longer make a profit. As a result, the company stopped making cars in 1938 to concentrate on trucks and trolley buses.

This work continued throughout the Second World War. Post war there was a brief attempt to re-enter the car market with the lowly 615cc Aero Minor but this lasted only from 1949-1950 before the firm decided to concentrate on its core commercial vehicle business. That lasted until 1971 when company merged with Osterreichische Automobil Fabriks (OAF) AG before being taken over by MAN AG later in the year. The Graf and Stift name was still being used on trolley buses built until 2001.

1910 Graf and Stift 28/32 PS Double Phaeton

The Archduke's car was a Graf & Stift 5.8 litre 28/32hp Double Phaeton (engine number 287). The car had been ordered by Count Franz von Harrach new on 15 December 1910. At this stage Graf & Stift used four cylinder engines with "T" headed cylinders cast in separate blocks of two cylinders and welded together.

Although this might have been considered "state of the art" in terms of design at the time, there was nothing remotely advanced about the woeful 32hp power output from 5.8 litres of cylinder capacity. The car was both thirsty and slow—built for comfort rather than speed. The car's transmission was rear wheel drive via a propeller shaft and differential (further sapping the meagre power output) coupled to a four-speed crash gearbox requiring double-declutching skills to change gears smoothly.

The "Double Phaeton" body style was a throwback to the lightweight horse drawn carriages of the preceding century. Phaeton traditionally was the term used for a four wheeled open carriage with low coachwork. This bodywork style would have been reassuringly familiar to a Royal passenger in 1914 and would undoubtedly have appealed to the Archduke.

Unlike a convertible, a phaeton has no windows in the doors or bodywork and no permanent roof. The folding roof on the Graf and Stift was detachable and difficult to erect and stow. This meant that there was more room for seats—two rows in this case—hence the use of the word "Double" in the model's name. Even when raised, the roof left the sides of the car open to the elements. This made Phaetons lighter, though less practical, than convertibles.

The Double Phaeton remains on public display in Vienna's military museum and has not been run since 1914 making it not only the rarest example left in existence but also the one with the lowest mileage.

Chapter 3
1922 Ford Model T Touring

The photo is mildewed but dramatic. The 1922 Model T Touring is being driven at speed out of an entrance in the rock face by an Egyptian chauffeur wearing a fez. A small boy in traditional Egyptian dress sits on the running board holding onto the driver's door for dear life. In the passenger seat is a distinguished looking Gentleman with a white moustache clutching a rolled umbrella in one hand and holding on to the passenger door with the other.

In the back seat of the car are two figures—one female and one male—wearing black overcoats with their collars turned up and hats. It is clearly cold although the photo looks to have been taken in the desert. The car belongs to the rear passenger on the driver's side—Howard Carter. The front passenger is Lord Carnarvon, behind him his daughter Lady Evelyn Herbert. The location is the

Valley of the Kings in Egypt. The date is Saturday 17 February 1923 and the passengers are travelling from the newly opened (on 16 February 1923) tomb of King Tutankhamun.

The photograph was taken by Harry Burton, the official photographer of the expedition. Somewhat extraordinarily by modern standards the opening in the rock that the car is emerging from is a neighbouring ancient Egyptian tomb that was used as a garage by Carter during the excavations of Tutankhamun's tomb. The car looks almost new, indeed, according to Carter's diary, he had only recently taken delivery of the Model T on Saturday 6 January 1923. The entry simply read: "motor and chauffeur arriving 10 am" followed by "motor and chauffeur arrived".

However, he had made extensive use of the vehicle since then, ferrying Lord Carnarvon and his daughter from the Winter Palace Hotel in Luxor where they were staying to the excavation site in the Valley of the Kings and back again. Carter seems to have been very pleased with his new found mobility. Harry Burton's wife, Minnie's, diary records on 9 January 1923: "H (Harry) and I rode Mr Carter's donkeys to his house, and then with him in the new Ford Car to the river bank.

"To Winter Palace for a moment and then shopping and to lunch—Mr C (Carter) brought us back in the Ford to the door". Being chauffer driven around Luxor and the Valley of the Kings was a far cry from the wilderness years Carter had experience following his resignation as Chief Inspector of the Egyptian Antiquities Service in 1905 following the Saqqara Affair.

It was not until late 1907 that, on the recommendation of Gaston Maspero the famous French Egyptologist, Lord Carnarvon offered him new employment supervising the excavation of tombs in Deir el-Bahri. While Director General of the Egyptian Antiquities Service, Maspero had been impressed by Carter's structured systems and methods of recording finds.

Carter had been born on 9 May 1874 in Kensington, London. His father was an artist and encouraged and nurtured his son's considerable talent in this area. Carter's interest in Ancient Egypt was sparked by the collection at Darlington Hall, the family seat of the Amherst's, close to Seafoam in Norfolk where he spent his childhood summers staying with relatives. Indeed, his first expedition to Egypt in 1891 came about with the assistance of Baroness Amherst. The Baroness—an only child—had succeeded her father, the first Baron Amherst of Hackney, to the title by 'Special Remainder' of Parliament.

Unfortunately, she had inherited very little financially as a result of her late father having been defrauded by his solicitor. Much of her father's collection had had to be sold to settle debts. Nevertheless, the Baroness was a passionate Egyptologist and recommended to the Egypt Exploration Fund—a fund set up by novelist Amelia Edwards and Reginald Poole in 1882 specifically to fund archaeological excavations in Egypt—that the 17-year-old Carter should assist Percy Newberry in the excavation of tombs at Beni Hasan.

Carter's work was excellent and he was invited the following year to assist Flinders Petrie in excavations at Amarna. This led to further work with Edouard Naville at Deir el-Bahari. By 1899 he had caught the attention of Gaston Maspero who appointed him Chief Inspector of the Egyptian Antiquities Service. By this time Carter had learned Arabic and had built up a good relationship with the local staff working on the excavations.

Carter had spent seven years working for Lord Carnarvon on various excavations before the latter obtained a permit in 1914 to begin excavations in the Valley of the Kings. By this time, it was widely believed that there were no more major discoveries to be found in the Valley. The American archaeologist Theodore M Davis who had previously had the excavation permit for the Valley had discovered several Royal and noble tombs, including he believed all that remained of Tutankhamun's tomb. Davis wrote in 1912 that: "the Valley of the Kings is now exhausted".

Fortunately, for Carnarvon, Davis had become ill in 1914 (he subsequently died in early 1915) allowing Carnarvon to obtain the permit. Unfortunately, for Carnarvon, the First World War broke out at the end of July 1914 meaning a suspension of excavations. Carter left Carnarvon's employ to work for the British Government as a translator—given his fluent Arabic—and diplomatic courier.

It was not until late 1917 that the excavations resumed. There then followed almost five years of fruitless searching and digging. Frustrated, Carnarvon had reluctantly concluded by the 1922 season that he was throwing good money after bad. He informed Carter that 1923 would be the last opportunity to find anything.

On 1 November 1922 Carter decided to return to some earlier excavations to the Northeast corner of the entrance to the tomb of Ramses VI, digging a trench southward. At this point there were a row ancient stone huts of the Necropolis workmen. On 4 November 1922 a boy hired locally to carry water tripped up on a rock on the site of the hut they were excavating. The rock was the corner of the top step of a flight of stairs leading down into the rock. Carter's diary records:

At about 10:00 am, I discovered beneath almost the first hut attacked the first traces of the entrance of the tomb. This comprised the first step of the N.E. corner (of the sunken-staircase) Quite a short time sufficed to show that it was the beginning of a steep excavation cut in the bedrock, about four metres below the entrance of Ramses VI's tomb and a similar depth below the present level of the valley. And, that it was of the nature of a sunken staircase entrance to a tomb of the type of the XVIIIth Dynasty.

Carter immediately shifted his workers to dig out the remainder of the staircase. At the end of it, he came to a mud plastered entrance stamped with oval seals with hieroglyphics of the Royal Necropolis. The fact that the workmen's huts dating from the later construction of Rameses VI's tomb had been built on the concealed entrance that Carter had just discovered meant that it was likely that what lay at the end of the staircase was undisturbed.

Carter knew this was significant. He found a small gap in the top corner of the sealed doorway and enlarged it to a small hole that he could shine a torch through. On the other side was a passageway filled in with stones and rubble from floor to ceiling. Carter refilled the hole he had made. It was getting late so he had the staircase re-filled in by moonlight and hurried home to telegraph Lord Carnarvon to come immediately. The next day was spent covering up and securing the site until the time came for its formal opening.

Carnarvon arrived in Cairo on 20 November and in Luxor on 23 November. Carter began the re-excavation of the staircase, spending the night at the site on 24 November. The full excavation of the debris revealed the seal of Tutankhamen and also that the upper part of the doorway had been re-opened and re-closed on at least two occasions.

The presence of fragments of pottery, broken boxes bearing the names and seals of various kings led Carter to worry that the tomb had previously been raided and had subsequently been used as a hiding place for looted Royal treasure. Carter had a heavy wooden door made to secure the first opening.

On 25 November, he opened the first door having photographed it first. This revealed a blocked passageway completely filled with rubble that descended sharply. Here again there was evidence that a corner of the passageway had previously been excavated and re-filled as the stones used were of a different type.

On 26 November, he and Carter travelled to the—by now re-excavated—staircase in the Valley of the Kings. More than nine metres of the blocked passageway had by now been excavated, revealing a second sealed doorway. This doorway too showed evidence of re-opening and re-closing. Carter used a chisel his grandmother had given him for his 17th birthday to break a hole in the corner of the mud plaster.

He lit a candle and held it at arm's length through the hole—a wise precaution against poisonous gases that could sometimes gather in ancient underground excavations. The escaping air inside the tomb caused the candle to flicker. Carnarvon asked if he could see anything. Carter famously replied, "Yes, it is wonderful". What he also saw however were two statues either side of a further sealed doorway—the latter was a sure sign that what he had discovered was a tomb rather than just a cache.

The next day electric lighting was rigged up allowing the Inspector of the Department of Antiquities to inspect the finds. The objects in this chamber had been disturbed, many were overturned and there were broken fragments on the floor. Beneath a bench in the southwest corner of the tomb Carter spotted an opening in the rock wall which proved to be another sealed doorway which had been broken through by an ancient raider.

Carter and Carnarvon crawled under the bench and, using an electric torch, were able to see a passageway leading to another chamber. This chamber was in even greater disarray and was piled high with furniture that had been rifled through in a search for valuables. However, nowhere was there any sign of a mummy.

Nevertheless, there remained a further sealed doorway between the two statues. This too had been breached at some point—presumably by an ancient grave robber—and re-sealed with the cartouche of the Royal Necrolopolis. Carter and Carnarvon decided to wait until the antechambers had been cleared and catalogued (a painstaking process which took until mid-February 1923) before opening the next sealed doorway.

The official "opening" of the antechambers of the tomb to the public took place on Wednesday 29 November. To secure the tomb for the winter, Carter measured the entrance and had a steel gate made which was fitted in place on 17 December 1922.

With the antechambers finally cleared and Lord Carnarvon and Lady Evelyn back in Luxor, on 16 February 1923 Carter was finally ready to open the sealed doorway he had found inside the tomb. The doorway led to a burial chamber with a sarcophagus. Having removed the remainder of the mud plaster sealing the entrance Carter realised that he was looking at the best-preserved, undisturbed, burial chamber he had ever seen.

It was not until 28 October 1925—two years since the opening of the burial chamber that Carter and his team were able to open the innermost of three coffins to reveal the 3250-year-old gold and lapis lazuli mask. Sadly, Carnarvon never saw this, having died in Cairo from blood poisoning from an infected mosquito bite in the early hours of 5 April 1923. Carter's achievements went unrecognised by the British Government. He died from Hodgkin's disease in his London flat next to the Albert Hall on 2 March 1939.

1922 Ford Model T

The Ford Model T was produced from 12 August 1908 to 26 May 1927 and turned motoring from being solely the preserve of the ultra-rich to being within reach of ordinary middle-class Americans. Its revolutionary assembly line production (introduced by Ford in 1910 at his new Highland Park factory after 12,000 Model T's had been assembled using traditional methods and production was failing to keep pace with demand) made the car both available—since large volumes could be assembled simultaneously—and affordable—since the mass production of standardised components drove down costs.

By the time production ceased in 1927, over 16.5 million examples had been produced. Its pioneering and mass market-creating role won it the epithet "car of the twentieth century" in a 1999 competition. Aside from being cheap, the Model T was also reliable and easy to fix.

Famously Henry Ford is said to have told his management team that: "any customer can have a car painted any colour that he wants so long as it is black". This enforced monotone not only made production simpler but also bodywork repairs and replacements easier for owners. However, less well known is the fact that this policy took a while to introduce.

Indeed between 1908 and 1913 black was not available and instead Model Ts were grey, (town cars) green (touring cars, town cars and coupes) red (touring cars) 1912 saw the introduction of dark blue with black wings across the range. It was only in 1914 that Ford finally got his way and everything was only available in black. However, it is worth noting that even then no fewer than 30 different shades of black were used during the Model Ts production run.

The car was designed by two Hungarian immigrants: Joseph A Galamb and Eugene Farkas along with Childe Harold Wills and with the help of a wider team including C. J Smith, Henry Love, Peter Martin and Gus Degner. Such was the public's enthusiasm for the new car that Ford took 15,000 orders within the first week after its launch. Mechanically the car was simple.

The engine was a 20hp 2.6 litre, straight four cylinder, water-cooled, cast iron unit with a giddy top speed of between 40 and 45 mph. Despite the large cylinder capacity the car was capable of doing 25 miles to the gallon of petrol. In keeping with its rugged credentials the vehicle would also run on ethanol or kerosene.

This was possible because the electrical system was similarly basic—a low voltage magneto in the flywheel supplied alternating Current to trembler coils that powered the spark plugs. The car had no battery—because the magneto was part of the flywheel hand cranking the engine produced enough electricity to start the car. The early Model Ts had acetylene headlamps before the changeover to electric power in 1915. Hand cranking remained the only method of starting the car until 1919 when electric ignition was introduced.

The car featured a three-speed transmission—two forward gears and one reverse—and operated by means of three pedals and a large lever on the road side of the driver. Driving the car was complicated—perhaps why Carter chose to have a chauffeur. To engage the transmission the driver depressed the left pedal and moved the lever forward—fully forward engaged low gear with the pedal depressed or high gear with it released, if the lever were placed in the middle position neutral was engaged.

When in neutral, reverse could be selected via the middle pedal. The right pedal operated a transmission brake (the wheels themselves were un-braked) There was also a parking brake operated via the lever beside the driver's seat. Acceleration was controlled by a hand throttle on the steering wheel. The car was rear-wheel drive with the power transmitted via a single universal joint and a propeller shaft to the differential.

Suspension was via semi elliptical transversely mounted leaf springs for each axle allowing a large amount of wheel travel and therefore making the car well-suited to rough, unsurfaced roads. Wheels were wooden artillery wheels until the introduction of welded steel wheels in late 1926. Tyres were Pneumatic

"Clinchers", size 30 × 3.5 inch, running at 60 psi pressure to avoid leakage at the joint with the wheel rims. This made flat tyres a depressingly frequent event. Balloon tyres were not introduced until 1925.

The Model T underwent numerous body changes during its production run. Howard Carter's car was a 1922 "low hood" Touring—a design that was first introduced in 1917 and ran until 1923. The bodywork was the standard black. Wheels were the standard wooden rims with high pressure tyres—something which must have caused problems with the sharp limestone fragments on the floor of the Valley of the Kings. The cost of the car in the US was $319 however it is not clear what the shipping cost and import duties to Egypt would have been at that time.

The Ford Motor Company

The Ford Motor Company was not Henry Ford's first car company. In November 1901 he had founded the "Henry Ford Company" but this was rapidly taken over by Cadillac (see Chapter 17) and on 22 August 1902 Ford left the company albeit—and crucially—taking the rights to the use of his name with him.

Undiscouraged, Ford set up a new company—"The Ford Motor Company"—the following year using $28000 of cash from a group of twelve investors including, interestingly, the Dodge brothers (John and Horace—see Chapter 5). Following the failure of his earlier venture, Ford was not the chairman of the new company.

Early production, in common with Ford's competitors, was bespoke and small volume and characterised by the assembly of parts made by sub-contractors rather than manufacturing. Ford was astute enough to see the potential in this and gradually bought up his suppliers. Thus, by the time he introduced his revolutionary assembly line concept Ford was able to count on reliable supplies of components as and when required to keep the line running at optimum efficiency.

The first Ford production car was the Model A in 1903. In the following five years Ford introduced various short-lived new models—imaginatively named Model B, C, F, K, N, R and S. For this reason, the new car introduced in 1908 was called the Model "T". When replacing the, by then antiquated, Model T in 1927, Ford reverted to the beginning of the lettering sequence, calling the new car the Model "A".

Ford bought Lincoln (see Chapter 12) in 1922 to compete with Cadillac with whose management he still held a grudge given Cadillac's takeover of his original company. Ford added to its sub-brands in 1939 with the creation of Mercury in 1939 to take market share from General Motors' Buick (see Chapter 7) Oldsmobile and Pontiac brands.

In the interwar period, Ford set up plants in the Soviet Union—the Gorky Automobile Plant—assembling Model As; in Japan—in Yokohama—assembling Model Ts and then Model As; in Germany—in Cologne—producing cars and trucks and in the UK—in Dagenham—producing cars. At the outbreak of the Second World War Ford switched its US factories and assembly lines to wartime production.

However, following the fall of France in June 1940, according to published accounts quoted in the Washington Post, Henry Ford personally vetoed (his son Edsel Ford was President of the company by this time) a government-approved plan to produce Rolls-Royce engines under license for British fighter planes.

Meanwhile, Ford's German operation was building military vehicles for the Nazi regime. Hitler greatly admired Ford's mass production techniques. Indeed, two years before his rise to power, Hitler was quoted in the Detroit News as saying: "I regard Henry Ford as my inspiration" and adding that he kept a life-size photo of Henry Ford next to his desk.

This admiration was not entirely unrequited. Henry Ford was an anti-semite whose newspaper, The Dearborn Independent, had published a string of antisemitic articles. As the Washington Post noted in a 1998 article "in July 1938, four months after the German annexation of Austria, he (Henry Ford) accepted the highest medal that Nazi Germany could bestow on a foreigner," the Grand Cross of the German Eagle for his "distinguished service to the Reich".

Things changed after Pearl Harbour. The US government's subsequent declaration of war on Japan and Germany on 11 December 1941 made it illegal for U.S. motor companies such as Ford and General Motors to have any contact with their subsidiaries in German-controlled territory. Edsel Ford built a huge new factory—which became fully operational in 1942—at Willow Run to build the B-24 Liberator bombers using a mile long assembly line.

The factory produced one plane per hour and by 1945 Ford had built 86,865 complete aircraft, 57,851 aircraft engines, 4,291 military gliders and thousands of engine components. Ford also built 280,000 tanks, armoured cars and Jeeps (see Chapter 9). Edsel Ford's premature death in 1943 from stomach cancer raised the alarming possibility of, the by then senile, Henry retaking control. Ford was losing $9 million a week at this point and it was the major shareholders who insisted that Henry Ford's grandson, Henry Ford II should take over that saved the company from a US Government takeover.

Chapter 4
1922 Rolls Royce 40/50 Silver Ghost

The Rolls Royce is travelling at a steady pace through the woodland on the outskirts of Moscow to the Gorky Mansion. At the wheel—the car is right hand drive—is Adolphe Kegresse, the French engineer and former chauffeur to Tsar Nicholas II. In the passenger seat sits a stern looking bodyguard in a Red Army uniform.

In the rear seat is a tired, ill looking, bald man and his traditionally dressed and head-scarfed wife. They were gazing in the opposite direction from their Red Army bodyguard. The weather is mild and the hood of the Rolls has been folded down so that its passengers can appreciate the beauty of the countryside. Six months later the male passenger would be dead but the Rolls would continue to transport his wife until it was replaced with a newer Phantom II model at the end of the decade.

The car's rear seat occupants were none other than the hero of the October 1917 Bolshevik Revolution Vladimir Ilych Ulyanov, a.k.a "Lenin" and his wife Nadezhda "Nadya" Krupskaya. The car was one of, it transpires, three—all Rolls Royce Silver Ghosts—allocated for their personal use. Indeed, despite being a committed Marxist who considered property as theft and the elite or "super structure", as having cheated the proletariat out of the value of their labour, Lenin and his fellow Bolsheviks had a surprisingly soft spot for the "finest motorcar in the world".

There is a great deal of confusion about which cars were linked to Lenin with at least three currently on display in Moscow, St Petersburg and at the Lenin Museum at the Gorki Mansion respectively. The fact is that all three were Lenin's Rolls-Royces. The story of how this came about is an interesting one and unravelling it is not straightforward.

The first Rolls Royce cars associated with the Bolsheviks were those expropriated by the Soviet State from the Tsar. Nicholas II was a fan of luxury cars and owned somewhere around 40 at the time of the Revolution. Of these a proportion were Rolls Royce Silver Ghosts including four supplied from Paris coachbuilder Kellner (Chassis #2283—a 1913 Limousine, chassis #47AB—a 1914 cabriolet; chassis #49 RD and #57 PB—both 1914 limousines) and at least two others bodied by Barker—chassis #21 CB and #27 PD—both 1915 tourers.

However, while the requisitioning and use of these symbols of capitalist excess was arguably justified in the economic chaos and international isolation immediately following the Revolution, more interesting is the fact that, so taken with the quality and reliability of the vehicles were the Bolsheviks, that they decided to order brand new replacements in the early 1920s. This was done via the All-Russia Co-operative Society (ARCOS) and at least three of those ordered were pressed into service for Lenin's personal use.

The first of these cars was a 1921 Silver Ghost 40/50 six-seater Barker bodied tourer—chassis #17 KG featuring in a number of photographs bearing the registration number 236 which is now on display in the Russian History Museum in Moscow.

Despite the trade restrictions placed on the Soviet Union after the Revolution, the Rolls Royce factory records that this car was ordered on 11 July 1922 by the head of the Soviet Trade Delegation in London, N. Klinsko, for

ARCOS as part of a deal to buy a consignment of British made aero engines. The car reportedly cost 1850 GBP—a small fortune at the time—but came with a 15% discount as a sweetener to the deal. On 17 August 1922, the chassis went to Barker's for the construction of the body.

The second Ghost is chassis number #79YG which is now in the Lenin Museum at the Gorky Mansion and is fitted with a Kegresse half-track conversion. The factory records show that this car was bought as a rolling chassis with a motor and a kit of parts on 28 September 1922 by ARCOS and sent on 13 December 1922 to London's East India Dock for loading on a steamer to Petrograd.

The open tourer bodywork was added on arrival in Russia by the 4th State Automobile Plant in Moscow (formerly Petr Ilyin's carriage and automobile factory) according to the Soviet State archives and not by Mann Egerton of Norwich prior to shipping as widely believed. During 1923, Lenin used this Rolls-Royce 40/50hp as his everyday car in both summer and winter and it is likely that this is the car in the photograph, although it could equally be #17YG.

It was not until 1928, four years after Lenin's death, that chassis #79YG was converted at the Putilov plant in the by then renamed Leningrad to a half-track using designs by the legendary French engineer Adolphe Kegresse who had been both Tsar Nicholas II's and Lenin's chauffeur. The Kegresse modifications added a half—track arrangement at the rear and fitted skis to the front wheels to enable the car to be driven in snow. The car was only installed in the museum in 1949 and retrospectively described as "Lenin's winter car".

A third Silver Ghost rolling chassis, number #40YG, engine and kit of parts was bought on 19 October 1922, by ARKOS and shipped with #79YG on 13 December 1922 from East India Dock. This was bodied at the Ilyin factory as a limousine. This car was also put at the disposal of Lenin and his family from 1923 to 1929. After this, it too was converted into a half-track but the limousine body was too wide and fouled the tracks so it was re-bodied as an open tourer.

In 1949, #40YG was moved to Saint-Petersburg and was re-converted back to a four wheeled car for film use and had its engine and transmission removed and replaced by those of a Zil truck. It was subsequently acquired by the St Petersburg historical museum and put on display in a glass case in the museum as "Lenin's Rolls Royce". The original engine and Kegresse track system were destroyed in the 1990s.

The Soviet Rolls Royce buying didn't end with Lenin's death. Stalin was also a keen consumer—as the photographs of him on a hunting trip in the Steppes show—placing an order via ARCOS for five new six seater identical Phantom II open tourers by Park Ward (chassis #131 XJ; #165 XJ; 203 XJ; 204 XJ; 118 GY) all equipped with extra-large fuel tanks.

Although luxury cars may have come late in life to Lenin, he had not been poor prior to the Revolution. He had been born Vladimir Ilych Ulyanov—the nickname "Lenin" came later perhaps from the River Lena—on 22 April 1870 to a wealthy middle-class family in Simbirsk. His father had risen from being a serf to the middle class by being clever and had studied maths and physics at Kazan Imperial University before becoming a teacher employed by the Russian nobility.

By contrast, his mother, Maria Alexandrova Blank, who his father had married in 1863, was from a solidly middle-class background and was the daughter of a Russian Jewish doctor who had converted to Orthodox Christianity. Lenin's father's hard work and contacts saw him promoted to become Director of Public Schools for the Simbirsk province, responsible for setting up 450 new schools and resulted in his being awarded the Order of St Vladimir making him a hereditary nobleman.

Lenin was one of eight children and was the third eldest. Lenin had a happy childhood until the age of 16, spending summers in Kokushkino and studying hard at the Simbirsk Classical Gimnazia. It was following his father's death and the execution of his adored elder brother Alexander, for plotting to assassinate the Tsar, that Lenin's path to becoming a revolutionary began.

Having graduated from school with a gold medal for academic excellence, he followed his father studying law at Kazan University but was expelled after only three months later and exiled along with his family to Kokushkino for taking part in a student protest against government restrictions on student societies. With little else to do he read extensively and was particularly influenced by the writings of Nikolay Chernyshevsky and Karl Marx.

Lenin's mother was alarmed by his self-radicalisation and persuaded the authorities to let the family return to Kazan. This only made things worse as Lenin joined a revolutionary circle further fuelling his interest in Marxist ideology. Realising her mistake, his mother bought a country estate in Alakaevka in the Samara Oblast in the hope that Lenin would become interested in farming. The plan failed and she ended up moving the family to Samara.

Lenin produced a Russian language translation of Marx and Engel's 1848 Communist manifesto and joined a socialist discussion circle. His mother meanwhile persuaded the Russian authorities to allow her son to take his University Examinations at the University of St Petersburg as an external candidate. He was awarded a First with honours. To his mother's relief Lenin seemed to settle down staying in Samara and working as a lawyer. Nevertheless, in his spare time he remained active in radical and revolutionary circles.

The trouble began again when he moved to St Petersburg in 1893 to become a barrister's assistant. In his spare time, he became the leader of a Marxist workers' circle but, mindful of what had happened to Alexander, was careful to keep this a secret from the authorities. It was here that he met Nadya Krupskaya a fellow Marxist and his future wife. His mother paid for him to travel to Switzerland and Germany for him to stay at a health spa and to study.

In fact, he used the trip to meet other revolutionaries and to collect revolutionary publications which he smuggled back into Russia. Finally his luck ran out when he was arrested in St Petersburg on charges of sedition. He was held on remand for a year before being sentenced without trial to three years exile with his family in Siberia—a journey of 11 weeks.

By 1901 he was living in Pskov, followed by Munich and then London—where he met Trotsky—and had adopted the nickname of "Lenin", was active in the Russian Social Democratic Labour Party (RSDLP) and had published a subversive newspaper called Iskra ("Spark") Lenin's belief in strong leadership led to a split in the RSDLP between his followers who were in the majority—hence Bolsheviks—and those of Julus Martov who were in favour of individual expression and action but were in the minority hence Mensheviks.

The dominance of Lenin's supporters by the time of the 1905 massacre of protesters in St Petersburg meant that Lenin and the Bolsheviks played a key role in fuelling the insurrection. The October Manifesto of liberal reforms set out by Tsar Nicholas II following the uprising allowed Lenin to return to St Petersburg. But the government's crackdown of May 1907 meant that he had to flee to Switzerland.

Lenin and the Bolsheviks subsequently relocated to Paris which he hated, describing the city as "a foul hole". By 1913 Lenin was living in Krakow in the Austro-Hungarian Empire. This proved to be a problem when the First World War broke out the following year since the Russian and Austria-Hungarian

Empires were on opposing sides. Fortunately for him, as an opponent of the Tsarist government he was allowed to remain free and to move to Zurich in 1916.

Lenin was still in Switzerland when the February 1917 Revolution, fuelled by food shortages and poor working conditions, led to the Tsar's abdication and the transformation of the Russian Empire into the Russian Republic. Despite the ongoing war, he and Nadya were famously allowed to travel through Germany with 30 other dissidents on a sealed train carriage to Sassnitz to take the ferry to Sweden and then to cross into Finland and on by train to, the by then renamed, Petrograd (St Petersburg).

Lenin's health was not good and having stayed in Petrograd for a few months he left for the Finnish village of Neivola to recover. He was still in Finland in August when the Commander in Chief of the Russian Army launched an unsuccessful coup against the new government prompting its head Alexander Kerensky to turn to the Petrograd Soviet, which included the Bolsheviks, for help.

Lenin returned to Petrograd in October and called at a meeting of the Bolshevik Central Committee for the Bolsheviks to lead an armed insurrection against the government. He got his wish and by the end of October the provisional government was no more and the Bolsheviks were in power.

For a man already in poor health before 1917, the stress and workload of the Revolution and its aftermath, including making peace with Germany and the ensuing civil war took a terrible toll on Lenin. Having survived an assassination attempt in 1918 when he had been shot, by 1921 Lenin was seriously ill. In 1922 he suffered a stroke and convalesced at Gorki. By July—the time of the photograph—he had largely recovered such that he was able to go back to Moscow in October.

A second stroke followed in December forcing him back to Gorki. Lenin's third stroke in March 1923 left him temporarily mute. Having again recovered to a large extent he made his last visit to Moscow in the Rolls Royce in October 1923. On 21 January 1924 he died at Gorki having slipped into a coma.

Rolls Royce

Rolls Royce began life in 1904 when Charles Stewart Rolls decided to partner with the existing, Manchester-based, engineering business of Frederick Henry Royce. Royce had produced his first car, the two-cylinder Royce 10, in early 1904 before meeting Rolls at Manchester's Midland Hotel in May of that year. Rolls owned a motor car dealership in Fulham and signed an agreement on 23 December 1904 to act as sole dealer for Royce's cars.

The range not only included the Royce 10—so named because of its two-cylinder 10hp engine, but also a three cylinder 15hp car, a 20hp four cylinder car and, most importantly a 30hp six cylinder model—which would become the Silver Ghost. All cars were badged as Rolls-Royce. The company was formally incorporated in 1906.

With business rapidly expanding, the decision was made to move from Manchester. Various locations including Coventry were considered but eventually Derby was chosen because its City Council offered the inducement of subsidised electricity. Accordingly a 12.7 acre site was bought to the south of the city and a Royce—designed factory built. Production began in early 1908.

It was in this factory that both the Tsar's and Lenin's Rolls Royce would be manufactured. The original six-cylinder Royce 30 was redesigned to generate more power and named the 40/50hp. Claude Johnson, the Managing Director of the new company persuaded its founders that production should be focused exclusively on the production, development and refinement of this car alone rather than the other smaller and cheaper Royce models. Rolls-Royce's reputation was therefore founded on the engineering excellence and reliability of this car—the Silver Ghost.

During the First World War the Silver Ghost Chassis was used as the underpinning of the first armoured car. Silver Ghosts were used in a number of different theatres—including the Middle East where T E Lawrence of Arabia was a big fan. The First World War also led to Rolls-Royce's involvement in the manufacture of aircraft engines—notably the Rolls-Royce Eagle engine which was used in the first non-stop transatlantic flight in 1919 by Alcock and Brown in their converted Vickers Vimy bomber.

Between the First and Second World Wars, Rolls-Royce's motor car division went from strength to strength while rivals such as Bentley—founded in 1919—went bankrupt despite considerable racing success. As a result, Rolls-Royce was able to acquire Bentley in 1931 and set up a separate company under its ownership.

The aero engine business existed side by side with the motor car manufacturing—the reason that ARCOS was able to get a discount on one of Lenin's Silver Ghosts as part of a wider deal. Rolls Royce's aircraft engine business features elsewhere in this book (see Chapter 10) when, during the

Second World War, the British government was forced to broker a swap of shadow factories between Rolls-Royce and Rover who had initially given the task of developing Frank Whittle's jet engine before falling out with its designer.

The accidental acquisition of this project and the Barnoldswick factory led directly to Rolls-Royce's post war dominance in the jet engine sector.

In common with many British companies Rolls Royce suffered from poor management in the 1960s and spiralling development costs of its advanced RB211 jet engine led to its financial collapse in 1971 and the establishment of a new company Rolls-Royce (1971) Limited. The car division was sold to Vickers in 1980 while the rest of the company was nationalised. In 1987 the Thatcher government (see Chapter 19) sold its shares in Rolls—Royce to the public.

The car division which also included Bentley was sold by Vickers to Volkswagen in 1998 for 430 million GBP who sold the Rolls-Royce brand to BMW the same year. Ironically the current Rolls-Royce Motor Cars company has no rights to the vehicles produced from 1906 onwards—these rights are owned by Bentley which Volkswagen still owns. The new company built a new factory at Goodwood in West Sussex in 2003 where it still manufactures Rolls Royce motor cars.

1922 Rolls Royce 40/50 Silver Ghost

The Rolls Royce Silver Ghost was designed by its makers to be the "finest motor car in the world". Production began in 1907 and ran until 1925. There is some disagreement as to the origins of the "Silver Ghost" name. Some say it was the result of the extremely smooth and nearly silent engine, others say that it stems from the fact that the first production car to be made in 1907 was fitted with a silver painted open tourer body.

The six cylinder, 80 bhp, side valve, 7.5 litre engine was both quiet and powerful. It was fitted with a seven bearing crankshaft including full pressure lubrication and an extra-large centre bearing to eliminate vibration. Ignition was via twin spark plugs per cylinder coupled with the choice of a magneto or a coil. The car was capable of a respectable, though probably terrifying, seventy miles an hour.

The chassis had fixed front and rear axles and leaf springs. Braking was via drums on the rear axle and a transmission brake on the propeller shaft. Early cars such as those used by Lenin featured a red "RR" logo which was changed to black after the death of Sir Henry Royce in 1934. All Rolls Royce Silver Ghosts were ordered as a running chassis for their future owners to choose a suitable coachbuilder to have bespoke bodywork built to their preferred specification. A total of 7874 Silver Ghosts were made before the model was replaced by the Phantom in 1926.

Chapter 5
1922 Dodge Touring Car

It is Friday 20 July 1923 in Parral, Chihuahua, Northern Mexico. A large crowd has gathered to view a grisly spectacle. Men and women look on with morbid curiosity at corpses hanging out of a 1922 Dodge Brothers Touring Car. In total five men had just been mown down in an ambush. There was only one—badly wounded—survivor Ramon Contreras, a bodyguard of the main target.

That target was one of the heroes of the Mexican Revolution—General Francisco "Pancho" Villa. A man who lived by the sword had died in a hail of dumdum bullets. The one time darling, but later scourge, of the US had died instantly not at the hands of his cross-border enemies but because there was a risk that he might have been about to re-enter Mexican politics, upsetting the vested interests of the President Alvaro Obregon.

There was no hero's funeral for the dead revolutionary—instead he was buried in the city cemetery in Parral the day after being assassinated—indeed his earthly remains would go on to suffer the defilement of being exhumed and his skull removed by American treasure hunter Emil Holmdahl.

This was an undignified end by any standards but particularly for a man who had been a key ally of Emiliano Zapata, central to the revolution that overthrew the government of Victoriano Huerta and, who had once been considered so important he had been the subject of a cross-border US Army expedition led by General Pershing with George Patton (See Chapter 9) to capture him.

Villa had been a legend in his own lifetime—starring as himself in Hollywood films and giving interviews to the international press. However, this fame and recognition not only made him popular with the general public but also dangerous to the ruling regime—notably Generals Obregon and Calles. As such he was largely airbrushed from the history of the Revolution—an inconvenient maverick with populist appeal.

The events of the fateful day began with one of Villa's regular banking trips from his Hacienda to the neighbouring town of Parral. For some reason he was not accompanied as usual by his personal cavalry but drove with only a handful of bodyguards in the black Dodge Touring Car. The purpose of the trip was to pick up gold to pay his ranch staff. As the car passed a school en route to the bank a pumpkin seed seller rushed towards it shouting "Viva! Villa!" twice.

This was a pre-agreed signal to a group of seven assassins armed with Mauser rifles—by repeating the name twice the Pumpkin seed seller had told the gunmen that Villa was in the rear of the car. They fired a total of forty "dumdum" rounds—nine of which hit Villa in the head and chest killing him instantly. The steel bodywork of the Dodge, which survives in the Historical Museum of the Mexican Revolution housed in Villa's hacienda in Chihuahua, still contains the many bullet holes.

While it has never been proven who ordered Villa's assassination, the fact that the telegraph service to his hacienda had been cut to prevent any potential uprising, coupled with the number of assassins and the forward planning points clearly to government involvement. A state legislator from Durango, Jesus Salas Barraza, claimed responsibility and Obregon had him arrested and sentenced to twenty years in prison which was subsequently commuted to three months by the governor of Chihuahua. Barraza suspiciously went on to become a colonel in the Mexican army.

Born on 5 June 1878, Villa grew up on a large hacienda—the Rancho de la Coyotada (today a museum) in Durango state. He was christened Jose Doroteo Arango Arambula but later changed his name claiming that he was the illegitimate son of the Mexican bandit Augustin Villa. He was literate but left school early after his father died and went on to do a range of jobs to make ends meet including working as a foreman for a US railway company.

By the age of 16, he was living in Chihuahua but returned to Durango to kill a hacienda owner who had raped his sister. He stole the dead man's horse and fled to the Sierra Madre mountains where he became a bandit. Thanks to influential friends he escaped death having been arrested in 1902 for stealing mules.

His punishment was to be press-ganged into the Federal Army but he deserted a few months later, killing an army officer and stealing his horse. He became a supporter of Francisco Madero, a landowner turned politician, who was opposed to the increasingly corrupt Porfirio Diaz regime and sought to foment a revolution.

The arrest of Madero for standing in the 1910 Mexican Presidential election against Diaz, sparked a revolution by pro-democracy forces in Mexico. Villa, by this time 32 years old, joined the revolutionary forces and used the expertise he had gained as a bandit to defeat the Federal Army in Naica, Camargo and Pilar de Conchos.

This impressive track record brought him to the personal attention of Madero who enlisted his help in defeating the Mexican Liberal Party who had challenged his leadership. Villa's successful arrest and neutralisation of the Liberals resulted in his promotion to Colonel in the Revolutionary Army. A gifted commander, Villa went on, in 1911, to defeat the Federal Army at the battle of Ciudad Juarez on the Mexican US border. The net result was both a victory and ultimately a disaster for Villa.

On losing the battle of Ciudad Juarez, Diaz resigned on 25 May 1911. But in doing so he persuaded Madero to sign the Treaty of Cuidad Juarez which removed the President but left the regime in place. This meant that the senior military commanders that Villa had routed remained in office with a sizeable grudge against a man they viewed as a bandit. Added to this, Madero then refused Villa's request that hacienda land seized during the fighting should be distributed amongst revolutionary soldiers.

Villa would later tell a story of a conversation he had with Madero after the Treaty of Ciudad Juarez in which he said that Madero had killed the revolution, been made a fool of by the regime and presciently that the decision to make peace with the regime would "eventually cost us our necks, yours included".

Although Madero became President in 1911, it proved to be a disaster with him spurning his revolutionary comrades and instead surrounding himself by the deep state of the old regime. Madero's decision to appoint former Diaz loyalist Venustiano Carranza as Minister of War instead of fellow revolutionary Pascual Orozco was to cost him dear. Orozco conspired to overthrow Madero.

In response, Madero re-enlisted the help of Villa who once again delivered some stunning military victories for the President including the capture of Parral and, by joining forces with the Federal Army, Torreon.

As a result, the head of the Federal Army named Villa an honorary Brigadier. But Villa was immune to flattery and saw through this empty gesture. In response Huerta tried to discredit Villa having him accused of theft and ultimately put before a firing squad where the latter only escaped by persuading Madero's brothers (both Generals in the Army) to contact the President to spare his life.

In prison, Villa came into contact with followers of Emiliano Zapata. Villa escaped on 25 December 1912 and fled across the border to El Paso from where he tried to warn Madero of an impending coup led by Huerta. He was unsuccessful and Madero was murdered in February 1913. Villa gathered together seven men and headed back to Mexico in early 1913 to fight Huerta. He was not alone—Zapata who led the revolutionary peasant movement in Morelos also opposed the new regime.

Villa joined forces with Venustiano Carranza and army Generals Pablo Gonzalez and Alvaro Obregon to form the Constitutionalist Army of Mexico to fight Huerta. This was the high point of Villa's military career. He enlisted the support of talented soldiers from the army and bandit groups, financed his operation through a series of robberies, extortion of wealthy Hacienda owners and won spectacular victories against Huerta's forces at Ciudad Juarez, Tierra Blanca, Chihuahua and Ojinaga.

In 1913, Villa was elected as provisional governor of Chihuahua by local military commanders—albeit against Carranza's wishes. Villa used the role to strengthen his military capabilities. Such was his prowess as a military commander that the US Army arranged a contract with Hollywood to film his tactics with 50% of the profit being paid to Villa. Villa was even invited to Fort Bliss to meet Brigadier General John Pershing.

Villa's skill extended beyond the battlefield to fundraising. His traditional sources of campaign finance—robbery and extortion, were supplemented by the issuing of his own currency. The net result was that he amassed a huge war chest with which to hire more soldiers and to buy more equipment and animals. He even created mobile hospital units from train carriages and rebuilt the railway to the south to transport his troops and supplies to the front.

The resulting "Division of the North" was the most powerful and well-organised fighting force in Mexico.

After Villa's capture of the city of Torreon, Carranza became worried that Villa would capture Mexico City so threatened to withhold his coal supplies unless he diverted to attack Saltillo. Villa, unhappy at the clearly politically motivated interference with his military campaign, reluctantly agreed. He captured Saltillo and then tendered his resignation but was persuaded by his staff officers to withdraw it, to defy Carranza's orders and instead to attack Zacatecas—the centre of Mexican silver production.

This was a strategically vital location and was heavily defended. Villa took it at considerable cost to both sides, triggering the flight of Huerta on 14 July 1914.

However, getting rid of Huerta was the beginning rather than the end of Villa's problems. In his absence, of the common foe, factional divisions between the various revolutionary forces spilled out into the open. An attempt to share power between political groups and deliberately excluding armed groups brought Villa and Zapata together against Carranza—who they thought was planning to become a dictator—and Obregon the Commander in Chief of the Constitutional Army in the Northwest.

Although Villa and Zapata managed to occupy Mexico City and Villa had the strongest army, Obregon undermined his credibility in the press by painting him as a psychopath. Coupled with this, Carranza controlled Mexico's two largest ports and was able to amass considerable funds. Villa had to retreat from Mexico City in 1915 following a breakdown in discipline amongst his troops.

Carranza sent Obregon north to cut off his retreat, defeating Villa at Celaya in early April 1915, Trinidad between April and June 1915 and Agua Prieta in October 2015. Each battle involved huge casualties for Villa's forces. Carranza captured and executed several of Villa's most trusted and experienced commanders.

By November 1915, the once mighty Villa was reduced to an army of 200 loyal men and retreated to the mountains near Chihuahua. At the same time and partly as a result of Oberon's successful smear campaign, the US not only refused to sell Villa weapons but also recognised Carranza as the legitimate leader of Mexico. The US allowed Carranza to move his troops using its railways.

Feeling betrayed, Villa turned bandit against his former backers, hijacking a train with the resulting death of 17 Americans, recruiting a new guerrilla force to bring his total forces to 500 men and launching a cross-border raid against the town of Columbus in New Mexico. The latter allowed Villa to seize 100 horses and military supplies from the 13th US Cavalry Regiment stationed there. He also burned the town to the ground for good measure.

The raid infuriated US President Woodrow Wilson who ordered a cross-border US Army expedition to capture Villa. The effect of 5000 US troops led by John Pershing using motorised units—ironically employing the same type of Dodge Touring Cars that Villa would eventually be assassinated in—commanded by George Patton (see Chapter 10) as well as aircraft and trucks, served only to strengthen local support for Villa and to renew his credentials as a modern-day Robin Hood type figure.

The operation was eventually abandoned in February 1917 without success but claimed the lives of some of Villa's closest allies and 190 of his men. Villa by this stage was marginalised as a guerrilla leader in his regional stronghold of Chihuahua and Carranza focussed his attention on the threat posed by Zapata in the South instead.

Following Carranza's assassination on 21 May 1920, Villa seized the opportunity to negotiate an end to hostilities and his retirement with the interim President Adolfo de la Huerta. Villa was given a 25000 acre hacienda just outside Parral in Chihuahua as well as half a million gold pesos as a pension and a personal bodyguard of 50 cavalry by the government in return for laying down his arms and disbanding his militia.

1922 Dodge Touring Car

Villa's 1922 Dodge Touring Car was an excellent choice of transport for the retired revolutionary. Larger, faster, better engineered and stronger—thanks to its all steel bodywork as opposed to steel and wood—than its contemporary the

Ford Model T (see Chapter 3), the Dodge had a reputation for reliability and durability.

Indeed, Dodge's slogan during this period was "Dependability!" Powered by the tried and tested Dodge Brothers "L head" 35hp four cylinder engine, the car incorporated some advanced features such as 12 volt electrics, a vacuum pressurised fuel system and three speed manual sliding gear transmission. Braking was on two wheels, the wheels themselves being surprisingly robust wooden spoked rims with skinny 32" × 4" tubed tyres. The car had a canvas hood and no side screens so was relatively open to the elements.

It was presumably these qualities that led the US military to make the 30-35 Dodge Touring Car the first US Army Command Car during the Pancho Villa Expedition. Indeed, Lt George Patton (see Chapter 9) used three Model 30 Touring cars to carry out the first motorised raid in US military history.

Two different versions were built in 1922—a low radiator/bonnet model— as the Villa car—and a high radiator/bonnet which was produced from the summer of 1922. Patton had made good use of the low bonnets of the Touring Cars he used on the famous cross-border raid, using them as a means of transporting the dead bodies of the six of Villa's men he killed by draping them across the top and tying then down with rope to the running boards.

Villa's car survives in the museum created out of his hacienda in Chihuahua complete with bullet holes in the radiator and through the rear seat and bodywork where he was sitting. By 1922 the model had been in production, more or less unchanged since 1914 when it was first launched as the Model 30. The Model 30 sold 45,000 units within a year of its launch and catapulted Dodge to the third largest manufacturer in the US from a standing start.

Dodge

Brothers John and Horace Dodge were born in 1864 and 1868 respectively in Michigan. Their father Daniel had taken over his father's boat engine repair business in Niles, Michigan and his sons were apprenticed in the marine engineering trade from an early age. The family moved to Detroit in 1886 and the brothers took up engineering jobs at a boiler works and a typography company.

In 1896, they set up a bicycle company with Frederick Evans. These bikes were an early demonstration of Horace Dodge's genius as they featured ball bearings—something he invented to make the wheels more reliable and less likely to seize up with dirt. The bicycle company was a success and the sale of their stake in the business gave them $3700 of capital with which to set up their own engineering workshop. Here they began making components for the newly emerging automotive industry.

The quality of their workmanship and design meant that they won large contracts with both the Olds Motor Vehicle Company and, crucially, the Ford Motor Company to makes chassis, axles, engines and transmissions. After the failure of his first company (See Chapters 3 and 17).

Ford was short of money so rather than pay the brothers for the rolling chassis they were building for him he instead offered them a 10% stake in the company. In what was to prove to be a very shrewd business move, the brothers accepted the offer. Dodge began building rolling chassis complete with brakes, engines and transmissions for the Model T to help Ford to keep up with demand. John meanwhile became Vice President of the company.

In 1913, they founded Dodge Brothers Motor Car Company. They expanded their factory and built a test track—something which no other manufacturer had at the time. Their first car, launched in 1914, was the Model 30/35 Touring Car of which John Dodge is quoted of having said: "someday people who own a Ford are going to want an automobile".

Despite this, Dodge remained a key supplier to Ford until 1916 when Henry Ford's refusal to pay a dividend and instead to invest all profits in building a new factory at River Rouge led to them suing Ford for damages. Ford decided to settle out of court by buying out all of his shareholders. The Dodge brothers' 10% netted them a whopping $25million in cash.

At the same time Dodge was picking up lucrative contracts to supply the US military with trucks—notably an order from Pershing for 150–250 for the Mexico expedition. But that was only the beginning and a total of 12,800 Dodge manufactured vehicles would subsequently be used in the First World War.

Sadly, the Dodge brothers never got to enjoy their vast wealth—John died of pneumonia from Spanish Flu in January 1920 at the Ritz Carlton in New York and his distraught brother Horace drank himself to death by December of the same year. Their widows promoted Frederick Haynes to be President of the company. Haynes introduced the new Series 116 and also expanded truck production. The lack of model development on the car side of the business meant that Dodge had dropped to fifth place in terms of sales in the US market by 1925.

This prompted the Dodge widows to sell the company for $146 million to an investment bank Dillon, Read & Co who immediately floated it on the stock market netting a $14 million profit while retaining control of the company. A new model with a six cylinder engine was introduced in 1927 and the four cylinder model was dropped in 1928. However, declining sales meant that by 1927 Dillion Read & Co were actively looking for a buyer for the company. Dodge was sold to the Chrysler Corporation in 1928.

Dodge survived as premium brand in the Chrysler range above DeSoto—something that would be reversed in 1933—and the range was fitted with a new eight cylinder engine. When Chrysler built a new factory in Los Angeles in 1932 Dodge production was shifted there along with DeSoto and Plymouth. As part of Chrysler, Dodge produced over 400,000 light trucks for the US military during World War Two. Civilian car production was restarted at the end of 1945.

Throughout the 1950s and 1960s, Dodge formed part of the Chrysler range with worthy but unexciting offerings. The 1970s muscle car boom saw a renaissance in the shape of the legendary Dodge Charger R/T—a car later immortalised as the General Lee in the television series the Dukes of Hazard. The brand survived the DaimlerChrysler merger of 1998 as well as the Fiat (see Chapter 18) takeover of June 2009.

Chapter 6
1936 Mclaughlin-Buick 90 Limousine

The image is slightly grainy—taken with a flash at night whist the car was moving. The close-up is through the driver's window on the right-hand side of the vehicle through the glass partition of the face of the rear passenger. The man in the rear seat looks tired and has raised his right hand in an unsuccessful attempt to cover his face.

The photo was taken late on Friday 11 December 1936. The passenger is the, soon to be former, King Edward VIII who had just abdicated the throne to marry his fiancée, the American divorcee, Mrs Wallis Simpson, triggering a constitutional crisis. The driver is Royal Chauffeur George Ladbroke. The car is not a Rolls Royce as you might expect but a 1936 5.2 Litre McLaughlin-Buick limousine registered CUL 421.

The question as to why the King of the United Kingdom and the Dominions of the British Empire and Emperor of India preferred a Canadian-built US Buick to the more traditional Derby-made Rolls Royce is a good reflection both of his desire to be "modern" coupled with his love of all things transatlantic. The combination of the two when extended to human relationships was ultimately to cost him his throne and to pitch his capable, but less extroverted, younger brother into the role of Monarch just as the storm clouds of the Second World War were gathering.

CUL 421 was registered in central London in 1936 to HM the King, St James's Palace, SW1 and was a specially built Buick Series 90 limousine which had been ordered late in the summer of 1935 by the then Prince of Wales from Lendrum and Hartman in London and delivered in February the following year. The car was one of a pair ordered: the other was registered CUL 457 and used by Mrs Simpson.

It had been coach built to the King's personal specifications by the McLaughlin Motor Car Company of Oshawa, Ontario, Canada. There have been many conspiracy theories about the choice of Registration numbers for the cars. The word "cul" in French translates as "bum" in English or "ass" in American. Given that the cars were registered nine months before the abdication crisis this is just an unfortunate coincidence (not least because the cars would remain in service in France for three years after it).

The registrations are part of a Central London series that featured on a number of London Transport vehicles registered at the same time. Nevertheless, it does seem unlikely that the link was not made and perhaps was a source of amusement to the car's owner. CUL 421 was not the first car the Prince of Wales had ordered from McLaughlins—in 1924, in a break with precedent whereby Royal visitors had always used British cars, he had ordered nine for a Royal visit to Canada.

This precedent was followed again in 1927 for a subsequent Royal visit and again in 1939 for a planned visit by King George VI. Being Canadian-built, the car benefitted from "Empire exemption" on import duties and was considered "British" since it originated in the Dominions. The future King's choice of a McLaughlin-Buick was entirely consistent with his almost film star status at the time. Other famous owners of the marque included Gracie Fields and George Formby.

McLaughlin had lengthened the General Motors 90 Series Buick chassis and designed a new luxury body for the King to give: "two passengers luxury and privacy". The specification included an almost endless list of extras with everything from drinks cabinets, vanity mirrors, a radio, reading lights, a jewellery cabinet, two silver-gilt cigarette boxes, six silver topped decanters, stowage for luncheon trays and even a special drawer to for the London telephone directories.

The exterior was finished in black with beige West of England cloth used for the interior. The car had been ordered whilst the heir to the throne was still the Prince of Wales. The long lead-in time however meant that by the time the car arrived in London, King George V had died and the vehicle belonged to the new King.

Following the visit to Downing Street and the public announcement of the Abdication, The McLaughlin was the chosen means of transport for the Duke's journey into exile in France. It was driven to Portsmouth and loaded onto a Royal Navy warship and taken to France where the, by then, Duke of Windsor, continued his journey to Austria while his future wife, Wallis Simpson, took its sister car with her to the South of France to await the finalisation of her divorce.

Following his marriage to Mrs Simpson, the car was once again pressed into service for the honeymoon. The Duke was so enamoured of the quality and style of the car that in the subsequent years, he ordered two more McLaughlin-Buicks—one in 1938 and another in 1939.

With the benefit of hindsight, the origins of the abdication crisis—the conflict between duty and love—were clear to see. Edward Albert Christian George Andrew Patrick David Saxe-Coburg and Gotha was born on 23 June 1894 at White Lodge in Richmond, Surrey, the eldest son of the Duke and Duchess of York and third in line to the throne. The Duke's father was the Prince of Wales (subsequently King Edward VII) and his mother was the daughter of the Duke and Duchess of Teck.

Known within his family as David, Edward was brought up by nannies and tutored by Frederick Finch and Henry Hansel until he was 12. At this point he took the exams to attend the Royal Naval College at Osborne on the Royal Estate on the Isle of Wight.

In 1909, after two, unhappy, years Edward went to the Royal Naval College at Dartmouth with the plan that two years later he would join the Navy. His grandfather's death in 1910 led to that being curtailed and Edward becoming the Duke of Cornwall and of Rothesay on 6 May 1910. In June 1910 he also became Prince of Wales and Earl of Chester.

As heir to the throne, the Royal Navy plan was abandoned and he was sent to Magdalen College Oxford where eight terms later he left with the ability to play Polo but no academic qualifications. His Investiture as Prince of Wales took place at Caernarfon Castle on 13 July 1911. At the outbreak of the First World

War he joined the Grenadier Guards but, by order of Lord Kitchener, was not allowed to serve at the front.

During the 1920s Edward carried out Royal duties at home and abroad on behalf of his father, the King. He was a celebrity due to his good looks, status and eligibility. He was a prolific womaniser with a string of affairs with married women. This hedonistic recklessness and refusal to act in a mature way infuriated his father who was loathe to see him become King, predicting that: "After I am dead the boy will ruin himself in twelve months".

It was not only the King that was worried by Edward's impetuous and adolescent behaviour it also caught the attention of the Prime Minister, Stanley Baldwin. The King had given Edward the lease of Fort Belvedere in Windsor Great Park, which he used to conduct his affairs with, amongst others, Lady Furness—the American wife of a British Peer. It was through this relationship that he was introduced to Mrs Wallis Simpson, a fellow American and a divorcee, who had left her first husband, US Naval Officer Win Spencer, in 1927 to marry Ernest Simpson an American businessman.

This was the last straw for the King who, despite the latter's denials, knew full well that Edward was having an affair with her. The British Establishment was equally outraged and sufficiently concerned to assign the Metropolitan Police to track the couple's movements.

The trouble deepened when, following George V's death on 20 January 1936 and his ascension to the throne, he chose to be accompanied by Mrs Simpson to watch the proclamation from St James's Palace. He spent the summer instead of at Balmoral as was traditional, on holiday with Mrs Simpson in the Eastern Mediterranean. By autumn of 1936 it was increasingly apparent that Edward planned to marry his American lover regardless of what anyone thought.

Mrs Simpson's divorce proceedings from her second husband began at Ipswich Assizes in October of the same year but a UK news blackout kept the King's affair and intentions from public consciousness until December.

Meanwhile, rumours in the American press were rife leading Edward's Private Secretary Alec Hardinge to warn him in writing on 13 November that the story was likely to break in the British press. In response to this advice, Edward decided to surface his marriage plans with Prime Minister Baldwin, summoning him to Buckingham Palace on 16 November. Baldwin was clear that from the point of view of public opinion, the marriage was a non-starter.

Added to this, if the King chose to ignore Ministerial advice the Cabinet was ready to resign en masse. The Church of England in the shape of the Archbishop of Canterbury, Cosmo Gordon Lang, was equally clear that marrying a divorcee was incompatible with being the head of a church that forbade allowing divorced people to remarry in church as long as their ex-spouse remained alive.

An added complication in the case of Mrs Simpson was that even when divorced from her current husband, Ernest, her first husband, U.S. navy Pilot Win Spencer, remained very much alive and, indeed, the grounds for that divorce—emotional incompatibility—were not valid under English law meaning that any future marriage was potentially bigamous.

Aside from these obstacles, the British Establishment shared little of Edward's enthusiasm for the divorcee. There were widespread rumours that she had some sort of sexual hold over the King as well as two-timing him with a married car dealer named Guy Trundle.

Even the US Ambassador Joseph Kennedy was heard to refer to her as a "tart". The generally accepted view in establishment circles was that she was a gold-digger only after the King's money and that she would desert him once she had secured it.

Meanwhile in intelligence circles, there was a belief that she was a Nazi agent after her name appeared in leaked diplomatic telegrams from the German Ambassador in London, von Ribbentrop. To say that she was not universally admired in government and society circles would be something of an understatement.

Edward had anticipated Baldwin and Lang's likely response and stated clearly that he intended to marry Mrs Simpson as soon as possible and he was ready "to go" if the Government was not willing to consent. In response Baldwin undertook to explore three options: a royal marriage; a morganatic marriage and abdication. It was clear that the first option would not fly for all of the reasons set out by Baldwin and Lang.

Edward's preference was therefore for the second option (some say originally suggested to him by Churchill) a morganatic marriage which he believed could work. Mrs Simpson wouldn't become Queen, nor would any offspring be in the line of succession. Surely, Edward argued, that might assuage public opinion?

The flaw in this scheme was that not only did the British Cabinet need to approve it, but so too did the infinitely more conservative and less broad-minded governments of the Dominions because what was being proposed changed the law governing the succession. Needless to say the Prime Ministers of Australia, Canada and South Africa were having none of it and nor was the British Cabinet.

Churchill at this point worked frantically behind the scenes to delay the point of decision, arguing that given time the romance might fizzle away. However, there was little support for this approach other than from Oswald Mosley. The King suggested to Baldwin that he make a radio address to the nation setting out the issues and unveiling his plan for a morganatic marriage to Mrs Simpson and for the British people to decide if they could accept this or he would need to abdicate.

Keen to minimise the crisis, Baldwin opposed this idea on the grounds that the Sovereign's freedom to act was constrained by the need to follow Ministerial advice. Faced with this roadblock, Edward decided that abdication was the only option. The instruments of abdication were drawn up declaring his "irrevocable determination to renounce the throne" for himself and his descendants immediately.

He invited his three younger brothers Albert, Henry and George to witness him signing them on 10 December 1936 at Fort Belvedere. His last act as King the next day was to give Royal Assent to his own abdication. In a broadcast to the nation the King said: "I have found it impossible to carry the heavy burden of responsibility and to discharge my duties as King as I would wish to do without the help and support of the woman I love."

McLaughlin Motor Car Company

In common with most coachbuilders, McLaughlin began doing just that, having been founded in 1869 as a carriage maker and rapidly becoming one of the largest manufacturers in the world. The company pioneered a unique fifth wheel arrangement that improved safety and comfort and became an international business turning out 25000 carriages a year by the turn of the century. McLaughlin even had an office in London at this point. By 1915, McLaughlin was building one carriage every 10 minutes.

However, in 1907, in parallel to the traditional horse drawn products of the company, the business was refocused to cater for the new and growing market for automobiles. The plan ran into difficulties when the in-house engine designer became ill.

As a result, McLaughlin began buying engines and gearboxes from Buick who were based in Flint, Michigan. The relationship with General Motors was formalised via a stock swap between Robert McLaughlin and William Durant General Motor's founder, whereby General Motors would supply McLaughlin with Buick engines and chassis.

Durant got heavily into debt buying up other manufacturers for General Motors including Cadillac, Pontiac and Oldsmobile and lost control of the company in 1910. With help from McLaughlin, Durant set up a new company— Chevrolet (see Chapter 16)—and by selling stock was able to regain control of General Motors in 1916. Sam McLaughlin became Vice President cementing the link between the two companies.

By 1918, McLaughlin was effectively the subsidiary of General Motors in Canada with the company also manufacturing Chevrolets for the Canadian market. The luxury coach-built cars produced by the company were badged as McLaughlin-Buicks—a practice that continued until the early 1940s and therefore covered CUL 421.

Buick Series 90

The Buick Series 90 used a 344 cubic inch (5.2 litre) version of the Buick Straight 8 overhead valve engine mated to a synchromesh transmission. The engine had alloy pistons, used downdraught carburettors, produced 104 brake horse power and featured automatic vacuum-operated spark advance replacing the earlier steering column mounted manual spark lever. Front suspension was independent by coil springs and shock absorber.

The car featured the latest Lockheed hydraulic brakes. CUL 421 featured two batteries—the second below the driver's seat with a double pole throw switch allowing the spare battery to be instantly used in an emergency. The car was also fitted with a Smith hydraulic "Jack-all" system to make changing tyres easier.

The Duke of Windsor kept the car for three years in France (despite its registration number) after the abdication including using it for his subsequent marriage to Mrs Simpson at a Chateau in the Loire, before selling it on and replacing it with a newer model. The car was first bought by Frederick Chivers of the Chivers Jam Company. Since then, it has changed hands several times never quite managing to find a permanent home.

By 1969, it was owned by Nicola Bulgari of the Bulgari jewellery family. He sold the car at Sothebys on 22 June 1987 to the Daily Mail who subsequently offered it as a competition prize.

Unfortunately, it was won by a reader who didn't have a garage and sold the car on. The car was reportedly bought by an antique dealer from Worcestershire, who advertised for sale again on eBay in 2003. The car failed to sell and was subsequently auctioned again by Bonhams on 3 December 2007 where it sold for £100,500 to three Midlands businessmen. According to the DVLA computer the car was last taxed in 2007 and is presumably in storage given the records indicate it has not been exported.

Chapter 7
1939 Horch 830 BL

The scene is one of total devastation. Smoke is rising from the wreckage of a vehicle. Miraculously the windscreen is still intact albeit with a bullet hole. The bonnet and front bodywork have been completely destroyed exposing what is left of the engine. One sun visor remains forlornly in the raised position and the hood frame in the background rests at a slightly skewed angle.

One of the onlookers is dressed in a German officer's uniform. The date is 17 July 1944. The place is the N179 just outside Livarot in Normandy, France. The smouldering wreckage is all that remains of Field Marshall Erwin Rommel's Horch 830 BL staff car. The Field Marshal himself is seriously wounded and has lost an eye. The damage is the result of his car having been strafed by a Royal Air Force Spitfire.

There are three different accounts of the attack on the Horch from three different pilots, two from 602 Squadron RAF and one from 412 Squadron RAF. What is not disputed is that Rommel was thrown from the vehicle suffering severe injuries to the left side of his face from flying glass and ended up in hospital where Doctors thought he might die having been diagnosed with three fractures to the skull.

Subsequent events bore this out: Rommel died of his injuries on the 14th October 1944 and was subsequently given a State Funeral with full military honours in Ulm. At least this was the "official" Nazi regime reporting of events: the true cause of Rommel's death was somewhat different.

On the 17 July 1944, Rommel was returning to his headquarters at the Chateau Roch Guyon after inspecting the front in Normandy. There he had met Oberst-Gruppenführer, Sepp Dietrich, commander of the 1st SS Panzer Division. As well as discussing the situation on the ground, Rommel had asked Dietrich an odd question—namely whether the latter would follow his orders even if those orders were at odds with those of the Fuhrer himself.

Somewhat surprisingly, given that Dietrich had been Hitler's chauffeur and bodyguard in the early 1930s, he replied in the affirmative. For Rommel, sounding out Dietrich was the latest in a series of discreet conversations he had had with senior members of the Wermacht. However, that was not the primary purpose of the visit and he was anxious to get back to his Headquarters to update Field Marshall Gunther von Kluge on the deteriorating situation on the ground in Normandy.

Dietrich suggested that Rommel should take a Kubelwagon, so as to be less conspicuous from the air and to avoid main roads given Allied air superiority. Rommel politely declined the offer, preferring his large and comfortable 830BL Horch staff car. This was to prove a costly decision.

In the open top Horch were General Field Marshall Erwin Rommel, sitting in the front passenger seat—a position he much preferred to sitting in the rear. Alongside him was his chauffeur, Sergeant Karl Daniel. In the back of the car were Major Neuhaus, Captain Hellmuth Lang who was acting as spotter for any enemy aircraft, along with Sergeant Holke who was kneeling on the rear seat to keep look out of the road behind.

All was well for the first two hours of the journey and at 18h00 the car was travelling at speed along the N179 (now D579) towards Vimoutiers. Eight RAF fighters had been attacking any traffic on the road near Livarot for most of the afternoon and the ditches were littered with the smouldering remains of burned-out vehicles. Mindful of Dietrich's advice, Daniel left the main road to follow a side road.

At the same point, Lang spotted two enemy planes flying very low and approaching at full speed. Rommel ordered Daniel to turn into a tree-lined driveway 300 feet on the right further up the road. However, the pilot of the first aircraft already had the Horch in his sights, he opened fire with his 20mm cannon on the left-hand side of the car.

Daniel was fatally hit and slumped over the steering wheel, making the car swerve to the right where it hit a tree and ricocheted back onto the road before rolling and landing in a ditch. Rommel was thrown hard against the bullet-proof windscreen before being thrown out of the car altogether, landing on the side of the road. Lang and Holke were also thrown clear but were uninjured and ran to where Rommel had landed.

Neuhaus broke both his pelvis and his spine. Rommel had been severely wounded by glass from the windscreen as well as shrapnel, which had hit him on the left temple and cheek, fracturing his skull in three places and puncturing his left eyeball.

The injured were taken to St Joseph hospital in Livarot, 8km away. Rommel was transferred to the Bernay Luftwaffe Hospital before being transported on 23 July to a hospital in Vésinet east of Saint-Germain. However, it was not until 3 August that it was officially announced that Rommel had been the victim of a car accident. At Rommel's request, no mention was made of having been strafed by enemy aircraft.

Johannes Erwin Eugen Rommel was born on 15 November 1891 to middle class parents in Heidenheim a provincial town near the Black Forrest in the South West German state of Baden Württemberg. His father was a Lieutenant in the artillery and, aged 18, Rommel followed in his footsteps enlisting in the 124th Wurttemberg Infantry Regiment.

During the First World War, he fought in France, Romania and Italy, where he perfected his trademark tactic of penetrating attacks under covering artillery fire coupled with rapid flanking manoeuvres. After being awarded the Iron Cross second class, he was promoted and transferred to the Alpenkorps as a company commander. Here he distinguished himself in the campaigns in the mountains against Italy where, following this his capture of 10,000 men at Longarone, he was awarded the Blue Max (Pour le Merite) as well as promotion to Captain.

For most of the 1920s Rommel was based in Stuttgart in command of the 13th Infantry Division. In the early 1930s he was promoted to Major and transferred to the Dresden Infantry Training School. Like Patton (see Chapter 10) he used this time to write a manual on Infantry tactics. A further promotion in October 1933 to Lieutenant Colonel in command of the 3rd Jager Batallion followed before a move to the War Academy in Potsdam in 1935 where he wrote a bestseller "Infanterie greift an".

This not only earned him a further promotion to Colonel but also brought him to Hitler's attention and he was assigned as the War Ministry's liaison responsible for the military training of the Hitler Youth in February 1938. Hitler arranged for his transfer to the Furherbegleitbatallion—his personal escort— along with another promotion—to the rank of Generalmajor—in August 1939.

Closely involved in the invasion of Poland as the commander of the Furherbegleitbatallion, Rommel lobbied for command of a panzer Division which Hitler duly granted, promoting him to General and making him commander of the 7th Panzer Division in February 1940. In this position Rommel played a central role in the 1940 invasion of the Netherlands, Belgium and France for which he was awarded the Knight's Cross.

Again, like Patton (see Chapter 9) Rommel's focus on the advance using highly mobile Panzer Divisions made him a formidable opponent. At times he found himself deep inside enemy lines supported only by his vanguard but the shock and disarray this caused worked to his advantage.

Although much has been written of Rommel's alleged "chivalry" it was during this campaign that he was responsible for the destruction of the historic centre of Rouen by refusing to allow access to the fire brigade as a punishment for the city's resistance or as he put it: a 'fire demonstration' to discourage similar attempts to resist the German advance. Following the city's fall, 100 black citizens and French colonial troops were executed. The murder of 50 surrendering French Officers at Quesnoy was also directly attributed to his 7th Panzer Division.

After his military success in France, Rommel was promoted to Lieutenant General and appointed commander of the Afrika Korps on 6 February 1941. Although technically subordinate to the Italian Commander in Chief, Italo Gariboldi, Rommel effectively assumed military control of Axis forces in North Africa, launching a surprise offensive against the British on 24 March 1941 which forced the British to retreat to Mersa El Brega, resulted in the fall of Benghazi on 3 April and the besieging of Tobruk on 11 April.

Here again, Rommel's track record is questionable. The Afrika Korps under his command were involved in the deportation of Jews from Libya for forced labour in Italy following the capture of Benghazi, although Yad Vashem's International School for Holocaust Studies attributes primary responsibility to the Italians rather than the Germans. Added to this, some historians cite Rommel as having used Jewish prisoners to clear minefields by walking ahead of his forces.

As a result of his success, Rommel was appointed commander of the newly created Panzer Group Africa in August 1941 under Field Marshal Albert Kesselring. On 26 May 1942, he launched an offensive in what was to become the Battle of Gazala which would last for over a month and during which he would outflank the British, capture Tobruk on 21 June with 32,000 prisoners and vast quantities of supplies. In response, Hitler promoted Rommel to the rank of Field Marshal.

Although the British had been forced to retreat to El Alamein, by mid-July the tide had begun to turn. On 8 August, Montgomery became the new Commander of the British Eight Army and showed himself to be more than a match for the "Desert Fox". When Rommel launched an attack in late August, Montgomery had anticipated this his likely tactics and fortified his positions. Rommel was defeated and, suffering from a liver infection, flew to Germany handing over control to General Georg Stumme.

The British launched the second Battle of El Alamein on 23 October. Stumme suffered a heart attack and died the following day forcing Rommel's return on 25 October. By 2 November when Montgomery launched a new offensive—Operation Surcharge—Rommel was down to just 35 operational tanks, Montgomery was victorious and Rommel was forced to retreat to Tunisia.

After the defeat, Rommel's spate of bad luck continued. He was moved to Greece on 23 July 1943. However, the day he arrived—25 July—coincided with the overthrow of Mussolini and he was diverted to Italy to command Army Group B only for Hitler to change his mind and to give overall command to Kesselring instead. Rommel was then side-lined by Hitler and redeployed to Army Group B in Normandy where he was made "General Inspector of the Western Defences" but relieved of any operational command.

Despite finding the defences in disarray, Rommel was thwarted by his lack of an operational command from making major improvements until, with von Rundstedt's grudging support, he was given command on 15 January 1944. Despite Rommel's energy in having millions of mines laid, bunkers built and obstacles erected on the beaches and in fields where gliders might land, work was far from complete by the time of the 6 June invasion.

To compound his problems, Rommel's sector lacked quality troops and ammunition because von Rundstedt expected the invasion in the Pas de Calais area. This then is how he came to be travelling by car from the front in Normandy on 17 July 1944 when his staff car was attacked. However, his subsequent death was not—as was claimed—as a result of the injuries he had suffered. Instead, it was the result of his growing disillusionment with Hitler.

The Prussian aristocracy, who made up the senior ranks of the Wermacht, had never fully accepted Hitler. By late 1942 and the impending defeat of the German 6th Army at Stalingrad had made it clear to many senior officers that Germany could not win the war. That said, the plotters of July 1944 were far from peace-loving liberals looking to bring Germany back into the family of nations.

There had been a number of failed attempts to kill Hitler with the closest being a bomb placed on his personal plane (disguised in a Cointreau bottle) following a visit to the Eastern Front in March 1943. The attempt involving Rommel centred on Hitler's Headquarters in East Prussia, the Wolfsschanze (Wolfs Lair) and was masterminded by Colonel Claus Schenk Graf Von Stauffenberg.

Von Stauffenberg had been an officer in Rommel's Afrika Korps before being badly wounded in Tunisia in 1943. His distinguished record, physical injuries and disillusionment with Hitler made him the perfect choice for Rommel and other senior plotters who arranged for his transfer to a staff job at Hitler's HQ at Rastenburg in East Prussia.

The initial plan was to carry out the bombing on the 15 July but events conspired to frustrate von Stauffenberg's plans. On the 20th, he had another chance, preparing two devices before entering the conference room. However, he was disturbed and only had time to set one of the timers which he placed in his briefcase and entered the meeting room.

Fate had already intervened at this point as the meeting was held in one of the wooden huts in the compound rather than in one of the bunkers which would have contained the blast making it more deadly. Stauffenberg placed the briefcase on the floor under the heavy wooden table close to Hitler. He then left after a pre-arranged phone call summoned him from the room. At this point one of the other officers noticed the briefcase and moved it placing it next to the heavy table leg on the side away from Hitler.

Stauffenberg immediately left the building with his adjutant and made their way out of the compound in a staff car to the airstrip. At this time the bomb exploded causing the building to be destroyed and leading Stauffenberg to believe that there was no way that Hitler could have survived.

The plan had been to initiate "Operation Valkyrie" to mobilise Wehrmacht units to disarm SS units and arrest leading Nazis. But the plotters could not confirm that Hitler was dead. Only when Stauffenberg returned late in the afternoon was the plan put into operation. Stauffenberg, his adjutant were arrested and shot by firing squad in the courtyard of the Wehrmacht headquarters on the orders of General Fromm, a co-conspirator, in an attempt to save his own life (this failed). Over 4,500 people were subsequently arrested and many condemned to death.

Under interrogation, conspirators such as German General Kommandant in Paris General von Stulpnagel and others mentioned Rommel's name. It also featured as a potential "Reich's President" on a list recovered from another plotter. Rommel was judged guilty in absentia while recovering from the 17 July attack.

Two Generals were sent to his home on 14 October 1944 to confront him with the evidence and to give him three options: return to Berlin and explain himself to Hitler, surrender to the People's Court for a show trial or take cyanide and be given a hero's funeral and have his family provided for. Rommel left home with the officers drove up the road, stopped by a forest, walked into the woods and took the cyanide.

Horch 830 BL

Rommel's staff car was a popular choice amongst the upper echelons of the Wermacht. Constructed in 1939, it featured a powerful 3823cc V8 engine with a bore and stroke of 78 × 100 mm capable of producing 92 bhp (67.6KW) However, it had a prodigious thirst for fuel at 20 Litres per 100km (14 mpg) Although the car weighed a hefty 2.6 tonnes, it was capable of a credible 125kph

(78mph) and this was the speed that Rommel's 830 BL would have been cruising at en route from Normandy back to his Headquarters when the attack happened.

The 830 BL was a big, sleek, car 5050 mm long and 1780 mm wide but only 1650 mm high with a wheelbase of 3350 mm. The model had first been introduced at the February 1933 International Motorcycle and Motor show in Berlin. The car was built at the Zwickau Horch factory until production stopped and was switched exclusively to military vehicle production in early 1940. Horch also produced a military variant—the 830R which had rigid front and rear axles as well as the Horch 108—an off-road version supplied to the Afrika Korps.

Before his move to BMW in 1932, Horch Chief Designer Fritz Fiedler (see Chapter 20) had been responsible for the design of the engine which was based on side valve V12 Horch engine fitted to the 670 model. The new V8 featured a triple mounted crankshaft and a bank angle of 66 degrees.

A central chain driven camshaft drove both banks of cylinders. Fuel was provided by a twin double downdraft Solex carburettors. Transmission was via a four speed ZF helical gearbox with synchromesh on all gears and an overdrive. The six-seater 830BL featured a stiffer box section chassis, cable operated drum brakes and modern double wishbone independent suspension at the front and a de Dion double joint axle at the rear.

Horch

Horch was founded by August Horch and Salli Herz on 14 November 1899, in Ehrenfeld, Cologne. Horch had begun his career in the automobile industry with Benz (see Chapter 8) and in 1904, he established the Horch and Cie. Motorwagenwerke AG in Zwickau in Saxony. Following a financial scandal the company was re-founded in July 1909 as August Horch Automobilwerke GmbH.

Unfortunately, "Horch" had already been registered as a brand by a rival company and as a result he was forced to establish another company. Horch's solution was ingenious. Horch translates as "listen" in old German so instead he opted for the Latin translation of the word: "Audi". Thus, the Audi Automobilwerke was founded on 25 April 1910. The first Horch car featured a 4.5hp engine capable of a feeble 20 mph (32kph) and an open body design with headlights featuring candles inside. Public reaction was, to say the least, uninspiring.

As a result, Horch designed a new 20hp four cylinder model in 1902 which was subsequently unveiled at the Frankfurt Fair in 1904. The vehicle was technologically superior to Daimler and Benz models of the time. Horch went on to develop the first six-cylinder engine in 1904 which first appeared in a vehicle in 1907. This technological leadership was to continue with Horch being the first to design and fit an eight-cylinder engine to their vehicles in 1923. By this time the company had moved upmarket thanks to clever artistic advertising.

However, Horch himself had been forced out of the company in 1909. Audi was amalgamated with Horch in 1928 when both were bought by Jorgen Skafte Rasmussen the owner of DKW (Dampkraftwagen) The result was the formation of Auto Union on 29 June 1932 amalgamating the Audi, Horch, DKW and Wanderer brands.

Auto Union produced a hugely successful range of grand prix cars—the Types A-D in the mid to late 1930s, winning no fewer than 25 international races between 1935 and 1939. At the same time the company became a key supplier to the Wermacht producing the Horch 108 heavy standard passenger car, the Horch 901 medium standard passenger cars and the SdKfz 11 half-track. With the outbreak of the Second World War, the company's production facilities switched rapidly to military vehicles and the last civilian cars—including the 830 BL—were produced in early 1940.

After the war the original Auto Union factory in Zwickau—or at least what remained of it—was in the Soviet occupied sector which subsequently became East Germany. A new 6 cylinder Horch—the P240—was produced from 1955-1958.

Meanwhile on the other side of the Iron Curtain, a new Auto Union company was set up in West Germany to produce two stroke engine DKWs. The Audi name was revived in 1964 when the company was bought by Volkswagen. But Horch was never revived—at least in part because the brand name belonged to rival company Daimler Benz (see Chapters 1, 8 and 19).

Chapter 8
1940 Mercedes Benz 770k W150 Type II
Grosser Offener Tourenwagen

It is 19 July 1940—outside the Kroll Opera House in the central Tiergarten of Berlin, a crowd of flag-waving Nazi supporters have turned out to catch a glimpse of their Fuhrer, Adolf Hitler. As the Mercedes Benz 770K Grosser Offener Tourenwagen glides into view they raise their right arms in the Nazi salute. The gleaming black paintwork and shining chrome of the car sparkle in the sunlight.

Yet, the dark coachwork and unyielding metal with hooded headlights and rigid Nazi penant give a clue to the evil that lies within. In the front passenger seat Hitler raises his right forearm to return the crowd's salute. At the wheel of the car is Erich Kempka, Hitler's personal driver. The two rows of seat behind him are occupied by Heinz Linge his valet and Rudolf Schmundt and Julius Schaub his Adjutants.

All four are part of the elite Waffen SS *Führerbegleitkommando*—Hitler's personal bodyguard. Hitler himself is dwarfed by the massive and intimidating scale of the car, which is presumably intended to act as a projection of its occupant's power.

This was the first day that the recently delivered Mercedes—registered IA [V] 148697—had been used by the Fuhrer and although Hitler was photographed in a series of different Mercedes 770K Grosser Offener Tourenwagen in the late 1930s and early 1940s this one was of a unique specification built specifically for him.

That two of the car's occupants would be dead before the end of the war, one in a Soviet prison for 10 years and the other two captured by the Americans and that the car itself would go on to serve briefly as a US Army staff car tells you everything you need to know about the fate of the supposedly 1000-year Reich—

Hitler's day had begun as usual. Rising at 11 he had been served breakfast in bed by Linge before having the latter use a stopwatch to time his getting dressed. The armoured Mercedes had arrived from the Daimler-Benz factory in Stuttgart on 8 July and had been delivered to the Reichs Chancellery carpool. The car had a number of distinctive features. It had 2.5 cm bullet-proof glass and 0.6 cm armour plating in the doors and floors. It weighed in at a colossal 4.1 tonnes.

The dash compartment contained stowage for two machine pistols and there were two similar compartments in the rear. Externally the car differed from other 770 Grossers in the carpool used by Hitler in that it featured rounded rear, bullet-proof, quarter windows, four vents below the windscreen, a plain grille with a starting handle (although probably ornamental) hole and 20 ventilation louvres on each side of the bonnet top.

The louvres were to keep the 230 bhp 7.7 litre straight eight engine cool. Due to its huge weight, the cars top speed was 150 kph (93 mph) Using the newest car was very much in tune with Hitler's plan for the day which was a celebratory mass promotion of twelve of his Generals who had distinguished themselves during the recent victory in the Battle of France, to the rank of Field Marshall. The car duly arrived at the Chancellery driven by Kempka and travelled via Potsdamer Platz to the Kroll Opera House in the Tiergarten.

This was a symbolic as it marked the final repudiation of the restrictions placed on Germany by the Treaty of Versailles after World War I. A month earlier on 22 June Hitler had forced France sign an armistice in the same railway carriage that Germany had been forced to sign in in 1918. The Treaty of Versailles had placed strict controls on the German Army including a prohibition on the appointment of Field Marshalls.

Although Hitler had already breached this condition as early as 1936, the 19 July ceremony was intended to bury it definitively. Following the military success in France and the Low Countries Hitler had decided to raise morale by promoting 12 Generals to the most senior rank. This was more than just an honorific title. Field Marshalls were entitled to a tax-free salary of 36,000 Reichsmarks for life.

By promoting individuals for their success on the battlefield Hitler boosted the prestige of his armed forces—something which following the string of defeats from 1943 onwards he would move away from, instead taking decisions himself. Given this it is not surprising that two of the twelve promoted that day would become involved in the von Stauffenberg 20 July 1944 plot to assassinate Hitler.

One—Gunher von Kluge committed suicide by taking a cyanide capsule while the second—Erwin von Witzleben was stripped of his rank, tried in a civilian court and executed. Goering—who was already a Field Marshall—was given an extra promotion to the newly created rank of Reichsmarshall making him the most senior member of the military while at the same time avoiding putting him in command of either the Army and Navy.

The choice of venue—the Kroll Opera House—the temporary seat of the Reichstag following the 1933 fire—provided a powerful reminder of Hitler's rise to power. By setting fire to the Reichstag and blaming it on a Dutch Communist Marinus van der Lubbe, the Nazis had persuaded the German President, von Hindenburg, to pass an emergency decree under Article 48 of the Weimar Constitution suspending civil liberties and leading to mass arrests of Communist Party delegates.

Thereby giving the Nazis a majority in the Reichstag which Hitler subsequently used to pass the Enabling Act of 23 March 1933 making himself Chancellor and effectively dictator. The Reichstag was transferred to the Kroll Opera House from 1933–1942.

Both buildings were scheduled for demolition as part of Albert Speer's Welthaupstadt Germania redevelopment plans. The Kroll itself was to be replaced with a Fuhrer's palace. The Reichstag itself was suspended on 26 April

1942 when Hitler passed a decree making himself "supreme judge of the German people". While Hitler laid waste to Germany's democratic structures, RAF Bomber Command devastated the Kroll building in a raid on 23 November 1943. The ruins were eventually demolished in 1951.

What then of IA ^{V} 148697? The car was one of at least seven used by Hitler but as stated previously had many special features. With the Soviets advancing on Berlin in early 1945, it was loaded onto a flat-bed railway truck and taken south to Berchtesgaden in the upper Bavarian Alps, presumably for safe storage or perhaps as an escape vehicle.

The area famously was the site of Hitler's summer retreat in the Obersalzberg above the town—the Berghof. And where Hitler went other prominent Nazis were sure to follow. Hermann Goering, Joseph Goebbels, Martin Bormann, Heinrich Himmler and Albert Speer all also chose to purchase and requisition land in the area: something that would subsequently lead to confusion as to the identity of the original owner of IA ^{V} 148697.

On 6 May 1945 in the last days of the war the US 20th Armoured Division was fighting in the area north of Salzburg when technical Sergeant Joe Azara noticed a large car on a flat-bed railway truck in a siding near the town of Laufen. The car was tied down with wire cables to stop it moving in transit. In the ensuing firefight, the car was hit by various stray bullets—three to its bullet-proof windscreen, one to its dashboard and five or six to the bullet-proof side passenger window.

Nevertheless, once the US troops had mopped up the remaining German resistance Sgt Azara was able to get the car unloaded from the truck. The engine was also damaged but fortunately Sgt Azara was able to locate a spare of the same specification in the garages of the Berghof. On making enquiries he was, erroneously, informed by a Dutch prisoner that the car was broken and had been sent from Berchtesgarten because Goering no longer wanted it.

Sadly, for Sgt Azara he was not allowed to keep his find. It was passed to headquarters where it was repainted olive drab with stencilled US five pointed white stars on its rear doors and pressed into service as a VIP staff car. The car was subsequently shipped to the US for a tour of the country as "Herman Goering's car" as part of a fundraising drive for US War Bonds.

Having been put into storage, the car eventually emerged in a US Army surplus auction held at the Aberdeen Proving Ground in Maryland in the autumn of 1956. It was advertised as "Herman Goering's car" and was bought by R J Rumble for H J O'Connell a collector from Montreal for $2725.

O'Connell had the car restored at a cost of $5000 Canadian dollars by a Toronto specialist Rumble Motors back to its 1945 colour and specification using photographs of similar cars—hence the subsequent incorrect addition of a centre spotlight in front of the radiator. Mr O'Connell sold the car to Claude Pratte, a Quebecoise industrialist, who eventually offered it to the Canadian War Museum in Ottawa in 1969 in return for a tax break.

The museum was distinctly unenthusiastic given the car's doubtful provenance as "Herman Goering's car". As a result, Lee Murray from the museum wrote to R J Rumble noting that the car was, in fact, one of seven delivered to the German Army in 1940 and used by Hitler in his public appearances.

Rumble replied maintaining that the car was Goering's but included two crucial pieces of information: its chassis number 429334 embossed on a plate on the bulkhead of the engine bay; and its original registration number IA ^{V} 148697. Murray wrote to Mercedes Benz in Stuttgart with this asking them to check their factory records.

Getting no response, he contacted the German Ambassador in Ottawa who passed the request to the German Defence Ministry who contacted Mercedes-Benz. Murray received a reply from the Military Attache at the Embassy on 12 June 1970 that the car had been "delivered to the Chancellery of Adolf Hitler on 8 July 1940". Added to this the car had been sent to Daimler-Benz for repairs on 19 April 1943 and returned to the Chancellery on 15 September 1943. The museum proceeded with the acquisition yet oddly, given this information, decided to display the car as having belonged to "Herman Goering".

A German named Ludwig Kosche who worked at the Museum as its librarian was not convinced. Using his meticulous and methodical librarian skills and his German language he decided to investigate further. Kosche discovered that the car's link with Goering had long been in doubt. It had perhaps been perpetuated as a result of a mistake at the auction by R J Rumble who was bidding on O'Connel's behalf.

This happened because the auction featured two other cars captured by the 101st Airbourne—a 540K "the Blue Goose" and a 770 Offener Tourenwagen which had both been used by Goering. It is reasonable to assume that Rumble believed it was this 770 that he had purchased for O'Connell and that when the car was subsequently stripped of its 18 layers of paint, Rumble assumed that the US applied Olive Drab was in fact Luftwaffe grey.

However, Kosche spoke to Kempke, Hitler's driver who confirmed that the armoured 770 Grosser was never used in battlefield situations and would not therefore have been painted in camouflage at any point in its period of service. Kosche also went back through the Museum's files finding Lee Murray's correspondence and a letter dated 1971 from a member of the public casting doubt on the link with Goering given that Goering's Mercedes was owned by a museum in the UK and had three door hinges whereas the Ottawa car had only two.

This suggested that the Ottawa car was more heavily armoured, suggesting it was used by someone more important. By 1979 the Museum had dropped the reference to Goering all together and simply labelled the exhibit as "German Army Staff Car".

Kosche's investigation definitively proved the car to have been used by Hitler. The original rear number plate had been painted over during the restoration to make it appear that the car had a Luftwaffe series registration plate (beginning with WL instead of IA). He also trawled through photographic archives to unearth photographs of Hitler in the car thereby proving that the car in the museum was the same car and that Hitler, not Goering, used it.

The Kroll Opera House photos are the first record of the car being used but Kosche also found photographs of Hitler travelling in the car on 10 September 1941 during a visit to Marienbad; on 28 November 1941, when he attended the funeral of Werner Mölders; and on 15 March 1942, when he gave a speech in Berlin.

On top of this Kosche found photos of the car painted in US Olive Drab being unloaded from the troopship George Shiras in Boston early August 1945. These photos showed the distinctive bullet damage to the passenger window and twin heavy duty door hinges. Despite Kosche publishing his findings in 1982, it took until 1984 for the public information about the car to be altered in the museum. The car remains on permanent display.

Mercedes 770 Series Grosser

The Mercedes-Benz 770 Grosser was a model built between 1930 to 1943 and is closely associated with senior members of the Nazi Party. The car was the replacement for the Mercedes 630 and was targeted at the top end

Royalty/Presidents and Heads of Government market. The price was "auf anfrage" (by request) and it was the most expensive German car of its era. Before Hitler's rise to power in 1933 the German President Paul von Hindenburg used one.

Hitler, seeing the prestige and power-projection potential of the car, had adopted the model as early as 1931. The first series, known as the W07 was built up until 1938. This was succeeded by the Series II W150—of the same type as IA ^{V} 148697. In total only 205 cars were made over the thirteen year period. Three body styles were offered—a four door, six seat, hard top Pullman; a six seat Touring car (as Hitler's) or a Cabriolet.

The car was rear wheel drive and powered by the legendary 7655cc overhead cam straight eight-cylinder supercharged Mercedes engine. The engine featured aluminium pistons and for the Series II cars was capable of producing 155bhp in un-aspirated format and 230bhp with the aid of a Roots supercharger. The un-armoured Series II had a top speed in excess of 100 mph.

The basic construction of the Series I cars was robust with a steel box girder chassis and suspension by semi-eliptic leaf springs and beam axles. A new improved chassis was designed for the Series II cars made of tubular construction with coil springs all round, independent suspension at the front and a de Dion axle at the rear. The W150 model was fractionally longer than its predecessor and nine inches wider.

In addition, it had a five speed gearbox (with an overdrive fifth) as opposed to the four speed of the earlier cars. IA ^{V} 148697 is one of only 88 W150 Series II cars built. The most recent of Hitler's 770 Grossers-IA ^{V} 148461: the car that carried Hitler and Mussolini through the streets of Munich in 1939—to be offered at auction was bought by an anonymous buyer in March 2018 for a reported $7 million. 10% of the proceeds of the sale were donated to Holocaust education.

The Grosser model was revived in the 1960s with the Mercedes 600 (W100) luxury limousine. Although this vehicle attracted pop star buyers such as John Lennon, David Bowie and Elvis Presley, its political customers often fell into the genocidal dictator category—Pol Pot, Kim Jung il, Idi Amin, Robert Mugabe and Saddam Hussein—rather like the keenest buyers of its first incarnation.

Daimler-Benz

Daimler—Benz was formed by an "Agreement of Mutual Interest" of 1 May 1924 between the German motor manufacturers Benz and Cie and Daimler Motoren Gesellschaft (see Chapter 1) Under the agreement both companies continued to manufacture their own models and engines until 28 June 1926 when the formal merger took place.

The economic climate in the Weimar Republic and hyperinflation resulting from Germany's decision to fund the First World War exclusively from debt and the crushing reparations payments imposed on the country after its defeat in 1918 created tough conditions for luxury car manufacturers. The merger made economic sense and, from that point on, all products were badged "Mercedes-Benz".

The name "Mercedes" came from the most important Daimler model—the Mercedes series—designed and manufactured by Wilhelm Maybach. Mercedes was in fact the name of the engine of a race car that Daimler had produced in 1900 for Emil Jellinek to the latter's design. Jellinek insisted the name of his daughter—Mercedes—should feature in the name of the car's engine—Daimler-Mercedes.

The cars went on to considerable success in competition and were commonly known as the Mercedes 35hp. As a result, Daimler had begun producing cars from 1902 bearing the Mercedes name—indeed, bizarrely, Daimler had sold the rights to the Daimler marque after Gottlieb Daimler's death in 1900 to the Daimler Motor Company in the UK (see Chapter 1)

Following the merger, the new company unveiled an entirely new model range at the October 1926 Berlin Motor Show including the 8/38hp two-litre car (W 02) and the 12/55hp three-litre model (W 03) The famous three-pointed star logo—used as a radiator cap ornament—had been trademarked by Gottlief Daimler's sons, Paul and Adolf, as early as 1909. In 1927 the model 'K', a short wheelbase, supercharged variant of the W03 became the fastest touring car in the world. These models were constantly improved and updated.

In the interwar period Mercedes achieved considerable success on the racetrack. The Mercedes Benz 150 (W30) sports saloon of 1934 featured a light weight mid mounted 55bhp 1.5 litre engine making it a formidable race car. By 1937 the Mercedes W125 effectively dominated international motorsport and the company was poised to try to take the land speed record with the Porsche designed T80—a 650km/h twelve-cylinder, 44.5 litre, 3450 bhp monster—before the outbreak of the Second World war.

During World War II the company not only produced luxury cars such as the 770K but also built engines for German aircraft—notably the Messerschmitt 109 fighter—U Boats and tanks as well as making barrels for Mauser rifles. During this period the company used the labour of more than 40,000 concentration camp prisoners. Mercedes subsequently paid more than $12 million in reparations to the surviving families of the prisoners.

After the war Mercedes rebuilt its shattered manufacturing capacity. The W186 four door limousine of 1951–1957 re-launched the company into the luxury car market. This was replaced from 1957 by the WW189—the so called "Adenaur" after the West German leader of the period. As well as limousines, during the 1950s Mercedes-Benz launched a new range of stylish cars including the 190 and the 300 SL. "Gullwing"—the first production vehicle to feature fuel-injection. Mercedes' success continued in the 1960s with the 220, the 230 and the new 600, (W100) Grosser.

However, the revival of its pre-war racing success was brought to an abrupt halt in 1955 when a catastrophic incident led the company to close down its Competitions Department for forty years. The accident happened at Le Mans in 1955 when Pierre Levegh's Mercedes 300SLR crashed into Lance Macklin's Austin Healey, causing a fireball that not only killed Levegh, but also 80 spectators. It was 1995 before Mercedes re-entered competitive motorsport, supplying engines for the McLaren Formula One team.

In 2010, it bought out the Brawn Formula One team the reigning world champions and transformed it into a new Mercedes Benz factory team.

Chapter 9
1943 MB Jeep

It is 1 January 1945. There is snow on the ground—it is winter—yet the US Army MB Jeep is open to the elements. There is a man sitting in the front seat in a sheepskin Irvin flying jacket with a standard issue US army M1 steel helmet strapped tightly on his head. The helmet has three silver stars riveted to its front. In the rear of the jeep is a GI there to operate the M1919 .30 calibre Browning machine gun.

However, a closer look reveals that this is no ordinary Jeep. For a start the mudguards at the rear are a different shape. The passenger seat just has a higher, more curved, back than a standard Jeep front seat. Out of shot, there are two large Buell trombone air-horns mounted on top of the bonnet. The front wing has a rigid flag attached with three stars and an identical flag is mounted above the front bumper in front of the radiator grille. This is the Jeep of General George S

Patton and the location is Bastogne in the Ardennes. The man in the passenger seat is the General himself.

The fact that Patton's Jeep is there at all is testament to the talent and determination of one of the greatest US military commanders in history. The modifications are also an indication of the personality of its owner—part showman, part maverick but 100% a soldier's soldier.

Patton had been an early adopter—and customizer—of the Jeep. An earlier iteration—the "War Eagle"—had featured an elongated rear body tub, thickly padded leather front and rear seats and saloon car like sweeping rear wings. This vehicle survives in the General George Patton Museum of leadership in Fort Knox.

The Jeep in the photo is a later iteration with more restrained and subtle modifications carried out by Patton's personal driver and mechanic Francis "Jeep" Sanza. Sanza had been one of the original test drivers of the prototype Jeep when it had been delivered to the US Army for evaluation in 1941, earning his nickname after successfully driving the vehicle through a lake underwater and emerging dripping wet on the other side.

Sanza not only knew everything there was to know about driving a Jeep but was also a talented mechanic who could take the engine out of one in under 40 minutes and repair it in the field. Sanza's modifications to the Bastogne Jeep included bulletproof glass (windscreen and side screens) rear wheel arch flares, the customary twin Buell air-horns, a high-back leather passenger seat, a Browning M1919 machine gun and upgraded engine.

Patton believed strongly that as a Commander he needed to be visible to his men, leading from the front. His choice of clothing and weaponry—ivory handled Colt revolvers in Wild West style holsters (something he had adopted early on in his career after an Army issue Colt tucked into his waistband had accidentally gone off) a sheepskin Irvin flying jacket, sunglasses and a chrome plated steel helmet—were all designed to convey the image of a maverick.

The Jeep, with its blaring air-horns and three star red and white flags was a means of further enhancing his visibility—as much a showman's mount as a practical military piece of equipment. The Bastogne Jeep still survives today in the American Armoury Museum in Fairfield California.

Patton was old school—nicknamed "old blood and guts" by his men he commanded great respect as someone who would not ask his troops to do what he wasn't prepared to do himself. Born in 1885 in San Gabriel California, into a military family who had served on both sides of the US Civil War, Patton was greatly interested in classical military history as a child. He attended the Virginia Military Institute and West Point Military Academy where he graduated 46th of 103 cadets and was commissioned as a Second Lieutenant in the Cavalry.

In 1911, he was posted to Fort Myer where his leadership qualities caught the eye of Henry Stimson, the Secretary for War. Posted to the 8th Cavalry at Fort Bliss in Texas in 1915, Patton was on border patrol duty at the time of Pancho Villa's (see Chapter 5) cross border raid on the border town of Colombus and took part in the Pancho Villa Expedition, having lobbied its commander, John Pershing, to do so. Here he organised the first ever US Army motorised attack using three Dodge Model 30-35 touring cars, winning him a promotion.

During the First World War Patton was on General Pershing's staff and was promoted to Captain in May 1917 before being posted to France as part of the US Expeditionary Force. In November 1917 Patton was responsible for setting up the American Expeditionary Force's Light Tank Regiment. By August 1918, Patton had been promoted to Major and was in charge of 304th Tank Brigade, a part of the US First Army.

In common with the approach he would later take during the relief of Bastogne, Patton took personal charge of the logistics for the tanks during the battle of Saint Mihiel on 12 September. He was later wounded while leading six men and a tank during an attack on a German machine gun emplacement as part of the Meuse-Argonne Offensive. After the War, Patton became a key advocate of tank warfare. Both he and Eisenhower—who he befriended—advocated the development of US armoured capabilities.

However, budgets were tight and Patton was returned to the Cavalry and to the Command and General Staff College where he graduated in mid 1924. Following promotion to Lieutenant Colonel in 1934 he was posted to the Hawaiian Division in early 1935. He was promoted again to Colonel in July 1938 and caught the eye of the Army Chief of Staff George C Marshall who recognised his talent and spotted his potential as a future General.

It is fair to say that peacetime did not suit Patton's personality and the post September 1939 general mobilisation came both as a relief and as an opportunity for him to try to strengthen US Armoured Divisions.

During exercises in 1939, Patton worked closely with Lieutenant General Adna Chaffee Jr and together they drew up proposal for what became the 1st and 2nd US Armoured Divisions. As a result, he was promoted to Brigadier and put in charge of training the 2nd Armoured Division before being promoted to Major General and made Commanding General of the Division. There then followed months of large-scale exercises and training during which Patton learned how to fly to be able to observe the Division's movements from the air and to improve tactics and techniques.

His obsessive and meticulous approach to logistics coupled with bold strategy and rapid offensive movement earned him many plaudits as well as a key role in Operation Torch—the allied invasion of French North Africa in 1942—and a further promotion to Lieutenant General. However, his judgement was questioned when, during the invasion of Sicily in July 1943, his military success was marred by an incident where he slapped and verbally abused two soldiers suffering from Post-Traumatic Stress Disorder.

Partly as a result, Patton's subordinate Omar Bradley was put in command of the US First Army for Operation Overlord—the Normandy landings—while Patton was given command of the newly formed Third Army in England.

Nevertheless, Patton's genius was clear—and, if not always recognised by his own side, at least by his German counterparts including Rommel (See Chapter 7). His preferred mix of rapid offensive action backed by aerial reconnaissance and support, forward scout units and military intelligence and underpinned by excellent logistics made the Third Army both a unique and potent fighting force. It also made Patton particularly well informed and therefore able to spot patterns that his fellow commanders missed.

His innate understanding of the key US strengths in the campaign—air superiority and mobility—allowed the Third Army to advance further and faster than his Allied contemporaries at least until he ran out of fuel at the end of August 1944. To his great frustration and at the cost of US lives, supplies had been prioritised for Montgomery's unsuccessful "Operation Market Garden", leading to the Third Army being halted for most of the month of September 1944 and allowing the Germans time to regroup in the fortress of Metz.

Despite taking this objective—albeit at considerable cost—the lack of supplies continued to slow his advance between early November and mid December 1944. With time on his hands, Patton studied the intelligence and cross-referenced it with what he knew from his own aerial reconnaissance and forward scouts. So, when the Germans counterattacked with 29 Divisions and 250,000 men on 16 December 1944 in the Ardennes, Patton was both less surprised, but also crucially better prepared, than most.

Despite being engaged in fighting close to Saarbrucken, Patton had ordered his staff to make three separate plans to rapidly pivot his forces towards the "Bulge" which the German advance had made in the Allied front. Thus, when Eisenhower asked him at a meeting of senior Allied commanders on 19 December how long it would take to disengage six Divisions and to counterattack in the North to relieve the 101st Airbourne Division who were besieged in Bastogne, Patton was able confidently to reply: "As soon as you are through with me."

Unaware of Patton's prior contingency planning, Eisenhower didn't believe him. Patton revealed that he had already planned a counterattack by three full Divisions on 21 December. Eisenhower, still doubtful, proposed the morning of 22 December as the date for the counterattack. Such was the level of forward planning that, as Patton left the meeting, he needed only to phone through the order "Play ball" to his Headquarters to set one of the greatest feats of military logistics in history in motion.

The effect was immediately to trigger three Divisions to turn on their heels and move North to Bastogne. However, conscious of the risk of being out-flanked, in total Patton moved six Divisions along a line running from Bastogne to Diekirch to Eternach in Luxembourg. This involved the incredible feat of re-routing 133,000 vehicles and 62,000 tonnes of supplies in less than 48 hours.

The day before the offensive Patton and Bradley met to discuss the plan with Patton famously remarked in his inimitable style: "Brad, this time the Kraut's stuck his head in the meat grinder—and I have hold of the handle—"

On the ground in Bastogne, the situation was increasingly desperate. Having successfully halted the German advance on 19–20 December by the clever and bold use of paratroopers and four M18 Hellcat tank destroyers of the 705th Tank Destroyer Batallion, the US had not only managed to destroy more than 30 German tanks but also to inflict between 500–1000 casualties. This had led the German Commander to assume that the village was being defended by a much stronger force.

The ensuing delay had allowed the 101st Airborne Division to organise its defences in a circle around Bastogne. It had also meant that the 2nd Panzer Division had used up a great deal of precious fuel keeping its engines ticking over and would subsequently run out at Celles, en route to its objective of the Meuse, allowing the 2nd US Armoured Division and the British 29th Armoured Brigade to halt the advance and to destroy it.

However, the presence of so many units around Bastogne meant that remaining US troops in the area—notably the 1st Battalion—had to fight their way back into Bastogne through the encircling German forces at heavy cost. The stage then was set for a brutal siege that was to last six days. The 101st Airborne organised the 506th Parachute Infantry Regiment, the 327th Infantry Regiment and assorted engineers and artillery units to form a perimeter around the outskirts of Bastogne.

Almost all of the medics had been killed in a German raid on the first night of the siege and all units were suffering from losses. The remaining tanks—40 light and medium—plus a further eight tanks from Bastogne were organised into a mobile force. In addition, a temporary artillery group was cobbled together and their 155mm howitzers were deployed as direct fire against German armoured units.

All seven roads into Bastogne were blocked by German forces and US troops were outnumbered 5:1, short of ammunition, of medical supplies and of food. The appalling winter weather and full cloud made re-supply by air impossible. The one thing that went in the defenders' favour was the German decision to allow two of the halted three Panzer divisions to resume their offensive towards the Meuse leaving only the 26th Volksgrenadier Division behind. Nevertheless, the resourcefulness of the US troops in shifting their limited resources to repel attack after attack was crucial.

An attempt by the German Commander, von Luttwitz, on 22 December to persuade the US forces to surrender was met with a short response from his American counterpart, General McAuliffe, reading simply "Nuts". The Germans therefore planned a full-scale assault to take the village on Christmas Day 1944. The Luftwaffe bombed the besieged Americans on Christmas Eve to soften up the US defences.

Due to a shortage of troops, the German attack did not take the form of a simultaneous assault on all fronts. Instead, the Germans attacked with 18 tanks and an infantry Battalion at a point held by the 3rd Battalion of the 327th Infantry regiment. The attack was repulsed and the Panzers that had made it through the perimeter were destroyed by 502nd Parachute Infantry Battalion and the four M13 Hellcats of the 705th Tank destroyer Battalion. The fighting continued throughout the day and night at various points around the perimeter but the US defences held.

On 26 December, the day after the German assault had begun, Patton's Third Army 4th Armoured Division arrived and punched a hole through the German lines encircling Bastogne. This allowed reinforcement and crucially resupply of the defending forces. The US 101st Airborne was awarded a Presidential Unit Citation for its heroic defence of Bastogne.

Patton later wrote that the relief of Bastogne was "the most brilliant operation we have thus far performed" and viewed it as "my biggest battle". Little did he know it at the time, but this was to be the case due to his un-timely death on 8 December 1945 following being paralysed in a freak, slow motion, car accident involving his staff car. Patton was buried with his men in the US military cemetery in Luxembourg.

1943 MB Jeep

Described in its patents as a "cargo truck, personnel carrier, emergency ambulance, radio car, trench mortar unit, mobile aircraft machine gun unit or for other purposes" the Jeep was a flexible and ubiquitous piece of kit of the Allied armies in World War Two. Present in every theatre—with more than 30% of production being supplied to the British and Soviet armies—at a rate of 145 per infantry Regiment—the Jeep was a versatile, reliable and trusty workhorse.

Pressed into service in 1941, the Jeep was arguably the first mass-produced four-wheel drive vehicle and the ancestor of all of today's modern equivalents. Its origins lay in a 1940 wartime US government tender issued to 135 US companies to build a working prototype four-wheel drive reconnaissance vehicle. There were two responses—from the American Bantam Car Company and from Willys-Overland. The deadline—49 days—was impossibly short.

Bantam, with the help of the US Army, drafted in designer Karl Probst from Detroit and work began on 17 July 1940. Two days later by 19 July, Probst had drawn up detailed plans and designs for the "Bantham Reconnaissance Car". Probst's design was submitted on 22 July—a mere five days after he had begun work—complete with blueprints. The genius of the design was that it used readily available off the shelf components with only the four-wheel drive parts needing to be specially made by Spicer.

On 23 September 1941 a fully working prototype was delivered to the US Army's Camp Holabird base in Maryland for testing. Apart from being under-powered it passed on all counts. Given the Army's requirement for mass production and the small-scale of Bantham's operation, the blueprints were also given to both Willy's Overland and to Ford to improve with the resulting Willys "Quad" and Ford Pygmy prototypes being produced.

The Army commissioned 1500 from each of the three manufacturers for further testing in the field. A change of specification to double the weight to 110kg allowed Willys to install its powerful "Go Devil" engine to create the Willys MB. This extra power and huge torque was exactly what the army was looking for and the contract was awarded Willys-Overland.

The need for maximise production as quickly as possible led Willys to allow the US Government to produce the vehicle with other manufacturers, thereby making Ford the second supplier.

Despite having designed the Jeep, Bantham manufactured only 2700 before its production lines were switched over to making trailers. Early Jeeps had subtle differences depending on whether they were manufactured by Willys (welded slat grille) or Ford (pressed slat grille) Keen to advertise their brands, both companies initially embossed the rear panel with their company names until the US government banned this in 1942. Interestingly no Jeep produced before 1945—when Willys launched a civilian version—the CJ (Civilian Jeep)—carried the Jeep name.

Opinion remains divided as to the origin of the word "Jeep". One school of thought is that it derives from the Ford name for the vehicle—"GP" (where G denotes government and P 80" wheelbase) or a shortening of "General Purpose" to "GP" as claimed by Joe Frazer the chairman of Willys-Overland from 1939 to 1944. Others claim that it was named after Popeye's jungle pet "Eugene the Jeep". However, the term "Jeep" was First World War US Army slang for an untested vehicle which seems more plausible.

Willys Overland

Willys Overland was formed when John Willys bought the Standard Wheel Company's Overland Automotive division in 1908. The name Willys-Overland first appeared in 1912 although the bulk of the cars it produced between 1912 and 1918 were badged Willys-Knight in recognition of the designer of the side valve engine with which they were fitted. Amazingly, Willys was the second (to Ford) largest US automotive manufacturer during this period.

During the Great Depression, Willys went into receivership and was forced to sell off most of its factories and to axe its model lines. By 1936 the company had been streamlined and reorganised as Willys—Overland Motors. The success of its re-designed 1937 four cylinder model allowed the company to introduce new innovations such as Lockheed hydraulic brakes for its 1939 model.

This success was also crucial to the Jeep since it allowed Willys to hire Joseph Frazer from Chrysler as Chief Executive who in turn hired Delmar Roos the ex-Studebaker Chief Engineer to set about improving the four cylinder engine. Roos spent two years redesigning the engine using higher quality materials and finer tolerances to reduce its weight, increase its power and most importantly improve its reliability to be able to run for 150 hours without maintenance or failure. The end result was the legendary "Go Devil" engine which became the standard fitment of all production World War 2 Jeeps.

During the War Willys not only built Jeeps but also airframes for the JB-2 Loon—an American copy of the German V1 Flying Bomb which the US planned to use in the war against Japan. Willys Overland filed the trademark application for the "Jeep" brand in February 1943 but this was opposed by Bantham on the grounds that they had actually designed the vehicle.

The Federal Trade Commission initially found in favour of Bantham and were greatly irritated by Willy's shameless use of the Jeep in wartime advertising, even going as far as to serve the company with a "cease and desist" order on all claims that it "designed" or "created" the vehicle. Willys eventually got around this because it was the only manufacturer of civilian Jeeps after the War and was able to copyright the word "Jeep" in 1946. As a result, it was granted the trademark in 1950.

Post War, Willys concentrated its production exclusively on Jeeps—both civilian and military. The Civilian C2A spawned variants such as a station wagon and a truck. Willys re-entered the car market in 1952 with the Willys Aero. However, Willys was acquired the following year by Kaiser. This was also the same year it had established a production operation in Brazil which provided an important base both for Jeep production for the South American market and also later for Brazilian production of the Renault A108 Alpine under the brand name Interlagos.

In the US, the Willys brand survived until 1963 when it was dropped in favour of the "Kaiser-Jeep Corporation". The "Jeep" brand lives on having passed through the ownership of the American Motors Corporation (AMC) Renault, DaimlerChrysler and today resides with Fiat (See Chapter 18).

Chapter 10
1954 Series 1 Land Rover

It was a cold morning in the rolling Kent countryside, hardly surprising given it was Tuesday 30 November 1954. Christmas was in touching distance, but the presents had come early to the elderly gentleman in the heavy tweed overcoat with the large sheepskin collar.

It was his 80th birthday and he had risen, washed and dressed in a pinstriped suit as usual, put on the heavy overcoat and a Homburg hat and now walked across the gravel outside his country home, Chartwell near Westerham, towards the waiting bank of photographers and the brand-new Bronze Green Series 1 Land Rover, registration number UKE 80, that had been parked in front of the house.

As he made his way slowly to the car, he puffed a long Romeo y Julietta Cuban cigar making him look almost steam driven from a distance. He was followed by an energetic little poodle named Rufus. He stopped by the driver's door of the Land Rover and obligingly looked at the cameras, a twinkle in his eye as he drew on the cigar.

The man was of course the UK Prime Minister Sir Winston Churchill and the car was an 80th birthday present from the Rover company in Solihull. These after all were the days before strict ethics rules would forbid the acceptance of such a generous and valuable gift by a serving British Prime Minister.

The car was specially modified by Rover to have a separate wide passenger seat to accommodate the Prime Minister's ever-increasing girth and a separate seat for his driver rather than the standard front bench seat. In addition, the car was fitted with a special heater system for the passenger footwell to keep the elderly Sir Winston warm as he was being driven around the Chartwell grounds. Rover arranged for the car to be registered locally in Kent in the name of "Rt Hon Sir Winston Spencer Churchill KG. OM. CH. MP. Chartwell, Westerham, Kent."

The fact that the 80-year-old Churchill was Prime Minister or indeed that he was still alive at all, were due to a combination of toughness and good luck. Sir Winston was nearing the end of a long and distinguished political career and had, for a while, been receiving polite hints, including from the late King, that perhaps the time for retirement had come. Health-wise he had survived a second debilitating stroke the previous year so was lucky to still be living.

But this was a man not known for his propensity to give up in the face of unfavourable odds. Having defeated the Nazis in the Second World War, his reward in the 1945 UK General Election had been to suffer a crushing defeat when a country weary with the austerity and privations of war had voted by a landslide in favour of a Labour government headed by his former wartime deputy Clement Atlee.

Churchill had, briefly, thought this would be his last period as Prime Minister and had said as much to Anthony Eden his Deputy. Not one to quit easily—if indeed at all—he had not however stepped down as Leader of the Conservative Party as expected but had weathered five years as Leader of the Opposition.

In his spare time, he had written a six-volume history of the Second World War. But he also remained an influential and respected international statesman during the five years including famously coining the term "Iron Curtain", securing a permanent seat on the UN Security Council for France and, according to a declassified FBI memo, urging the President of the United States to launch a pre-emptive nuclear strike against Russia.

By 1951 the mood in the country had changed and the Conservatives under Churchill were victorious in that year's General Election. Thereafter, things had not gone entirely smoothly for the Prime Minister. His attempts to re-launch a 'special relationship' with the new US President Dwight D Eisenhower had largely been rebuffed with the US viewing Churchill's Imperial view of the world as outdated and irrelevant. Churchill's subsequent opportunistic attempt at rapprochement with the Soviet Union following Stalin's death in 1953 had also played badly in Washington.

Two major colonial foreign policy crises had also weighed heavily in this period—the Mau rebellion in Kenya and the Malaya crisis. In Kenya the Mau uprising had led to the imposition of a state of emergency in October 1952 with British Troops deployed. The escalating violence came to a head in 1953 when the Mau massacred the Kikuyu who were loyal to the British.

Churchill's response was a combination of a 'hearts and minds' campaign coupled with a hard military response in the shape of "Operation Anvil" in 1954 which defeated the rebellion in Nairobi. The Malaya crisis was one Churchill had inherited from his predecessor and had begun in 1948. The tactics employed by the Prime Minister were the same with 40,000 British and Commonwealth troops deployed on the ground.

In both cases the underlying cause was that the days of colonial rule were rapidly drawing to a close. The world had been changed radically by the Second World War and Britain's colonies were simply not prepared to pick up where they had left off in 1939. Like the Prime Minister himself there was a sense of "fin de siècle" in the air—the old order was changing and within a few years the last vestiges of it would be swept away forever.

As if all of this global change were not enough to deal with, Churchill's health was not what it had once been. On holiday in the South of France in 1949, Churchill had suffered a minor stroke which had been kept out of the news. The strain of being Prime Minister again coupled with a diet that included steak and kidney pudding, chocolate, Pol Roger Champagne and Cuban cigars on a daily basis made him a prime candidate for a repeat. In June 1953 while hosting a dinner at Downing Street the guests had left the table to adjourn for a nightcap, but he had remained motionless.

Fortunately, while none of the dinner guests noticed, his Private Secretary Jock Colville and his son in law Christopher Soames who were also at the dinner did. "I think the Prime Minister is ill," Soames said diplomatically to Colville—

by this time the left side of Churchill's mouth had dropped and saliva had begun to run from the corner. Churchill's Doctor was called and the Prime Minister moved and made comfortable upstairs. The dinner guests were simply informed that the Prime Minister sent his apologies but had been called away on urgent business.

The next morning Churchill had been moved to Chartwell and following a visit by his Doctor and a leading neurologist they had drawn up a short statement stating: "the Prime Minister has had no respite for a long time from his arduous duties and there has developed a disturbance of the cerebral circulation which has resulted in acts of giddiness."

The draft text was submitted to two of Churchill's most trusted Cabinet colleagues, R.A. Butler and Lord Salisbury, for approval. Reasoning that the original version would effectively end Churchill's career and could in turn trigger a General Election, they shortened the statement to read: "The Prime Minister has had no respite for a long time from his arduous duties and is in need of a complete rest".

The true state of Churchill's health was kept secret by this duo, including from the rest of the Cabinet.

When asked about the Prime Minister's health five days later, Churchill's spokesman said on the record that: "there is no suggestion that the Prime Minister is suffering from any specific ailment". Churchill's diary was cleared. Butler took on the day to day running of government business while high level meetings and summits, such as one scheduled with Eisenhower, were postponed. The general public spotted nothing amiss. June turned into July and behind the scenes Churchill was fighting hard to regain the power of speech and movement in his left side.

His recovery was remarkable by any standards but for a 78 year old man with an unhealthy lifestyle in post war austerity Britain it was little short of miraculous and reflected his inner strength and determination. By mid-July he was well enough to return to work and was photographed leaving Downing Street looking perfectly normal. The summer was as usual spent in the South of France convalescing further.

His formal return to public life and his Prime Ministerial duties came in October 1953 when he made a speech at the Conservative Party Conference in Margate. Many within the Party—and particularly Eden who had his eyes on the leadership and on becoming Prime Minister—expected this to be the point that

Churchill announced his retirement. They were disappointed. Churchill would serve for another year and four months. During this time Eden would become the heir apparent and a high-profile international statesman.

Following a dinner at Downing Street attended by the Queen and the Duke of Edinburgh on 3 April 1955, Churchill finally retired as Prime Minister on 4 April 1955 but remained an MP for Woodford until the 1964 General Election in the year of his 90th birthday. He became Father of the House in 1959 and was the only MP who had first been elected under Queen Victoria and was still serving under Queen Elizabeth II. Churchill spent most of his retirement after leaving Downing Street at Chartwell, his country home near Westerham in Kent where UKE 80 was used as a—chauffeur-driven—runabout in the grounds.

Land Rover

Rover had begun as a bicycle manufacturer and had produced the arguably the first modern bicycle in 1885—the Rover Safety Bicycle. About this time the company turned its attention to the emerging opportunities offered by the motorcycle and motor car. The result was a production switch beginning in 1899, which resulted in the advanced Rover Imperial motorcycle which featured a centrally mounted engine and sprung forks much like a modern motorbike. After a year of production and despite good sales, Rover switched its attention again to motorcars only resuming motorcycle production in 1910.

From 1901 Rover began making two seater Rover 8 cars. Rover added to the model range until 1912 when the success of the 12hp Tourer led to Rover adopting a one model policy. Production switched to trucks and ambulances during the First World War. The 1920s and 30s were not particularly good for Rover with the company paying no dividend to its shareholders from 1923 until the mid-1930s.

During this time, Rover was running at a loss and brought in new management in the shape of Frank Searle from Daimler and Spencer Wilks from Hillman to try to turn the company round. This duo was joined by Spencer Wilk's brother Maurice—a talented designer. Together they decided to re-orientate the business towards the more luxury end of the market introducing the Rover Ten 6 light saloon in 1936 and the Rover 16 (the "P3") in 1938.

The Second World War was kind to Rover with the company benefitting from the government decision to pursue rearmament and to build "shadow" factories for private companies to run. Rover was the beneficiary of two such factories—the first built in 1937 at Acocks Green in Birmingham and the second in Solihull in 1940. This was just as well given that the original Rover factory in Coventry was destroyed in a German bombing raid in 1940.

Rover built aircraft engines throughout the war and was given the task of developing Frank Whittle's jet engine from 1940 onwards. This was done in a disused cotton mill in Barnoldswick in Lancashire. Relations between Rover and Whittle broke down over the former's unhappiness at Rover's unauthorised modification of his design. The result was a swap of shadow factories with Rolls Royce (See Chapter 4)—the latter gaining the Barnoldswick jet engine factory in return for a tank engine factory in Nottingham which went to Rover.

After the war Rolls Royce continued to make jet engines for aircraft. Rover gave up its badly damaged Coventry factory and took advantage of the government's subsidised offer to buy the two shadow factories it had been operating. Thus, Rover continued making the Meteor tank engine used in the Centurion tank in the former shadow factory at Acocks Green until 1964. Car production was switched to Solihull—the other shadow factory it had been running where Bristol aircraft engines had been built.

It was in Solihull that the development and production of the Land Rover would be based and would become Rover's most profitable and successful vehicle through the merger with the British Motor Corporation to create British Leyland, the subsequent restructuring to form Austin Rover, the eventual formation of Rover and its subsequent sale to BMW who broke up the unwieldy and unprofitable company, selling Land Rover as a separate entity to Ford in 2000.

1954 Series 1 Land Rover

By the time UKE 80 was registered at the end of 1954, the Series 1 Land Rover had been in production for six years.

The original concept was dreamed up by chief designer Maurice Wilks as a stop gap model to generate some funds to allow Rover to resume its luxury car manufacturing once domestic demand recovered. Wilks, who owned a farm on the island of Anglesey in North Wales, saw a market for an agricultural utility vehicle which combined the attributes of the US World War Two Jeep with some of the functions of a tractor.

Wilks himself had tested out the usefulness of such a vehicle by buying a US army surplus Willys Jeep (See Chapter 9) at the end of the war to use on his farm which he rated highly for its versatility and ruggedness but less highly for its reliability. He also had an eye to Rover's Coventry based rivals Standard who had started production of the now legendary Ferguson TE20 tractor in a former shadow factory they had bought at Canley in Coventry.

Part of the Ferguson's appeal was its innovative power take off from the rear differential allowing a huge range of farm machinery and implements to be powered from a single machine. In Wilk's mind he conceived a Jeep-like vehicle capable of carrying livestock, grain, milk churns or any manner of farm implements, which also incorporated a power take off thereby delivering the best of both.

His starting point was to buy a decommissioned Jeep and give it to a team led by Rover's Chief Engineer Arthur Goddard to remove the body tub and replace the engine and transmission with that from the Rover P3 saloon car. Given the intended use the vehicle should be extremely robust and simple to repair. The bodywork was therefore to be of a simple sectional design with flat surfaces and compound curves so no specialist tools would be needed to mend it.

Post war steel rationing led to the use of an aluminium magnesium alloy, called "Birm-a-bright" developed for the wartime aircraft industry and consequently available in large quantities. This also carried the double advantage of being very light and also not susceptible to rust unlike steel, meaning that any knocks sustained by the vehicle during agricultural use would not need to be repaired and repainted.

The colour range was equally military surplus driven: bronze green, light green and mid grey were all RAF paint colours used to paint the outside and interiors of wartime aircraft and were readily and cheaply available.

The first prototypes were built by Goddard's team on a simple galvanised steel ladder chassis—again for durability and ease of repair. These were tested in 1947. The original idea of having the steering wheel in the centre of the vehicle, meaning that it would not need to be re-tooled for export markets, was dropped at this point in favour of a conventional right-hand drive arrangement.

By contrast, the innovative power take-off was retained. The tried and tested pre-war 1.6 litre Rover "P3" engine was used. At the same time, Rover developed its own transfer gearbox to allow the vehicle to switch to four-wheel drive. The, retrospectively-named, Series 1 Land Rover was launched at the Amsterdam Motor Show on 30 April 1948—less than a year from Goddard's first prototype.

The three cars for the show were driven to Amsterdam from London rather than being trailered there like modern day exhibits. The first batch of 48 cars were priced at £450 each.

UKE 80 is a late 1954 built Land Rover in the revised 86-inch (2.18m) wheelbase. It has the standard 1.6 litre Rover "P3" derived petrol engine producing 50 bhp coupled to a four-speed gearbox (again from the Rover "P3") and a two-speed transfer gearbox. This set up includes the Rover designed freewheel unit which disengages the front axle from the transmission on the overrun giving a form of permanent front wheel drive in addition to a differential lock mechanism in the driver's footwell allowing the freewheel to be locked.

It is a standard model fitted with the optional door tops with sliding windows, spare wheel, passenger seat cushions and the canvas tilt (all still extras in 1954) The car features the later headlamp arrangement where the headlights are mounted in front of the grille rather than behind it as for the very early cars.

UKE 80 passed to Christoper Soames Churchill's son in law following his death and was sold at auction and bought by a farmer from Sevenoaks, Frank Quay, for £ 320. Mr Quay used the vehicle for its intended purpose on his farm. By 1977, "UKE 80" was off the road and stored in the corner of Mr Quay's barn only to re-emerge in 2011.

The vehicle had covered a mere 12,932 miles by the time it was auctioned by Cheffins in 2012, which must make it one of the lowest mileage Series 1 Land Rovers in existence. The car was sold for £129,000 to the Emil Frey museum—whose founder was an admirer of the late British Prime Minister—in Switzerland where it was sympathetically restored and is now on permanent display.

Chapter 11
1957 Facel Vega FV3B

People are standing, hands in pockets, along the side of a tree-lined road. It is winter, the trees bare: the on lookers wearing coats. Confirmation that this is France comes in the form of two smartly dressed Gendarmes. They are stationed either side of the twisted remains of back end of a car that is wrapped around a, seemingly undamaged, Plane tree.

Six metres away in the foreground rests the front bulkhead, doors and dashboard of the car, its aircraft like central instruments still in place. The dashboard clock has stopped at 1:55 pm. The force of the impact is evident from the mangled wreckage. Ironically, one of the victims of this automotive carnage was a Nobel Prize winner who had famously been reported as saying that 'the most absurd way to die would be in a car accident': Albert Camus.

The accident had happened at 1:55 pm on 4 January 1960 on a long straight stretch of the Plane-tree-lined Route Nationale 5 (now the RN 6 or D606) twenty-four kilometres from Sens near the town of Villeblevin in the Yonne. The car's occupants—Albert Camus, Michel Gallimard (his publisher) Gallimard's wife Janine and their 18 year old daughter Anne—had stopped for lunch at the Hôtel de Paris in Sens and were back on their remaining 100km of their journey to Paris.

The day was cold but there was no ice on the road. That the 255 bhp car was travelling at speed—some estimate approximately 130 kph (over 80 mph) although more likely between 100–110 kph (65–70 mph)—is clear from the massive extent of the damage. The vehicle ended up in four parts after skidding, turning sideways and hitting a first Plane tree before the chassis and rear end wrapped around a second.

The dashboard and front bulkhead ended up 6 metres (20ft) further on; the huge Chrysler V8 engine a further 20 metres (60 ft) away on the road and the once impressive front panel with the words 'FACEL VEGA' in chrome letters, was found lying forlornly on the ground amongst the leaves. The occupants, with the exception of Camus, were thrown clear of the wreckage as the car broke up. Camus was killed instantly. The Plane tree survives to this day.

Camus was only 46. He and his family had spent New Year with his publisher, Michel Gallimard and his family at their house in Lourmarin in the Vaucluse—which Camus had bought with his winnings from the 1957 Nobel prize for literature.

Camus's body was taken to the nearest town of Villeblevin where it was laid in state for the night in the town hall. Gallimard, who ran the Editions Gallimard concern in Paris, died five days later in Montereau hospital from the head injuries he sustained. Janine and his daughter survived. Camus's body was taken back to Lourmarin where his burial took place on 6 January 1960.

The remains of the car—a Gris Richelieu (dark grey with a hint of green) 1957 Facel Vega FV3B registered in Paris 5379 GH 75—were removed from the crash scene using a crane. The subsequent accident investigation was unable, definitively, to determine the exact cause of the crash other than 'excessive speed'.

As the Police noted, the road was straight and it was neither icy nor wet at the time of the accident. Contemporary accounts, including an analysis of the accident in "L'Automobile" of February 1960 suggest that the rear left-hand tyre lost pressure when the car was travelling at speed. Gallimard, the car's owner from new and someone who had previous owned a Facel, was an experienced driver and had attempted to slow the almost two tonne car without braking hard.

However, whilst commendably stable in a straight line, the Facel was prone to some understeer when cornering. The vehicle skidded, pushing the front wheel off the road into the rain gutter at the edge of the carriageway, which in turn caused the car to spin, hitting the first Plane tree before disintegrating and coming to rest wrapped around the second.

The service records of Gallimard's Vega reportedly showed that it had two rear wheel bearings replaced due to failure in the preceding two years of his ownership. The tyres were also the originals and were due to be replaced after the trip. It is also possible that one of the 48 splines of the Robergel wire wheels, had worked lose and punctured the tyre from the inside.

Whatever the cause, a titan of French philosophy and literature had been killed in what fellow philosopher Jean Paul Satre described as an 'absurd' situation and a nation mourned. This was almost a stereotype—for Camus not only to have been killed in the passenger seat of a French supercar that embodied the post-war renaissance of French prestige; but also to have had in his briefcase the first 150 pages of the hand-written manuscript of his latest masterwork.

This was his unfinished autobiography, "Le Premier Homme", later edited and published in 1995 by Catherine his daughter. This was truly the stuff of Gallic legend.

Camus had not originally intended to return to Paris by car at all. Indeed, he had put his wife and teenage twin children on the train at Avignon on 2 January and the return half of his train ticket was found in his jacket pocket at the crash site. He had planned to travel back to Paris via the SNCF in the company of his friend René Char. Quite why he decided to travel by car with Gallimard remains a mystery, but Gallimard was his friend and perhaps the chance to spend time with him and his family on a road trip was irresistible.

Gallimard loved cars and was an accomplished driver even if, occasionally as Janine Gallimard later recalled, Camus sometimes had to encourage him to slow down. The party had left Loumarin early on 3 January and had stopped in Orange for lunch. They drove on before stopping overnight at Paul Blanc's Michelin starred 'Chapon Fin' in Thoissey where they celebrated Gallimard's daughter Anne's 18th birthday. After breakfast on 4 January, they hit the road again for the final leg of the journey to Paris.

A future Nobel Prize winner, Camus was born on 7 November 1913 in French Algeria into a poor family of 'pieds noirs' (See Chapter 14) His father, a farm labourer, was killed in the First World War a year later at the battle of the Marne in 1914. As a result, his mother was left, more or less, destitute and he grew up in a dirt-poor household in the central Belouizdad district of Algiers. However, despite being poor, Camus had one advantage—that of being a French Citizen—which in turn gave him access to the French education system.

He was a bright child and won a scholarship to the Lycée. He excelled at school, but his home living conditions remained poor. By 17, he had contracted tuberculosis and as a result, he moved out of the city to live with his uncle Gustave Acault. This experience, along with tutoring from his teacher encouraged his love of philosophy.

It was no surprise then when he chose to study Philosophy at University in Algiers. Here he met his future first wife, Simone Hié—a morphine addict. Camus married Hié in 1934 but subsequently discovered she was having an affair with the Doctor who prescribed her the morphine. Thus, in 1936, he not only graduated, but he also got divorced.

Politically, Camus was naturally inclined towards the Left. Having joined the French Communist Party in 1935, he rapidly became disillusioned with its hard-line Marxist stance. He left the following year to join the Algerian Communist Party (PCA) whose main focus at the time was on independence rather than ideology.

However, he also flirted with the moderate Algerian People's Party (PPA) who were also involved in the independence struggle. For a while he was able to ride both political bicycles. However, a fork in the road appeared when the increasingly acrimonious relationship between the PCA and PPA led to his expulsion from the former.

By 1938 he was a journalist writing for the anti-Fascist, anti-colonialist 'Alger Républicain' newspaper. When the paper was closed down by the French authorities in 1940, Camus took up a new job as editor of the Paris Soir in France. During this period he wrote his first novel 'The Outsider', the essay 'The myth of Sisyphus' and the play 'Caligula', which framed his 'absurdist' philosophy.

The outbreak of war saw him attempting to join the army, only to be refused on the grounds of his tuberculosis. With the German Army advancing on Paris, he relocated to Lyon where he met and married—in December 1940—his second wife the mathematician, Francine Faure. They initially moved to Algeria where

Camus found work as a teacher but his illness flared up again with the climate and the couple soon moved back Europe to the French Alps on health grounds.

Here, he wrote a further novel—'The Plague'—and a play—'The Misunderstanding'. With the growing fame of his earlier works, he moved back to Paris in 1943 and joined the circle of leading French intellectuals including Simone de Beauvoir and Jean Paul Satre. He also became active in the Resistance and took on the dangerous job of writing for and editing, the French Resistance newspaper 'Combat'.

By 1945 Camus had achieved international fame as a writer and philosopher. While still on the Left, he renounced the totalitarian communism of the Soviet Union in favour of revolutionary syndicalism (syndicalisme révolutionnaire) where groups of workers establish trade unions and pursue their interests and workers' rights through strikes. This not only estranged him from Satre but also brought him into conflict with Moscow. Herein lies the origin of the main conspiracy theory surrounding his death.

This theory was expounded in an article in the Italian Corriere della Sera newspaper in 2011 by Giovanni Catelli and in a subsequent book 'the death of Camus' in 2019. Catelli claims that Camus's death was not accidental but rather the result of the actions of a KGB cell with tacit support from the French government.

The theory runs that the assassination was ordered by a Soviet Minister, Dmitri Shepilov, in response to an article Camus had written in March 1957 in *Franc-tireur* denouncing the 1956 'Shepilov Massacres' in Hungary during the suppression of the uprising. Camus had compounded Moscow's anger the following year by publicly backing fellow Nobel Prize winner Boris Pasternak, the author of Doctor Zhivago, which was banned by the Soviets.

So, while it is fair to say that by 1958, Camus was well and truly off Stalin's Christmas card list, whether this translated into an order being given to the KGB to assassinate him is another question.

It is certainly true that Camus's 'absurdist' philosophy which places individual liberties at its heart and draws a clear distinction between 'revolution' and 'rebellion', was ideologically at odds with Soviet communism and therefore—at least intellectually—a threat.

Camus noted that the revolution of a rebel could easily turn into totalitarian oppression if it were not underpinned by strict and clear morals. In his view, the historical rebellion—the harnessing of the abstract spirit of metaphysical rebellion (i.e., that between the sentient humankind and the unintelligent universe—which creates the absurdity resulting from the meaninglessness of man's need for justification and the inability of the universe to satisfy that need)—could easily result in the release of intrinsic evil.

Camus recognised that this was inherent in the act of rebellion and, if unchecked, could lead to immense human suffering. Camus's rejection of the Soviet model was based on precisely this: that the Soviet Union had failed to put in place the moral checks and balances that would have prevented it from turning into the brutal and oppressive regime it had become.

Catelli's theory argues that on instruction from Shepilov, KGB agents had rigged the interior of one of the tyres of Gallimard's Facel Vega with a special device which would bore its way out at speed causing a blow-out. Catelli formulated his theory in response to an entry in the, posthumously published, diary of Czech poet Jan Zábrana:

I heard something very strange from the mouth of a man who knew lots of things and had very informed sources. According to him, the accident that had cost Albert Camus his life in 1960 was organised by Soviet spies. They damaged a tyre on the car using a sophisticated piece of equipment that cut or made a hole in the wheel at speed.

The theory is at least consistent with the circumstances of the crash, which was the result of excessive speed coupled, with either a tyre blow-out or broken axle. However, it is clear that Camus had originally intended to return on the train with his family on 2 January and had only, relatively late on in the holiday, decided to stay and to travel back to Paris with Gallimard the following days.

For this theory to work, either Gallimard would have needed to be complicit—in which case he was prepared to risk sacrificing not only his own life but also the lives of his family which seems, at best, unlikely; or the KGB would have had to interfered with Gallimard's Facel Vega the on the night of 3/4 January by which time the car was already en route to Paris. If the car had been tampered with prior to this then Gallimard, rather than Camus, must surely have been the intended target?

While it is fair to speculate that nobody in the Kremlin is likely to have shed a tear on hearing the news of Camus's untimely death, the handling capabilities of the almost two tonne Vega in a high-speed tyre blow-out situation triggered by a defective tyre or debris in the road, seems a much more plausible explanation.

Indeed, it is interesting that Catelli's theory has not been endorsed by Camus' daughter Catherine. Others, including Cambridge French literature professor Alison Finch, have also raised doubts about Catelli's claims of French government assistance, arguing that De Gaulle (see Chapter 14) had far too much respect French intellectuals to have countenanced their assassination.

Facel Vega FV3B

According to the factory records, Michel Gallimard's FV3B was chassis number: FV3B 58-228 and was delivered on 26 September 1957 to 'Michel GALLIMARD', Paris. In the rare colour of 'Gris Richelieu' (a dark grey with a hint of green) with a contrasting beige leather interior, it must have been the embodiment of understated French good taste.

Beneath its beautiful and sophisticated coach-built bodywork, the car featured a massive piece of Detroit iron in the shape of a 4.9 litre, 255 bhp, Chrysler V8 Engine. The wheels were Robergel—a bolt on 15 inch × 5J chromed, 48 spoke, wire wheel—with Michelin tires. Crucially, given the weight and power of the car, the manufacturer's advice was to change these tyres at least every 18,000 km (11,000 miles) something that Gallimard almost certainly had not done by the time of the accident, which might help to explain the blow-out.

The car was registered 5379 GH 75—a 1957 series Paris registration number. Price new was FFr3,250,000—almost €100,000 today. The Facel Vega was very much a luxury car for the very wealthiest and most discerning customer.

The FV3B was the latest evolution of the Facel Vega launched at the 1964 Paris Salon de l'Auto. Designed by Jean Daninos, the name Vega was the idea of Daninos's brother Pierre—a famous writer and amateur astronomer. 'Vega' was the brightest star in the Lyra constellation (named after the instrument played by Orpheus in Greek mythology). The Chrysler (see Chapter 16) V8 engine along with the Torqueflite automatic transmission were sourced from the US company in the absence of any domestically produced alternative being available.

The chassis was designed by former British racing driver Lance Macklin, who had retired from the sport following his part in the 1955 Le Mans disaster (see Chapter 8). Suspension was via coil springs and double wishbones at the front coupled with leaf springing and a live axle at the rear. Bodywork styling was by Daninos and based on his earlier styling for the Ford Comète with additional, albeit restrained, tail fins. The dashboard was deliberately evocative of an aircraft with a bank of centrally mounted two-inch dials and heater control levers that resembled the thrust levers of a jet fighter.

Despite looking like finest burr walnut, the dashboard itself was made of steel which was painted by hand with a woodgrain finish. This helps to explain the survival of the dash assembly of Gallimard's car—had the dash been made of walnut it would have been reduced to matchwood by the impact instead of remaining intact.

The interior was trimmed in finest Connolly hide with Wilton carpets and west of England cloth headlining. The rear seats folded flat to allow long items to be stowed in the boot when there were no rear passengers. All brightwork was in aircraft quality stainless steel. The engine size of Gallimard's car was 4.9 litres and 255 bhp. This grew with the FV4 to 5.8 litres and a massive 325 bhp.

Gallimard's FV3B was made as a special order in a period of changeover to the FV4 model. During this period—September 1957—June 1958—FV3Bs were made in batches of eight cars in between batches of FV4s. When production of the FV3B ceased in June 1958 a total of 90 cars of this model had been made. Gallimard's FV3B—the 58th produced—was of the later, wider-bodied, type which were four centimetres wider and two centimetres longer than the first 12 made.

The car weighed in at somewhere around 1800 kg—nearly two tonnes. The engine was 4.9 litre, 255 bhp monster with a top speed of 203 kph (126 mph) Half of the cars were manual transmission with a 2.93 axle ratio: the remainder were fitted with Chrysler's Torqueflite automatic transmission.

Interestingly, only half were also fitted with power steering which became standard from the beginning of 1957 and was something which Gallimard's car therefore had. Disc brakes on the other hand were optional until 1960 and it is not known if Gallimard had chosen this safety feature. In total only 357 of all variants of FVs (1-4) were built before the model was replaced by the HK500 in 1959.

FACEL

Despite the cachet of Facel cars and their association with the late 1950s/early 1960s jet set—Picasso, Ava Gardner, Tony Curtis, Ringo Starr and the Shah of Persia (see Chapter 15) were amongst the list of celebrity owners—the company's origins were far from glamourous. Facel was as an industrial firm that dealt in metal pressings from fridge doors, Vespa scooters, to automobile bodies.

The company was formed on 20 December 1939 by one of the French Air Force's suppliers, Bronzavia, as a subsidiary to boost aircraft production as part of the French war effort. The Forges et Arteliers de Constructions d'Eure-et-Loir—hence the acronym FACEL—was initially headed by former motorcycle manufacturer Marcel Koehler and made aircraft components.

After the war in 1945, Jean Daninos took over from Koehler. Daninos had been a designer at Citroen (See Chapter 13) before moving to Bronzavia in 1937 as Technical Director. He had spent the Second World War in the US working for the General Aircraft Company.

In the post-war years, Facel produced finished body-shells and automotive body panels from its pressing plant, for a number of leading French manufacturers such as Panhard, Simca as well as Ford France. Facel was also responsible, as a coachbuilder, for the design of cars such as the Panhard Dyna X and worked with leading design houses such as Farina. Special one-off styling exercises such as the Bentley Cresta as well as the production Ford Comète and Simca Sports provided the styling cues for what was to come.

Daninos remained a designer at heart and this, coupled with the precision engineering inherent in aircraft production, provided the inspiration for Facel to begin production of its own cars. This move was also spurred on by economics resulting from the progressive shift away from the separate chassis and bodywork components in production cars, to unitary 'monocoque' construction, amongst the high-volume manufacturers who had formed the bulk of Facel's body pressing customers.

Thus, the Facel Vega brand was created in July 1954, headquartered in Paris at 19 Avenue George V—a glamourous address in the Plane-tree lined avenues of the 8th Arrondissement. The factory was further north at 132 Boulevard de Valmy in the distinctly unglamorous district of Colombes.

The brand was launched at the 1954 Paris Salon de L'Auto with the first cars featuring a tubular chassis, seductive bodywork, opulent interior styling and trimming and a huge American DeSoto (Chrysler) Firedome, 4.5 litre engine mated to either a two speed Chrysler Powerflite automatic transmission or a 4 speed Pont-à-Mousson manual box. These first-generation cars produced 180 bhp with a reported top speed of between 170–190 kph depending on the transmission.

The early models had a flat windscreen which was replaced with a more modern wrap-around in 1956 for the FVS 2. This model also featured the new

4.9 litre Chrysler V8 engine and three speed automatic Torqueflite transmission. The 5.8 litre HK500 launched in 1959 was basically a rebadged and lightly tweaked FV4. More power followed in the shape of Chrysler's 6.3 litre 360 bhp V8 raising the top speed to a 237 kph (147 mph) The final incarnation of the model came in 1962 with the restyled, lower and lighter Facel Vega II. However, by this time the seeds of Facel's demise had already been sown.

In 1960 Daninos had taken the fateful decision to enter the crowded mid-priced sports car—segment with a new model called the Facellia. Launched in 1959 as a cabriolet, coupe or 2+2 coupe. The plan was to compete with the likes of Alfa Romeo and Porsche (see Chapter 15).

The decision—driven by the desire to circumvent the French horsepower tax—that the Facellia was to have a four cylinder rather than a Chrysler V8 engine proved disastrous. The dual overhead cam, 1.6 litre engine designed by ex-Talbot—Lago chief engineer Carlo Machetti was fundamentally flawed by the decision to have only two main bearings rather than the usual four. The result was built-in unreliability, high failure rates and a tidal wave of warranty claims. Daninos was forced to resign in August 1961. Despite a switch to a stock Volvo engine, by 1963 Facel was losing money on every car it built.

In October 1964, the factory gates closed for the last time.

Chapter 12
1961 Lincoln Continental
Convertible Limousine

It is one of the most arresting images of the twentieth century. It is a scene of both horror and of chaos. The woman in the pink suit and hat desperately trying to escape out across the rear deck of the speeding Lincoln Continental Convertible, in the passenger seat beside her legs the slumped figure of a man.

The figures in the forward row of seats are crouching down, the driver and front passenger leaning forward into the windscreen. A man in sunglasses and a suit is climbing on to the rear bumper of the car using a handle welded to the boot lid to pull himself aboard. A police motorcycle outrider on a Harley Davidson flanks the other side.

The photo was taken at 12:30 pm on 22 November 1963 in Dallas Texas. The man in the rear passenger seat is the late President John F Kennedy who has just been shot twice, the woman on the rear deck his wife Jackie. The passengers in the row of seats in front are Governor John Connally who has been shot three times and his wife Nellie. The driver is Agent William Greer, the front passenger on the President's side of the car is Assistant Special Agent in Charge, Roy Kellerman. The car is SS-100-X, the US Presidential Limousine.

Although the events surrounding the assassination are well documented, the fate of the car is less well known. Particularly surprising is that it remained in Presidential service with the addition of a permanent hardtop and armour plating until 1978 and was used not only by Kennedy's successor President Lyndon B Johnson but also by President's Nixon, Ford and Carter.

The Presidential limousine—code named SS-100-X was the latest in a line of large American cars specially adapted for Presidential use. Presidents Eisenhower and Truman had used a pair of specially modified 1950s, stodgy, Lincoln Cosmopolitan saloons but with the arrival of the new, young, President these were beginning to look dated so the decision was taken in 1961 to order a new car.

The starting point, in a break with tradition, was a convertible and a standard example—a model 74A—was chosen from Ford's Lincoln assembly line in Wixom, Michigan in January 1961. The car was sent to coachbuilders Hess and Eisenhardt of Cincinnnati who transformed it by adding three and a half feet of extra length to the rear passenger area of the car to allow for an extra row of seats thereby converting it to what they called a "parade limousine".

The Secret Service who ordered the car really went to town on the other options—radio telephones, illuminated flagpoles on the wings, interior floodlighting and a hydraulically operated rear seat which could elevate by 11 inches. The piece de resistance was the choice of roofs—canvas, aluminium or a futuristic Perspex "bubbletop". All were interchangeable depending on the weather.

Every option therefore apart from any that might have enhanced the security of the occupants of the car, which, curiously given its intended use, was neither fitted with bullet proof glass or armour plating—something which the Warren Commission report would note later—namely that it "was neither bullet-proof nor bullet-resistant". This "insecurity by design" coupled with the last minute, weather related, decision taken on the ground to remove the Perspex bubble top gave Lee Harvey Oswald the clearest possible shot at the President from the sixth-floor corner window of the Dallas Book Depository.

The car was fitted with a hand-built 350 bhp seven litre engine and weighed 3,500kg—more than 700kg than the standard car. The list price of the car was $7,347 but the modifications cost an extra $200,000. It was registered to the Ford Motor Company who leased it to the Secret Service for a nominal $500 per annum.

The car, finished in a special shade of navy blue, was delivered to the White House on 15 June 1961 and immediately pressed into service. For the Dallas trip the car was flown by the US Air Force to San Antonio and then on to Dallas on 21 November 1963. The car was fitted with the "bubble top" as the weather forecast was mixed. The decision to remove the "bubble top" was only taken at the last minute on the morning of 22 November when the weather forecast proved to have been wrong.

After the shooting the car was impounded by the Secret Service and the FBI. The "bubble top" was refitted and the car was taken to the airport and loaded onto a US Airforce plane which took off back to Andrews Air Force Base at 15:30 the same day. The car was then returned to the White House garage and photographed and examined in detail for evidence.

The windscreen—which had a bullet hole in it—was removed. But instead of remaining locked away in storage or exhibited in a museum the car was sent back to Cincinnati to Hess and Eisenhardt to be rebuilt for further use. From a practical point of view, not least given the timescale to build a replacement, this made sense. But from a human perspective it looks rather callous.

The rebuild reportedly cost $500,000 dollars and involved work at Ford's experimental centre in Dearborn. The car was titanium armour-plated and fitted with bullet proof windows adding 1600 pounds of extra weight. The new glass was capable of stopping a 30-calibre rifle bullet—the same type that had been used to assassinate the President.

The convertible roof was replaced by a permanent, armour-plated, fixed one which included a bullet-proof rear window weighing 1500 pounds alone. The car was also fitted with bullet-proof tyres with aluminium sidewalls and the rear cabin was re-trimmed to remove any traces of the assassination. The car was pressed back into service, transporting President Lyndon B Johnson for the remainder of his term in office with one further rebuild in 1967 when the colour was changed to black and the air conditioning upgraded.

Following the 1969 Presidential elections, the new President Richard Nixon continued to use the car but had the roof modified to include a hinged glass panel so he could stand up and wave at the crowds. Following Nixon's impeachment and resignation, the car passed as a back-up vehicle to his successor Gerald Ford and then to his successor Jimmy Carter who retired it shortly after taking office in early 1977. The car is now on permanent display in the Henry Ford Museum.

The contrast between the long career and dignified retirement of the Lincoln and the short and brutal death of the young President it had been built to transport and protect is striking. Kennedy had been born into a political family in Brookline Massachusetts. His father Joe Kennedy was a businessman and politician, as were his grandfathers. Kennedy was a bright child who, thanks to his father's wealth, was privately educated at Choate in Connecticut.

Having originally wanted to study at the London School of Economics as his elder brother had, he was forced by ill health back to the US where he began studying at Princeton. However further ill heath caused him to pull out and he applied and was accepted for Harvard. In 1938 Kennedy went to England to work in the US Embassy in London where his father was US Ambassador.

This was followed by a tour of Europe and the Balkans ending on 1 September 1939—the day that the UK declared war on Germany. Returning to the US, he wrote his thesis on Britain's policy of appeasement of Hitler and became a strong advocate of US intervention in the war.

Kennedy's attempt to join the US army in 1940 was unsuccessful due to his lower back problems. Eventually by 1941 he was able to join the US Navy reserve thanks to the help of a friend of his father and was drafted into naval intelligence. He volunteered for the motor torpedo Boat Squadron in 1942. In 1943 he was sent to Tulai Island in the South Pacific and was on a night-time patrol in his torpedo boat on 1–2 August when the boat was rammed and cut in half by a Japanese destroyer.

Kennedy managed to save the lives of many of his crew despite sustaining a serious back injury. He was both decorated and promoted and went on to perform another daring rescue later in the year before being retired on medical grounds in November 1943.

In 1944, Kennedy's elder brother Joe was killed when the plane loaded with ammunition he was flying blew up over the English Channel. Kennedy's father had wanted Joe to run for the Presidency—after his death his attention switched to his next eldest son John. With financial backing from his father Kennedy was elected to Congress in 1946 representing Massachusetts—a role he continued to perform for six years before running for and getting elected to, the Senate in 1952.

Having married Jacqueline Bouvier in 1953 he spent the next two years undergoing successive operations on his spine. He also wrote a book while convalescing entitled "profiles of courage" which won the 1957 Pulitzer Prize for biography. Kennedy was re-elected by a huge margin in 1958 and began preparing to run for the Presidency in 1960 and secured the Democratic nomination over Senate Majority Leader Lyndon B Johnson. Kennedy won the subsequent Presidential election against Richard Nixon overturning the latter's six-point lead at the start of the campaign.

Kennedy's presidency made him many enemies—something which the conspiracy theorists around his assassination have made much of. It was marked by a break with the past in terms of his style of governing and decision making which concerned some in the deep state. Foreign policy crises abounded—Cuba—which he inherited from Eisenhower along with the CIA funded Bay of Pigs invasion plan.

The failure of this—due largely to his unwillingness to provide air support to the invasion for fear of being seen to be intervening directly to change the regime—left him deeply unpopular amongst the Cuban exile community which in some cases had strong links to the mafia. The subsequent Cuban Missile Crisis further compounded the sense among some senior figures that he was too young and inexperienced—something exposed during his 1961 Summit with Khrushchev when he had failed to prevent the signing of a treaty between Moscow and East Berlin and the subsequent partition of the city.

Added to all of these crises was his Administration's involvement in trying to prevent the rise of Communism in South East Asia where he had decided to support the South Vietnamese President Ngo Dinh Diem with military, political and economic assistance.

Here again, he was reluctant to fully commit himself, having raised the number of US military advisers and Special Forces to 16,000 by autumn 1963 he was unwilling to order a full-scale deployment of troops—something which greatly concerned the US politico-military complex. Indeed, it was not until after his assassination that US forces were finally deployed by Lyndon B Johnson his successor.

The trip to Dallas then was one that took place against this backdrop of underlying hostility and mistrust both within parts of the US government but also in the wider population. Texas had voted Republican in the 1960 Presidential election and part of Kennedy's aim was to soothe the local Democratic Party and to begin building support and raising funds for his re-election campaign in 1964. The trip had been pre-announced in September 1963 but the exact route for the Presidential motorcade was not settled until 18 November.

Nevertheless, the planned route to the Dallas Trade Mart was widely trailed in the press several days in advance of the visit, giving would-be assassins sufficient time to select the best lines of sight.

The route was selected to maximise the President's public exposure and was deliberately meandering and designed to take 45 minutes. A route that used Dallas's Main Street, necessitating a one block turn, rather than the parallel Elm Street which connected directly to the Stemmons Freeway, was selected because Main Street was the traditional route for parades with maximum viewing opportunities from both street and building level. The result of this choice was that the route passed by the Texas School Book Depository.

The motorcade was made up of three cars. First was a white Ford saloon with Jessie Curry the Dallas Chief of Police, Agent Win Lawson, Sheriff Bill Decker and Agent Forest Sorrels on board. The second car was SS-100-X carrying Governor Connally and the President and their wives. Third was a 1955 Cadillac convertible with Agent Sam Kinney, Assistant to The Special Agent in Charge Emory Roberts, two of the President's aides—Ken O'Donnell and Dave Powers, Agent George Hickey and PRS (Diplomatic Security Service personal protection) Agent Glen Bennett.

In addition, there were four Agents riding on the running boards of this vehicle: Clint Hill, Jack Ready, Tim McIntyre and Paul Landis.

The motorcade left Dallas's Love Field airport at 11:40 but was delayed by the huge crowds of between 150,000 and 200,000 people on the route. At 12:30 the motorcade slowed and made the turn from Houston Street into Elm Street to enter the Stemmons Freeway. At this point the vehicles were travelling at approximately 11 miles an hour. The governor's wife had turned to Kennedy and said, "Mr President, you can't say that Dallas doesn't love you."

Kennedy had just replied, "No, you certainly can't," when three gun shots were fired, the first entering his back and exiting via his throat before travelling on to severely wound Governor Connally, a second hitting him in the head and blowing the top of his skull off.

In the photograph Jackie Kennedy is seen trying to climb onto the rear deck of the car—although when interviewed later she had no recollection of this. She was then heard saying, "They have killed my husband. I have his brains in my hand."

Eyewitnesses traced the shots to the corner window of the sixth floor of the Book Depository where Lee Harvey Oswald had been working. Oswald was subsequently arrested having murdered Dallas Police Officer J D Tippit in the suburb of Oak Cliff three miles from the Book Depository. Two days after his arrest Oswald was shot by nightclub owner Jack Ruby and never stood trial.

Lincoln

Founded in August 1917 in Dearborn Michigan, by Henry and Wilfred Leland and named after the 16th US President, Lincoln was Leland's response to Cadillac (See Chapter 17)—the company he had founded, sold to General Motors in 1909 and resigned as an executive from in 1917 after a dispute with his boss. Funding to set up the Lincoln Motor Company factory came from a $10 million-dollar government contract to build Liberty V12 aircraft engines.

After the end of the First World War, the factory was re-tooled to build luxury cars powered by a V8 engine derived from the Liberty V12. The company was nearly bankrupt by 1922 when Ford stepped in to buy it for $8 million giving Ford a luxury brand with which to compete with Cadillac.

Aside from this, the purchase also provided a satisfying revenge for Henry Ford (See Chapter 3) who had been forced to sell his second company, the Henry Ford Company, because of an investor revolt led by Leland. The latter had then renamed the company Cadillac and sold it for a large profit to General Motors. Unsurprisingly the Leland brothers were rapidly removed from the company after the takeover.

Lincoln was managed by Edsel Ford and the company was successful producing 7,875 cars by 1923 and returning an operating profit. The Lincoln Model L was replaced by the Lincoln Model K in 1931 and 1933 saw the introduction of a 12-cylinder V12 engine—the first to power a US production car.

The origins of the Lincoln Continental lay in a one off commissioned by Edsel Ford for a holiday in Florida. He wanted the car to look more European than standard offerings so a bespoke body was specially built by the factory using a 1939 Lincoln-Zephyr Convertible chassis as a basis. The car was widely admired and its "continental" looks were reflected in the name that was eventually chosen.

Lincoln was formally merged into Ford in the 1940s and production was halted during the Second World War. After the war the brand was merged with Mercury. The first new post-war model—the LE—was unveiled in 1949 and used a modified Ford flathead V8 engine and rear hinged "suicide" passenger doors—a feature that would eventually re-emerge in the 1961 model.

In 1956, Ford launched a new "Continental" sub brand of luxury car into the range as the prestige brand. The Continental had restrained, European, styling and featured minimal chrome trim, no tailfins and a trademark spare tyre semi-circular bulge in the boot lid. At $10,000 the car was the most expensive offered by any US manufacturer. Unfortunately, the hand-built nature of the car meant that even at this price every car built returned a $1000 loss.

Lincoln introduced a single model policy from 1961 with the Lincoln Continental (the Continental sub-brand was killed off at this point) The 1970s started well for Lincoln but the 1973 oil crisis and the introduction of federal safety regulations hit it hard. The Continental was redesigned and the range expanded. The focus on large luxury cars continued throughout the 1980s and 1990s with bodies becoming more aerodynamic. In the early 2000s Lincoln switched to produce SUVs, pick-up trucks and sports sedans. The Lincoln Continental model was revived in 2017.

1961 Lincoln Continental Convertible

SS-100-X was a fourth generation Lincoln Continental Convertible—the model was brand new and an attempt to draw a line under the $60million losses of its predecessor. The new model was available only as a four-door saloon or four door convertible and, in an effort to maximise rear passenger space saw the re-introduction of rear-hinged "suicide" doors as featured on the first post war models.

Ford was committed to making the finest mass-produced car with the Lincoln and quality control was rigorous. Engines were individually bench tested and the car carried a two-year, 24,000-mile warranty. The car was styled in house by Elwood Engel and was originally intended to be a four door Ford Thunderbird—the basic platform of which the model shared. The car featured a 320 bhp seven litre V8 engine—the largest ever used in a Ford passenger car—capable of propelling the car from 0–60mph in 11 seconds.

The downside was terrible fuel economy at 14 mpg. Transmission was three speed "turbo drive" automatic. The car featured a power hood derived from the Ford Fairlane 500 Skyliner which retracted beneath a rear hinged boot lid. The model was designed to have a nine-year production life and survived with minor changes until 1971.

Chapter 13
1962 Citroen DS 19

On the evening of 22 August 1962 in the courtyard of the Elysee in Paris, President Charles de Gaulle and his wife Madame Yvonne de Gaulle were shown to their black chauffeur driven Citroen DS 19—registration number 5249 HU 75—for the drive to the military aerodrome at Villacoublay where a French Airforce helicopter would take them back to Colombey-les-Deux-Eglises their country home to complete their holiday.

De Gaulle had just chaired a meeting of the Council of Ministers—it had been a long week and he was looking forward to unwinding in the French countryside. At the wheel of the smart Citroen was de Gaulle's chauffeur Francis Marroux. In the front passenger seat was Colonel Alain de Boissieu, de Gaulle's son in law and Aide de Camp. A second identical DS contained the President's two bodyguards and a Doctor.

The convoy, flanked by two motorcycle outriders, set off at 19:45 across Place de La Concorde and toward the Porte de Châtillon towards the RN 306. By 20:10 as the sun was setting as the Presidential motorcade was entering the quiet suburb of Petit Clamart. The vehicles approached the crossroads of the D306 and Rue Charles Debry and Rue des Bois. Unbeknown to De Gaulle and his convoy this was the killing zone prepared by 12 members of the OAS.

In 1958, the Fourth French Republic of President Rene Coty collapsed in the wake of the Algiers crisis. The North African colony had been French since the capture of Algiers in 1830 and a full Département of the Republic since 1848. By the early 1950s more than one fifth of the population was of European origin. In common with other European colonial powers, France in the mid-1950s was faced with a growing number of struggles for independence from its overseas territories.

Perhaps because of its particularly high European population—sometimes referred to as "Pieds Noir"—or its geographical proximity to metropolitan France—being a mere 454 nautical miles from Marseilles—the fight for independence in Algeria was particularly bloody and bitter. Many former soldiers, including sympathisers of the wartime Vichy government, had settled in the cities of Algiers and Oran after the war.

An uprising in 1945 by the indigenous population had been brutally supressed by French forces but tensions had continued to grow before finally exploding into the Algerian independence war of 1954–59 waged by the FLN against the French authorities. The European Pieds Noir population of Algeria was neither supportive of independence nor neutral.

On the contrary, its military veterans were strongly opposed and felt they needed to mobilise. The *Organisation de Résistance de L'Algérie Française* was set up to stop independence and to counteract the FLN. The result was a cycle of tit-for-tat bombings, abductions and murders.

By 1958 the situation was at boiling point. The "Pieds Noir" feared that the French government was about to betray them by agreeing to independence as it had done two years earlier in the cases of Morocco and Tunisia. Perhaps because of his response to the uprising in 1945 or because he was a former soldier, the "Pieds Noir" began to call for the return of Charles de Gaulle as President of France.

De Gaulle, they reasoned would never sacrifice French honour to political expediency. The result was that on 13 May 1958 a coup attempt began in Algiers spearheaded by Pierre Lagaillarde, the future founder of a secret military organisation the OAS, four French Generals: Raoul Salan, Edmond Jouhaud, Jean Gracieux and Jacques Massu and the commander of the French Mediterranean fleet Admiral Auboyneau.

This group seized power in Algiers and demanded the return of de Gaulle and a guarantee that Algeria would remain French. The coup was supported by the former governor of Algeria Jacques Soustelle—a supporter of de Gaulle.

Despite having retired 12 years earlier, De Gaulle indicated his willingness to serve if required. By 24 May the crisis had escalated with French paratroopers from Algeria taking control of Corsica as a staging post to seizing Paris and removing the French government if it failed to resign and install de Gaulle.

On 29 May, Rene Coty went to Parliament to resign thereby averting a civil war and proposed de Gaulle as the only man who could re-establish the Republic. De Gaulle agreed provided he was granted extraordinary powers for six months to stabilise the situation and provided a new constitution was agreed creating a powerful President elected on a seven-year term. These changes were agreed by a referendum on 28 September 1958—the crisis was over and, in the eyes of the Lagaillarde and his associates, the future of Algeria as part of France had been assured.

Except it hadn't. The "Pieds Noir" had assumed that de Gaulle would be wholly opposed to Algerian independence, but they hadn't bothered to check. Faced with the unwinnable fight against the FLN and the risk to French oil and gas interests, the new President took a rather more pragmatic approach. De Gaulle began by offering a re-heated version of a peace plan first tabled in 1956 involving local self-government for Algeria while remaining within the French Republic.

The FLN rejected this and went on the offensive. De Gaulle launched the Challe offensive in response using a mixture of helicopter gunships and local level hearts and minds tactics. It failed and so in September 1959 he conceded defeat and offered Algeria a referendum on self-determination. The "Pieds Noir" felt completely betrayed since the outcome was a foregone conclusion.

In response to unrest in Algiers, de Gaulle made a televised speech in 1960 in which he accused the 'Pieds Noir' of prolonging a "100 Years War" that damaged France's international reputation. The referendum on independence was held in January 1961 with 5,993,754 to 16,478 in favour. De Gaulle indicated his intention to respect the result. The gloves were off.

In 1961 a new secret organisation—the Organisation de l'Armee Secrete (OAS)—was formed to fight for Algeria to remain part of France and to assassinate de Gaulle. A failed coup attempt that year on the 1958 model swelled the ranks of the OAS as hundreds of right-wing soldiers deserted the army and headed for Algeria. When Algeria became independent on 5 July 1962, the OAS held de Gaulle directly responsible.

Operation "Charlotte Cordray"—so called after the assassin of the French Revolutionary Jean-Paul Marat in his bath on 17 July 1793 who was subsequently guillotined as a traitor four days later—had been carefully planned and was the best yet organised attempt on de Gaulle's life (there would be no fewer than 31 in total).

Led by Jean-Marie Bastien-Thiry—a Lieutenant Colonel in the French Airforce whose father had been a member of the Gaullist RPF and an acquaintance of de Gaulle in the 1930s—the team was hand-picked and made up of former soldiers. Bastien-Thiry was positioned as advanced look out at a bus stop by the main Villacoublay road—the only route to the aerodrome.

On sighting the Presidential motorcade, he was to signal by opening and closing his newspaper several times to his five colleagues waiting in a yellow Renault Estafette van by the side of the road. Further along the road in a street on the opposite side to the van were more OAS in a stolen Citroen ID 19.

The plan was simple—Bastien-Thiry would signal that the motorcade was coming. The occupants of the van would take up firing positions and spray the convoy with machine gun fire. In the event that the convoy was still moving after this, the Citroen ID 19 would emerge from a side street blocking the road and allowing its occupants to deliver the coup de grace.

Fortunately for President and Madame de Gaulle things did not go entirely according to plan. The technological design brilliance of Presidential Citroen DS was to play a crucial role in ensuring his miraculous survival. The first problem for the OAS assassins was that the sun was setting rather faster than they had anticipated.

In the back of the van with a pair of binoculars and a loaded machine gun was Korean War veteran Serge Bernier. In the driving seat was Lazlo Vargahidden and in the back seat were Gerard Business and two Hungarians—Marton and Sari—all armed with automatic weapons. Bernier was looking through his binoculars out of the back window of the van in the vain hope of trying to see Bastien-Thiry's newspaper. But the dusk was rapidly turning into an all-enveloping gloom, which swallowed the shadowy figure of the Lieutenant Colonel and his newspaper.

The Presidential motorcade was suddenly speeding towards the van and Bernier shouted to his colleagues while kicking open the van's rear doors and opening up with his sub machine gun. The two Hungarians exited via the side door and assumed firing positions on the ground. A hail of bullets spat from the yellow van as de Gaulle's car streaked past at over 100km/h. Bernier ran round to the front of the van still firing.

Incredibly, a pedestrian strayed in front of Bernier at this point forcing him to stop firing and scream to get out of the way. By the time the bystander had moved the car was too far away. Its tyres had been hit and it swerved into the direction of the oncoming traffic, but the driver was able to regain control thanks to the brilliant design of the car's hydro-pneumatic suspension. Inside the car de Boissieu had yelled to the occupants to get down.

The convoy now loomed into view of the OAS Citroen but was nearly past it before its driver, La Tocnaye, floored the accelerator. The other occupant of the Car, Georges Watin, was only half in the passenger door at the time with his leg trailing on the ground as the car sped off after the President. Watin opened fire with his sub machine gun smashing the back window of the President's car and the bodywork of the rear pillar on the President's side.

La Tocnaye was convinced they had hit the President. But Watin's machine gun jammed allowing the car with de Gaulle's close protection team to cut in front of the OAS Citroen and the President's car to escape. Behind the two motorcycle outriders were gaining ground and un-holstering their pistols. Watin's gun cleared and he sprayed the motorcyclists' tyres with bullets. But it was too late—the President's and the security car were approaching the entrance to the aerodrome. La Tocnaye swerved the Citroen, its tyres squealing in protest and headed for the motorway.

At the airbase the President and Madame de Gaulle emerged from the DS showered in glass but otherwise unharmed. Over 150 rounds of ammunition had been fired and the President's DS was peppered with bullet holes. But the technologically advanced design of the car and cool reaction of his driver had saved the occupant's lives. De Gaulle was never to forget this, would always insist on a Citroen as his official car and would even eventually go to the lengths of securing government intervention to prevent the takeover of Citroen by Fiat.

As regards the conspirators he was mostly lenient—commuting death sentences to life in prison for all except Bastien-Thiry who showed no contrition and—unwisely—chose to mock the President during his trial. When cross-examined about his assertion that his aim had only been to stop the President's car and to capture him he was asked the question how he would have prevented the President from escaping. His flippant reply—by taking his glasses and braces away—sealed his fate.

De Gaulle used emergency powers to have him shot by firing squad within hours of his trial—making him the last man in France to be executed in this way.

Citroen

Citroen was founded in 1919 by Andre Gustav Citroen—a French industrialist whose factories had made armaments for the French Army during the First World War. Citroen began preparations for large-scale motor manufacturing during the war itself and in 1916 commissioned Louis Dufresne of Panhard to design a cutting edge 18hp car for production after the war. Citroen was an astute businessman and saw an opening in the market for relatively inexpensive but technologically sophisticated small cars.

With this in mind in early 1917 he enlisted the services of Jules Salomon— a famous automotive engineer—to further develop the work. As a result, four months after the end of the war in 1919, Citroen launched a new small car—the Type A. General Motors came very close to buying Citroen at this point but decided against on financial grounds.

As well as producing cars, Citroen used his links with the French military to develop a range of half tracked vehicles using the Kégresse track system (See Chapter 4) The US army bought several of these and eventually concluded a deal to licence the technology using it in the M2 and M3 White half-track vehicles used by the US Army in the Second World War.

Always innovative, Citroen not only pioneered front wheel drive—with the Traction Avant of the 1930s being the first mass produced car to employ this technology—but also steel and monocoque construction—dispensing with the need for a traditional (and heavy) chassis and produced the first commercially available diesel-powered passenger car—the Rosalie—in 1933.

The Traction Avant cemented Citroen's reputation for technological innovation with its combination of front wheel drive, monocoque construction and four-wheel independent suspension. But all of this was expensive and by 1934 Citroen was forced to file for bankruptcy and was taken over by the Michelin tyre company.

Pierre Michelin became the chairman in 1935, the same year that Andre Citroen died of stomach cancer. Michelin was killed in a car accident in January 1938 and was succeeded by Pierre-Jules Boulanger who maintained the Citroen tradition of technological innovation as a source of competitive advantage. After the German invasion, Boulanger refused to meet Dr Ferdinand Porsche and hid details of all technological innovation from the Nazis.

In a masterstroke he organised the sabotage of military trucks being produced on the Citroen production lines for the Wermacht by having the oil fill level on their dipsticks engraved too low resulting in frequent breakdowns and engine failures. In parallel, Boulanger and Paul Magès continued to work in secret on new designs and innovations to bring to market after the war. Gestapo records discovered after the war had Boulanger on a blacklist of the most prominent enemies of the Third Reich.

Post-World War 2 Citroen unveiled the 2CV at the 1948 Paris Motor show which with its unitary construction, simple air-cooled two-cylinder engine and amazing suspension became an instant best seller with over eight million rolling off the production line by the time it was retired in 1990. The revenue from this utilitarian workhorse was channelled into ever-greater technological innovation.

The culmination of this work was the Citroen DS—launched at the Paris Motor Show in 1955—a car that comprehensively re-wrote the automotive engineering rulebook. It was no coincidence that the name of this beautiful car—DS—was a play on the French word for Goddess—déesse.

Despite the success of both the DS and the 2CV, Citroen lacked a mid-market volume sales car and by the late 1960s was facing a takeover from Fiat (see Chapter 18). De Gaulle opposed this and ensured that the French government intervened to limit Fiat's stake to 49% in an agreement known as PARDEVI (Participation et Developement Industriels).

Michelin, by contrast had been in favour of the Fiat takeover and had been looking to divest itself of the company. Fiat's involvement provided the funding for the development of a much-needed mid-sized car—the GS. This was launched in 1971 and by 1972 was selling over half a million units. But Fiat was not convinced by the wisdom of its investment and decided to pull out by selling its 49% stake back to Michelin.

For Michelin, this was most unwelcome and, coupled with the 1973 oil crisis, Citroen's earlier decision to buy Maserati and, the ill-fated Comotor rotary engine project; by 1974 the company had once again gone bankrupt. The final nail in the coffin came in 1974 when US design regulations outlawed the main technological features of Citroen's model range. The French government stepped in and brokered the merger of Citroen and Peugeot which was successful from 1976–1979 but saw the successive dilution of Citroen's technological brand essence.

1962 Citroen DS 19

The Presidential DS 19 limousine was built at Citroen's factory at the Quai André-Citroën in the Javel district of Paris. Despite the model having already been in production for over five years by the time of its manufacture, the timeless styling of Italian designer Flaminio Bertoni and superb engineering of André Lefèbvre ensured that the car looked as space age and revolutionary as the day the first example had rolled off the production line in 1955.

The car featured the revolutionary hydro-pneumatic self-levelling suspension system developed by Paul Magès that had first been tested on the rear of the Traction Avant in 1954. This system employed four connected hydraulically pressurised (to 2400 psi) steel spheres containing pressurised nitrogen with a cylinder containing hydraulic fluid fitted to each sphere operating an internal piston.

Overall pressure for the system was created by twin pumps and accumulators—one for the suspension system and one for the other hydraulic systems. This ensured that the suspension of each wheel exactly corresponded to the road conditions. The system was filled with vegetable oil—liquid hydraulique vegetal (LHV) allowing the car's suspension to adjust its firmness and ride height automatically depending on load and what type of road the car was on.

This system meant the car would always remain level—something that was to prove vital in ensuring the continued directional stability and driveability of the President's car even after the OAS had shot out at least two of the car's tyres. Added to this, the 1962 DS 19 also featured all round hydraulic servo assisted disc brakes as well as hydraulic power steering—again allowing the President's chauffeur to steer his way out of danger.

The President's car was fitted with Citromatic semi-automatic transmission which used a hydraulic clutch to automatically shift gear eliminating the risk of the car being stalled in the aftermath of the assassination attempt. The car handled particularly well for its size thanks partly to its lightweight fibreglass roof helping to ensure that it had a low centre of gravity but also because of its different front and rear track widths and tyre sizes to prevent the understeer commonly associated with early front wheel drive cars.

Performance wise, the 1962 DS19 was no dragster. Under the bonnet was a 1.9 litre overhead valve water-cooled four-cylinder three bearing engine derived from the Traction Avant.

This had been updated with a new all aluminium cross-flow cylinder head with hemispherical combustion chambers. Fuelled by a single Weber 32 twin bodied carburettor and employing a compression ratio of 8.5:1, the Series 2 DS 19's engine produced a claimed 83bhp. The DS's designers had wanted a larger flat air-cooled six-cylinder engine but the French vehicle taxation system based on horsepower and budgetary constraints relating to the DS's development costs effectively ruled this out.

The 1962 model, known as the Series 2, incorporated a nose restyle to make the car more aerodynamic and optional driving lights mounted in pods on the front wings to the inside and in front of the Cibie headlamps. The cars internal ventilation was also improved along with some other minor revisions.

The car itself resides in the Charles de Gaulle memorial museum at Colombey-les-deux-Eglises and was recently loaned to China as part of a de Gaulle exhibition. However, some controversy surrounds whether the car on display carrying the 5249 HU 75 registration number is actually the same car as the one which saved the President's life. An investigative and satirical weekly French magazine believes the car to be a fake. *Ce véhicule prêté par la France est une faux. Plus précisément, une réplique.*

According to their sources two years after the attack and once the bullet holes had been repaired the car was sold to General Robert-Pol Dupuy, the former military chief of staff of the Elysee. He subsequently had an accident in the car many years later and the damaged car was stored in a garage before being donated in 1980 to the Charles-de-Gaulle Fondation. Given the extent of the damage to the car, the Foundation then decided to replace it with an identical model, while retaining the original interior layout. Whether this is true or not there are certainly photographs of the damaged car.

Chapter 14
1968 Lamborghini Miura

There is snow on the ground but the white-haired man wearing sunglasses, a patterned white jumper and a ski jacket is about to climb into the driving seat of the red Lamborghini Miura—a car completely unsuited to winter driving. A second, man of a similar age is holding the driver's door open flanked by a third man with receding hair. In the background are three stocky looking bodyguards—the first clue that the driver may be someone important. Then there is the registration number of the Miura—TEH 3986—not Italian or Swiss as one might expect but an Iranian number plate issued in Tehran.

The year is 1969; the driver of the car is the 50 year old Mohammad Reza Pahlavi, better known as Mohammad Reza Shah or the Shah of Iran. The photo was taken at the Villa Suvretta in St Moritz during an official visit to Switzerland with his family—hence the snow.

The Shah loved all luxury cars having a collection of over 600 by the time of the Revolution in 1979, but he had a particular penchant for Lamborghinis. This was no aesthetic infatuation: on the contrary the Shah liked to drive his cars hard and, particularly, fast. For him this was a year-round activity. As his nephew described his daily routine:

A 'spin' typically meant that he would drive by himself with a phalanx of armoured Mercedes 6.9's as chase cars. Due to the lack of freeways and tremendous congestion, some of these drives were in the early morning or late afternoon weekends on city streets. The preferred high-speed run was on an express artery on the west side of Tehran that linked to one of our first dedicated freeways. The other choice was to head for the mountain roads east of the Niavaran palace.

In the case of the Miura, the Shah had the car fitted with studded snow tyres for the Swiss trip and flown out especially by the Iranian air force. Chassis #3303 was built on 9 February 1968 and had production number 101. It was an early thin chassis example supplied new and built to order with Rosso red paintwork and his favourite white leather on the interior.

This Miura was the first of at least three and possibly four, that the Shah owned. One (A P400 S) remains in the national motor museum in Tehran. The other three are all outside of Iran with private owners. The reason there is more than one is simple: the Shah was not only fabulously rich but also easily bored. As a new model came out he had to be the first to own it before it was discarded and banished to the Imperial garage in favour of the latest model. Indeed, in the case of the last Miura he owned—a 1971 SJV—the factory only invented the model to keep pace with his insatiable desire for something new and different.

The 1968 P400 left Iran after the Revolution and according to the Lamborghini Miura Register's archives and found its way via a Swiss auction house into the ownership of the Shah's youngest son Prince Alireza Pahlavi.

The car was restored by Belgravia Service Garage in London for the Prince and re-painted orange. It was exhibited at the Louis Vuitton Concours d'Elegance at Hurlingham in London in 1993 and subsequently re-registered in the UK in May 1996 as WGC330F. The car remained in the Prince's ownership until 2010 when it was sold to a Geneva based Iranian collector. In 2015, it was sold again. The mileage at that point was a mere 10,545km. The car was restored a second time in 2017 in Italy.

After the P400 (chassis #3303) came a White P400S in 1970 chassis #4479, production number 496. This is the car in the Tehran motor museum and is currently fitted with the wrong wheels and sits on axle stands. However, this car was most likely not the Shah's and was ordered by the Shah's twin sister. The interior is in blue whereas the Shah's preference was usually for white leather. The car was delivered on 07/04/1970 to Dealer G Nations of Geneva.

Next up was a 1971 Miura P400 SV chassis #4870, production number 635, engine number 30622 in Blu Notte (Night Blue) with a white leather interior. This car was delivered on 02/07/1971 to Rome dealer S.E.A. having been ordered via the Iranian Embassy in Rome as was the case for many of the Shah's cars.

The Miura was a very early production P400 SV with a single sump built specifically for the Shah. The car was fitted with a tape player and air conditioning and was registered TEH 88847. After the Revolution the car was fitted with a locally made bonnet with permanently raised headlamps as sanctions made it impossible to obtain spare parts and the mechanisms had broken.

In the early 1990s, the car was sold by the Iranian authorities to Manfredi Sinistrario—a BMW dealer—and imported via Turkey to Italy where it was restored by ex-Lamborghini factory staff and re-painted in Ischia blue. It was sold in 1999 to new owners in California. The car won the Newport Beach Concours D'Elegance in October 2002.

The final Miura owned by the Shah was a 1971 Miura P400 SVJ—this was the first production "Jota" spec car ever made by Lamborghini. Chassis #4934, production number 678 and engine number 30685. The car was finished in metallic Bordeaux red with the usual white leather interior. As usual, the car was delivered to S.E.A. Rome having been ordered via the Iranian Embassy on 09/12/1971.

The Shah's desire for novelty inspired the design—as legendary Lamborghini automotive engineer Bob Wallace said: "The Shah wanted something special and he was willing to pay for it."

The car started life as a standard SV but was modified by Wallace to include brake vents behind the front and rear wheel arches, an external fuel filler, fixed headlights behind Perspex covers, a single windscreen wiper, an oil cooler, a front spoiler and a straight through exhaust system plus a race harness seatbelt for the driver and studded snow tyres at the Shah's request. The price new was a staggering L 13,000,000 more than double that of a standard P400 SV.

The car was delivered to St Moritz in January 1972 and the Shah drove it once in the Alps before getting the Iranian air force to take it back to Tehran. Like the other Miuras it was seized after the Revolution before finding its way to Dubai in 1994 where it was sold to Mohammed Al Sadek along with nine other cars.

In 1996, it was auctioned by Brooks in Geneva and bought by US actor Nicholas Cage for USD 497,500—three times its estimate after a bidding war. In 2003 Cage sold the car a London based collector before being sold to a collector in 2008 in Gstaad, Switzerland and again in 2009.

The story of the owner of this fabulous fleet of supercars is an interesting one. By 1969 when the photograph was taken, the Shah had been in power for 28 years. Ten years later he would be deposed by the Islamic Revolution, the Monarchy abolished and less than a year later he would be dead from cancer.

Mohammad Reza Pahlavi had been born on 26 October 1919 in Tehran, Persia, the eldest son of Reza Khan who subsequently became the first Shah of the Pahlavi dynasty. Mohammad's father had been a Brigadier-General in the Persian Cossack Brigade and was of Mazandarani and Georgian origin. He became Shah in 1925 following the 1921 Persian coup d'état which deposed Ahmad Shah Qajar. Mohammad became Crown Prince following his father's coronation in 1926.

The Crown Prince lacked confidence having been bullied by his overbearing father who deliberately refused to show him any affection. He was sent to Switzerland in 1931 to be educated at the Institut Le Rosey. In 1936 he returned to Iran to attend the military academy.

At the outbreak of the Second World War, Iran had declared itself neutral but Hitler's invasion of the Soviet Union in 1941 brought unwelcome attention. The Iranian state railways were run by German engineers who refused to cooperate with the Allies plans to ship arms to the Soviet Union via this network. Moscow and London's insistence that the Germans be sacked risked an invasion if it was ignored. The Crown Prince saw his opportunity and deliberately failed to inform his father of this risk.

The result was that British and Soviet troops occupied Iran and Reza Shah was forced to abdicate. By skilful manoeuvring and despite not having Soviet and UK support, the Crown Prince became Shah on 17 September 1941 although it was 1946 before the Red Army withdrew from Iran.

All was well until the early 1950s when, following the 1951 elections, the leader of the nationalist movement, Mohammad Mosadegh, was appointed as Prime Minister. Mosadegh was committed to nationalising the Iranian petroleum industry which was controlled by the Anglo-Iranian Oil Company under the terms of a highly disadvantageous agreement negotiated by the Shah's father. Mosadegh persuaded the Iranian Parliament to vote unanimously in favour of nationalisation.

This was a huge blow to the UK's economy and its prestige in the region and Churchill and Eden vowed to resist it. Initially the US were sympathetic to Mosadegh, indeed the US Ambassador in Tehran, Henry F Grady, was something of a mentor to the Iranian Prime Minister. But a change of Administration in the US from Democrat to Republican coupled with concerns about the risks of a Communist take-over led the US to align with the British.

The CIA were invited to London to work up a plan for a coup to remove Mosadegh from office—the first of a number of CIA regime-change operations led by Allen Dulles which would include the Bay of Pigs fiasco in Cuba (See Chapter 12). The result was the 1952 MI6 and CIA funded "Operation Ajax" which was to be carried out with the cooperation of the Shah—who was given a $1million bribe by the CIA in return for his support.

However, the plot went awry and the Shah had to flee to Rome before plucking up the courage to return in August 1953 for a second attempt. This was also a failure but luckily for the Shah, opposition against the Prime Minister from the Communists destabilised his position which, coupled with an appeal to the military to respect the Shah's wishes, led to Mosadegh's removal and replacement by Zahedi (the UK and US's preferred candidate).

Pro-Shah mobs orchestrated by Zahedi and bribed with $100,000 of CIA funding marched from South Tehran to the city centre where they joined gangs armed with knives and rocks to beat up anti-Shah, pro-Mosadegh, activists. Zahedi for his part was given $900,000 by the CIA.

Although successful in the short term from a US and UK viewpoint, the coup fuelled deep-seated and long-lasting Iranian resentment and contempt for the regime, the US and the UK—something that would eventually boil over in 1979. As the US Secretary of State Madeline Albright noted in 2000:

In 1953, the United States played a significant role in orchestrating the overthrow of Iran's popular Prime Minister Mohammad Mosadegh. The Eisenhower Administration believed its actions were justified for strategic reasons; but the coup was clearly a setback for Iran's political development. And it is easy to see now why many Iranians continue to resent this intervention by America in their internal affairs.

In the immediate period following the coup, the Shah feared being deposed by Zahedi. Mosadegh's National Front was banned and its supporters persecuted. The Shah, while wishing to be an autocrat, also sought to build a powerbase by promoting economic and social reform. He dismissed Zahedi in 1955 and started to re-invent himself as a "progressive Shah" determined to modernise his country and raise living standards. However, at the same time the Shah failed to pursue the secular policies of his father allowing the Mullahs to re-establish themselves and their influence in Iranian society.

The Shah's first clash with Ayatollah Khomeini came in 1962 when the Shah changed the law to allow local officials to be sworn in using the holy book of their personal faith rather than the Koran. The Shah backed down but relations grew worse when the Shah launched his "White Revolution" the following year empowering women. Opposition to the Shah began to be centred in the holy city of Qom. 1963–64 was marked by nationwide demonstrations with Khomeini emerging as leader of protests, giving speeches and sermons calling for the overthrow of the regime. The Shah had Khomeini exiled to Iraq in 1964.

In response to the threat posed by the Ayatollah, in 1967 the Shah decided to hold a coronation in Tehran and award himself the ancient title of Shahan shah—King of Kings as part of a drive to give greater prominence to Iran's pre-Islamic history.

Despite relying on the US for his position, the Shah manipulated the West and particularly America's reliance on his country's oil. Although Iran didn't participate in the 1973 oil crisis, it benefitted from it by increasing production afterwards at the new higher price. It was also the prime mover in encouraging OPEC to raise the price further.

As a result, Iran's GDP was 50% higher by 1974. The Shah was unrepentant. Iran was booming while the West was in economic recession. Both British Prime Minister Harold Wilson and his French counterpart Valerie Giscard d'Estaing contacted the Shah to beg for loans—the Shah gave $1 billion to each country because he *did not want the European world to which he belonged to collapse.*

The newfound, limitless oil wealth concentrated in his hands made the Shah more arrogant and less tolerant towards the West. In 1976 he famously remarked:

Now, we are the masters and our former masters are our slaves. Every day they beat a track to our door begging for favours—Do we want arms? Do we want nuclear power stations? We have only to answer and they fulfil our wishes.

This of course was the origin of Iran's nuclear programme which had begun in March 1957 with a US/Iran agreement signed under Eisenhower's "Atoms for Peace" program and had led to the setting up of the Tehran Nuclear Research Centre equipped with a U.S.-supplied, five-megawatt nuclear research reactor fuelled by highly enriched uranium.

By the early 1970s, the Shah had plans to construct up to 23 nuclear power stations and the US, UK, France, Germany and Sweden were falling over themselves to win contracts. The first reactor was at Bushehr near Shiraz and was due to be completed in 1981. The US Administration signed a directive in 1976 to allow Tehran to buy and operate a U.S.-built reprocessing facility for extracting plutonium from nuclear reactor fuel.

By the late 1970s the Shah's narcissism had turned into megalomania—he believed Allah himself had chosen him to create the "Great Civilisation" in Iran. His regime dominated every aspect of life and monopolised the country's wealth.

He abolished the two-party democratic system in 1975 and replaced it with a one-party state. No opposition was tolerated—so called "traitors" those with dissenting political views were sent to prison or expelled. This political repression coupled with the deep wealth inequalities in Iranian society, where ordinary people were confronted with poverty, inflation and having to pay bribes to corrupt officials created a powder keg of popular dissent.

The end of the regime began in 1977 with protests after the death of Khomeini's son. This was further fuelled by a regime-sponsored article accusing

Khomeini of being a British spy, a homosexual, a drug addict and Indian rather than Iranian. The regime had made a fatal error in antagonising a powerful and organised force that was able to tap into and channel the popular resentment.

To compound the situation, the Shah had been diagnosed with cancer in 1974, had disappeared from public view and was being treated with medication that left him unable to think clearly. On 8 September 1978, the effectively leaderless army opened fire on unarmed protesters. The situation continued to deteriorate with a march of six-nine million Iranians against the Shah in December.

Increasingly paranoid, the Shah spent his time devising conspiracy theories rather than addressing the underlying causes of the protests. Strikingly he failed to see the Islamic dimension, preferring instead to blame the KGB, CIA and MI6. When oil workers went on strike in October 1978, turning off the financial taps, the Shah's regime began to crumble. By late December, his military commanders were making approaches to the emerging leaders of the Revolution.

A meeting of the US and French Presidents, the German Chancellor and the British Prime Minister in Guadeloupe in January 1979 convinced the Shah that the game was up and his former allies were about to abandon him. On 16 January he left Iran for Egypt. Within hours the Prime Minister, Shapour Bakhtaran, had allowed the Ayatollah to return from exile in Paris. A plan to persuade Khomeini to create the equivalent of the Vatican State in Qom failed. He seized power and by 11 February the Monarchy had been abolished.

After leaving Egypt, the Shah travelled to Morocco before settling in Paradise Island in the Bahamas and Cuernavaca in Mexico. Nixon visited him in Mexico. Ravaged by cancer, the Shah was suffering from gallstones and required surgery.

The Shah was unwilling to do this in Mexico, preferring the US. US President Carter was decidedly un-keen on this idea but was blackmailed by Henry Kissinger—the latter making his support for the SALT II Treaty with the Soviet Union conditional on allowing the Shah to be admitted to the US for treatment. Against State Department advice—who believed the Iranians would storm the US embassy if the Shah were admitted—Carter agreed on 22 October 1979. Complications meant that six weeks later the Shah was still there. The Iranian authorities demanded his return to Iran.

In the absence of this, the US embassy in Tehran was stormed and hostages taken. The Shah left the US for Panama before taking up Egypt's offer of asylum in 1980. Following a splenectomy the Shah died in Egypt on 27 July 1980.

Lamborghini

Lamborghini was established in Bologna in 1963 by Ferruccio Lamborghini a wealthy Italian businessman who had a successful tractor manufacturing business. Lamborghini wanted to challenge the dominance of manufacturers like Ferrari in the lucrative luxury GT car market. With this in mind, Lamborghini began by commissioning a company called Societa Autostar headed by former Ferrari engineer Giotto Bizzarrini to design a refined V12 engine for road use in his new cars.

Lamborghini was unhappy with Bizzarrini's design—which featured a dry sump, 3.5 litres, a 9.5:1 compression ratio and a maximum output of 360 bhp at 9800 rpm—because it was too much like a race car engine. He refused to pay Bizzarrini until the latter took him to court.

The first Lamborghini—the 350 GTV—was created by former Ferrari Italian chassis engineer Gian Paolo Dallara along with Paolo Stanzani, New Zealander Bob Wallace and styled by Franco Scaglione and was displayed at the 1963 Turin Motor show to critical acclaim.

Building on this success, Automobili Ferruccio Lamborghini S.p.A. was officially established at the end of October 1963. The factory was built in Sant'Agata Bolognese after Lamborghini did a deal with the city's Communist leaders who promised a 19% return on any profits deposited in the bank along with zero tax on profits in return for allowing the workers to join a trade union. The choice was a good one not only because of these financial inducements, but also because it was the centre of Italy's automobile industry giving easy access to skilled labour and facilities.

The 350 GTV was modified for production and its styling revised by Touring of Milan and was a success. The Miura however took Lamborghini to a whole new level. All was rosy until the 1973 oil crisis—an irony given the Shah's devotion to the marque and his role in deepening the oil crisis and subsequent economic downturn in the West.

Orders plunged and Lamborghini sold the ailing company to Georges-Henri Rossetti and René Leimer. The company subsequently went bankrupt in 1978 and was placed into receivership. Jean Claude and Patrick Mimran purchased the company in 1984, invested and expanded the model range before selling it to Chrysler in 1987 who in turn sold it to a Malaysian investment company in 1994. In 1998, the company was sold to Volkswagen and placed under the control of Audi.

Lamborghini Miura P400

The Miura was produced by Lamborghini from 1966 to 1973 with 764 examples built. Styled by Marcelo Gandini at Bertone it was not only beautiful but also blisteringly fast thanks to lightweight bodywork and a V12 3929cc, 345bhp, engine coupled with a five-speed manual, transmission.

The car was developed secretly by three Lamborghini engineers: Gian Paolo Dallara, Paolo Stanzani and Bob Wallace, in their spare time because they knew that Ferruccio Lamborghini, the company's founder, was no fan of sports cars preferring grand tourers instead. The model was known as the P400—P for posteriori (the engine position) and 400 reflecting the four-litre engine cylinder capacity.

The chassis for the car with its mid-mounted V12 engine featuring a gearbox in the sump which shared the same oil as the engine—Alec Issigonis's innovation for the Mini—was first displayed at the Turin motor show in 1965 and orders were placed despite the car having no bodywork. It was eventually unveiled as a complete car at the 1966 Geneva motor show and went into production the following year. The Shah's P400 was one of the first production run.

The car was named Miura after a famous Spanish fighting bull breeder who Ferruccio had visited in 1962—hence the raging bull on the Lamborghini badge—which also happened to be his star sign: Taurus. The car was an instant hit and became Lamborghini's mainstay for almost a decade until it was replaced by the Countach.

In 1968, the P400 was updated as the P400S featuring minor stylistic changes—electric windows and chrome trim round the windows and headlights and a fractionally bigger boot—and engine revisions which raised the power output to 365bhp. 338 P400S were made. In 1971 the model was updated again to create he Miura P400SV. Power was again increased—to 380 bhp—and the single sump was replaced by a twin sump arrangement allowing for different types of oil to be used in the engine and the transmission.

The final production variant—the P400 SVJ—the "Jota" was the combination of work done by Bob Wallace on a track car that would comply with the FIA's "Appendix J" regulations for track cars and the Shah's request for something new and special. The car featured bodywork modifications including a font spoiler and faired in headlamps behind Perspex covers. Only six were built #4934 (the Shah's), #4860, #4892, #4490, #5084 and #5090.

Chapter 15
1971 Porsche 911 Targa

It is the morning of 1 June 1972 in a nondescript street in the Dornbusch district of Frankfurt. In the centre of the photo is an almost new, dark coloured, Porsche 911 Targa with Konstanz—a city on the German-Swiss border—licence plates and a 'D' sticker on the engine compartment lid. The frameless doors are wide open and two men are busy, one with some luggage, the other looking into the passenger side of the vehicle. They are detectives.

A uniformed man with a white peaked cap and a pistol in a holster looks on, arms folded. He is a German police officer. One of his colleagues is standing in the middle of the street in front of the car. In the distance, on the pavement on the left-hand side, a crowd is being held back by two more police officers.

The car 'belongs' to Andreas Baader, co-leader of the Red Army Faction (RAF)—the Baader-Meinhof terrorist group. He, along with three other members, including Holger Meins and Jan-Carl Raspe, have just been arrested. Although he doesn't yet know it, Baader has driven the 911—or indeed any car—for the last time.

Quite what the leader of a vicious, revolutionary Marxist, anti-capitalist terror organisation is doing driving around in such a symbol of conspicuous capitalist consumption is puzzling. Or, indeed, how the other car seized that morning—a silver Iso Rivolta—also a high-end luxury sports car—fitted with the groups' Marxist-Leninist beliefs is equally mysterious.

However, as earlier chapters of this book show, killers are often curiously drawn to luxury automotive brands, even if their underlying ideology happens, inconveniently, to be Communist. Baader was no exception. Despite never holding a driving licence, his and his accomplices' appetite for top of the range automotive exotica was limitless, to the point where a running German joke in the period was that BMW (see Chapter 20) actually stood for Baader-Meinhof Wagen.

The Porsche, as with all of the group's vehicles, was, of course, stolen—in this case two months earlier in April from outside the apartment of Rainer Schlegelmilch—a leading German motor racing photographer. The Police searching the car found homemade hand grenades and explosive devices in the luggage compartment. The car was Porsche Canary yellow when Schlegelmilch had last seen it but had been resprayed Porsche Burgundy—another 1971 Porsche colour—to help hide its identity.

Schlegelmilch had claimed on his insurance after the theft and had bought a replacement 911 by the time of the arrests, which he heard about on the radio. Little did he know that Germany's most wanted terrorist had been driving around in his former pride and joy. It was not until the Federal Police contacted him subsequently that he learned of his stolen car's fate.

The 1 June arrests were the culmination of months of painstaking work by the German Police and Intelligence Services. The operation that day involved 150 police officers and a shoot-out reminiscent of a Western.

Yet, the arrest of Baader, his girlfriend and fellow terrorist Gudrun Ensslin, Ulrike Meinhof and their associates marked the end only of the first generation of a terrorist group that would continue to exist in different forms until at least 1998, with three wanted members still committing armed robberies as recently as 2017. In the course of the 1970s and 1980s at least 30 people would lose their lives as a result of RAF bombings and shootings.

Berndt Andreas Baader was born into a middle-class family during the Second World War in Munich on 6 May 1943. His father, Dr Bernt Phillipp Baader, a historian, joined the German army, was captured on the Eastern front by the Russians and died as prisoner of war along with at least 700,000 others. Baader, an only child, was therefore brought up by his widowed mother. He rebelled, dropped out and left school without qualifications becoming more interested in fast cars and women than qualifications or a driving licence.

As a result, he did not attend university. After enrolling at Art College, he disappeared into Berlin's counterculture, which rejected the values of the wartime German generation, which they saw as the remnants of the Nazi regime. For him, the anti-Nazi struggle of the RAF gave his own existence meaning and, along with his relationship with Ensslin, became the central driving force of his life. By 1965, Baader had a daughter with an artist Ellinor Michel and was living in a flat with her and her husband. He had a number of girlfriends and a string of court appearances for speeding and car theft.

The turning point from petty crime to violent terrorism came when he met the daughter of an evangelical Christian pastor—Gudrun Ensslin in 1967. Unlike Baader she had gone to university and studied philosophy and had led a sheltered upbringing.

However, like him she had arrived at the same set of extreme beliefs— namely that the post-war German state was still dominated by the wartime generation of former Nazis and, as such, the forces of the extreme progressive Left were at war. Baader was everything that Ensslin was not—he was experienced in breaking the law but lacked the intellectual and ideological underpinning that she brought with her. Together they formed a fatal combination.

The trigger that drew them closer together came on 2 June 1967, when a 26 year-old named Benno Ohnesorg was shot in the back of the head by a police officer during a Left-wing protest march against a state visit by the Shah of Persia (see Chapter 15) in West Berlin. Ohnesorg, a college student with a pregnant wife, had never attended a protest before.

Despite being found to be a Stasi (East German secret police) informant, the police officer Karl-Heinz Kurras, was found not guilty by a court, sparking outrage amongst left-wing radicals. This spurred Baader and Ensslin to commit their first terrorist attack in response by fire-bombing a Frankfurt department store on 2 April 1968 both in protest for Ohnesorg's killing and the German government's support for the Vietnam war.

Baader, Ensslin and two others were subsequently arrested and sentenced to three years in prison for the arson but were provisionally released from custody in June 1969, 14 months later under an amnesty to allow them to appeal. They were unsuccessful, and, in November 1969, broke bail and went on the run to Italy, France and Switzerland before covertly re-entering West Germany on false papers. It was during this time that they lived for a few weeks with the left-wing journalist Ulrike Meinhof in her apartment.

Given his passion for fast driving, it was not surprising that Baader was caught in a car when he was stopped and arrested by German police on April 4, 1970. As usual, the vehicle was a stolen and he was using false papers claiming to be Peter Chotjewitz—a lawyer who he had met in Rome while on the run and who had tipped him off that his appeal was to be rejected earlier in February 1970. On 24 April, 24 Baader was transferred from remand in Moabit to Tegel prison.

Ensslin and Baader's associates plotted both his escape. Baader's extraction was carefully planned and involved Meinhof using her publisher to request an interview between Meinhof and Baader at the German Central Institute for Social issues as part of their joint work on a (fictitious) book.

The justification for the use of a neutral venue outside of the maximum security Tegel was that Baader would need access to Left wing revolutionary publications which were banned in the prison. A formal request made on 10 May 1970 but was initially—and wisely—refused. However, the prison authorities relented after lobbying by Baader's lawyer and the interview was approved for a three hour timeslot at the Institute on 14 May.

The team for the operation was assembled—Irene Goergen, Astrid Proll and Ingrid Schubert—and equipment sourced including a 6.35mm Beretta and silencer and other weapons as well as an Alfa Romeo Giulia Sprint which was stolen as a getaway car and fitted with false plates. A recce of the Institute was conducted by Goergens and Schubert the day before the interview.

On the 14th, Baader arrived with two armed guards and was shown into a room to be interviewed by Meinhof where he was un-handcuffed. Goergens and Schubert arrived at the Institute's front door with suitcases on the pretence of carrying out some research. They opened the door to allow a masked gunman to enter and together stormed the room where Baader was, allowing him, the gunman, Meinhof, Goergens and Scubert all to escape via a window to the waiting Alfa Romeo.

Once Baader was free, Ensslin called, in an article in an underground magazine, for the formation of a Marxist-Leninist 'Red Army' to pursue the class struggle and start an armed resistance against the authorities. This group would become the Red Army Faction (RAF)—the Baader-Meinhof terrorist group. Ensslin, Baader, Meinhof and their associates travelled to Jordan to attend a terrorist training at a camp run by the Palestinian Liberation Organisation (PLO). Here, they learned bomb making and automatic weapons handling as well as terrorist organisation techniques.

Outside of the core group, the Red Army Faction operated as cells—or commandos—which were supplied from the centre but operated on a strict 'need to know' basis in terms of hierarchy and contacts. The group's organisation was based on Meinhof's pamphlet 'The Urban Guerrilla Concept' which in turn drew its inspiration and modus operandi from South American terrorist groups.

Baader, a frustrated art student with a keen eye for publicity, paid a designer to create the group's logo—a red star with a Heckler and Kock MP5 submachine gun. He also actively courted the media—a smart move given that polling in the period revealed that over 25% of West Germans under the age of 40 felt some sympathy for and affinity with the group.

To boost funds, the group carried out a series of high-profile robberies. With the proceeds they attacked the US Army headquarters in Frankfurt with pipe bombs, killing one and injuring 13 (11 May 1972); the Axel Springer Verlag (the offices of Bild Zeitung—a tabloid hostile to the revolutionary left) in Hamburg, injuring 36 (19 May 1972); the US Army Campbell Barracks in Heidelberg, killing three and injuring five (24 May 1974) This wave of attacks led to a renewed manhunt for Baader, Ensslin and Meinhof, which culminated in the 1 June Police operation.

Acting on a tip off, Police had been watching a lock-up garage in Dornbusch which contained the group's bomb making chemicals and equipment. On 1 June, just before 06:00, the burgundy Porsche drew up outside the garage and three men got out and were about to go inside when one spotted a number of what looked like Police on the surrounding roofs. One of the three fired at the Police with a pistol but was overpowered. Baader and Holger Meins ducked inside the garage.

There was no back door: they were trapped. Tv crews filmed as Baader and Meins fired at the Police and the Police lobbed teargas into the garage. A further three hours passed before Baader emerged brandishing his pistol and was shot in the leg by a Police marksman. Meins surrendered and Police broke the garage doors down to arrest the wounded Baader. The Porsche was seized by the Police as evidence.

A few days later Schlegelmich got a phone call from the Police asking him to visit a Police storage facility in Wiesbaden. There he was met by a representative of the German Security Service who showed him Baader's Burgundy Porsche Targa and explained that it was in fact his stolen car. Checking in the door pocket he found a business card from a smart restaurant in France he had visited just prior to the car being stolen. He was told that the car was required for evidence—he never saw it again, nor is its subsequent fate known.

In the following two weeks, Ensslin was arrested in a shop in Hamburg after removing her jacket to try on a dress only for the pistol in the pocket to be spotted by the shop assistant. On 7 June 1972, Meinhof was also arrested at an apartment in Hanover-Langenhagen with another group member Gerhard Müller. Baader, Ensslin, Meinhof, Raspe and Meins were all held in solitary confinement in the newly constructed, maximum security, Stammhein prison outside Stuttgart.

However, the Baader-Meinhof group terrorism did not stop as a second generation of the RAF carried out attacks including the kidnapping of Peter Lorenz the CDU candidate for Berlin mayor in return for the release of other RAF members and the botched seizure of the West German Embassy in Stockholm on 24 April1975.

The 'Stammheim four' trial (Meins had starved himself to death on hunger strike) finally began on 21 May 1975. Meinhof hanged herself in her cell on 9 May 1976 during the trial. The RAF assassinated Federal Prosecuror Siegfried Burback on 7 April 1977. A former Nazi, Burback had stated publicly that he did not believe that Baader 'deserved a fair trial'.

Indeed, there was criticism of the Nazi past of a number of judges involved in the trial. Proceedings also invoked special laws such as the exclusion of defence lawyers and the searching of the defendants' lawyers' offices. On 28 April 1977, Baader and his co-defendants were sentenced to life and transferred to a new, specially constructed, maximum-security wing of the prison.

Here, they committed suicide on the night of 18 October 1977—Baader and Raspe using pistols smuggled into the prison by their lawyer and Ensslin hanging herself. Despite the founders of the group being dead, the RAF continued its operations until on 20 April 1998 when an eight page statement was faxed to Reuters announcing its dissolution.

1971 Porsche 911 Targa

Baader's (or more accurately Schlegelmich's) 911 Targa was the latest model in a long lineage stretching back to September 1964 when the 911 had first gone into production.

Designed (at least as sketches) by Ferdinand 'Butzi' Porsche in 1959, its smooth lines were the logical styling progression of the earlier 356 that it replaced. The model was originally to be have been called the 901—but Peugeot had exclusive rights to car model numbers with a '0' in the middle (something dating back to their early models which featured an 'O' shaped hole in the middle of the grille for the starting handle) and launched legal action.

As a result, only the first 82 cars were badged '901'—the remainder being badged '911' (although the part numbers continued to begin with a '901' prefix) The first commercially available 911s in 1965 featured a rear-mounted, air-cooled, two litre, flat six cylinder 'boxer' engine and rear wheel drive layout. Transmission was a four or five speed manual box. The car was technically a four-seater but the absence of rear legroom meant that it was designated as a 2+2.

Porsche introduced the 911 Targa at the International Motor Show in Frankfurt in September 1965. The model was introduced in response to growing rumours that US Federal safety legislation was about to ban convertible cars in the US—a traditionally lucrative segment and market for Porsche. The US Department for Transportation was concerned by data showing that accidents involving convertibles were often fatal for the car's occupants.

Other manufacturers such as Chevrolet (see Chapter 16) also began to make contingency plans for the Corvette, but Porsche was the first to find a solution. To head off the threat, Porsche designers came up with the idea of fitting the car with a permanent stainless steel roll bar as used on Porsche competition cars.

Behind this, the car was fitted with a traditional convertible type vinyl hood and clear plastic rear window. In front of the roll bar, a removable vinyl covered steel panel was fitted that could be unclipped and stowed in the luggage compartment. Thus, the model combined the open top motoring of a convertible with the safety and sportiness of a roll bar. This was the same system offered on Triumph TR4, 4a and 5, a decade earlier as a 'Surrey top'.

The model was named 'Targa' after Porsche's success at the Targa Florio Rally in Sicily, not realising that the word meant 'number plate' in Italian—In August 1965, Porsche patented the 'Targa top' and started offering it on 911, 911S and 912 models from late 1966. It was a sales success, but the rear vinyl hood was unsatisfactory and leaked resulting in a metal framed, heated curved glass rear screen being offered in its place from mid-1967—a feature that became standard the following year—and which featured on Baader's car.

The threatened legislation never came into force, but by then Porsche had created a whole new market segment with the Targa which remained an option on 911s until 1994.

Baader's 1971 911 was a D series of the model which was produced from August 1970 until July 1971 with a larger 2.2 litre engine producing 153 bhp at 6200 rpm. This was not the fastest in the range—the 911S produced 180 bhp—but it had the best acceleration.

Porsche

Porsche was founded in 1931 by Ferdinand Porsche, Adolf Rosenberger and Anton Piëch as "Dr Ing. h. c. F. Porsche Gmbh" which looks rather more like a computer password than the name of what was to become one of Germany's most successful car companies. Initially the Stuttgart based company did not build cars but instead offered design consultancy—'Konstruktionen und Beratungen für Motoren und Fahrzeugbau' to companies such as Wanderer.

It was also involved in design work for Auto Union, which was formed in 1934 from the ailing DKW, Horch (see Chapter 7) and Wanderer brands. Following Hitler's decision to focus the German motor industry on two main projects—high performance racing (a contract handed to Mercedes-Benz—see Chapter 8) and mass transportation, Porsche gained the contract to build a 'people's car'—the 'Volkswagen' Beetle.

It was from these humble underpinnings that the Porsche sports car range would subsequently be developed, the first of which being the all-aluminium bodied, streamlined Porsche 64 special which was developed using Beetle components for a, cancelled, Berlin-Rome road race in 1939.

During the war Beetle production line was switched to military variants—the Kubelwagen and the Schwimmwagen. Attempts by Porsche to compete for the design of the Tiger 1 heavy tank were unsuccessful with Henschel and Sohn winning the contract (despite Porsche coming up with the name) but the design work was recycled into the Panzerjäger Elefant tank destroyer.

Later in the war, the Wolfsburg plant was switched over to V1 rocket production. Like many large German industrial companies operating in World War Two (see Chapter 8) Porsche made extensive use of forced labour.

After the war, the Wolfsburg Volkswagen factory was handed to the British and run by Major Ivan Hiirst. On 15 December 1945, French authorities arrested Ferdinand Porsche, Anton Piëch his son in law and his son Ferry Porsche as war criminals. All three had been members of the Nazi Party and of the SS. Bail was set at 500,000 French Francs for each.

The Porsche family could only afford this amount for Ferry, who was released six months later. Porsche and Piëch were imprisoned in Baden-Baden before being transferred to Dijon. Porsche claimed this was an attempt to force his company to collaborate with Renault to design a new car.

However, the French government claimed that Porsche had not only been involved in the use of forced labour (by some estimates there were 10,000 forced labourers of Slavic origin at Wolfsburg at the stage it was converted to V1 rocket production, at least 500 of whom died), but had deliberately transferred machine tools from French car factories to its own factory in Stuttgart.

The French government therefore requested one million French Francs in compensation, for the release of Piëch and Porsche. Eventually Porsche's family raised the money through a contract with the Italian sports car manufacturer Cisitalia and Porsche and Piëch were released in August 1947.

Ferry, who had kept the company going in his father's absence, had started work, in an old saw-mill in Gmünd in Carinthia where the company had relocated at the end of the war to avoid the Allied bombing of Stuttgart, on the Porsche 356. This would become the first car to be badged as a Porsche. Designed by Erwin Komenda (who had designed the Beetle) the first 49 were hand built due to a lack both of equipment and funding.

These prototypes were used to secure sufficient pre-orders to begin full-scale production in Stuttgart in 1950. The company's logo was based on the inter war Weimar Republic coat of arms of the People's State of Württemberg whose capital was Stuttgart. Despite using a number of the humble Volkswagen Beetle's underpinnings, the 356 was a huge success and as the model evolved the Beetle components were replaced with Porsche's own manufactured parts.

The 356 provided Porsche's mainstay until the introduction of the 911 in 1965. This proved to be the most successful model in the company's history staying in production—albeit with regular modifications and updating—for over 50 years with the millionth 911 being built in May 2017.

In 1972, the Company structure switched from being a limited partnership to a public limited company run by an executive board with external members other than just members of the Porsche family. The Company remains one of the world's leading luxury car brands and produced a €2.2 billion operating profit in 2021.

Chapter 16
1972 Chevrolet Chevelle Station Wagon

It is 2 April 1974. A tired and unshaven man in military fatigues is getting out of a khaki painted Chevrolet Chevelle. His parka coat is on the seat behind him and his driver is discretely looking away from the camera. He is going home to his family after a long day.

The man is the former Chief of Staff of the Israel's armed forces, Lieutenant General David Elazar. He has just resigned his post following a Committee of Inquiry which, earlier in the evening, held him solely responsible for Israel's lack of preparedness for the Yom Kippur War. The fact that, despite having started at a disadvantage, Lieutenant General Elazar had led his forces to victory had made no difference. Somebody needed to take responsibility for Israel having been taken by surprise and that duty fell to David Elazar.

This was undoubtedly a great injustice, not least because none of his colleagues such as the Head of Israeli Military Intelligence or his political superiors—including the Israeli Prime Minister and Defence Minister—resigned. Given the stress and humiliation, Elazar's premature death just two years later from a heart attack at the age of 50 should have come as no surprise.

Elazar had been born in Sarajevo and had emigrated to what was then Palestine in 1940 to settle on a Kibbutz. He fought with distinction in many of the battles during Israel's war of independence. A talented soldier, he rose rapidly through the ranks becoming a Commander in the Harel Brigade. After independence he remained in the army becoming commander of Israel's Armoured Corps in 1961.

In 1964, he was promoted to become chief of the Northern Command, a post he held through the Six Day War in 1967 until 1969. On 1 January 1972, he was appointed Chief of Staff. His early tenure in this post was dominated by Counter Terrorism operations following the 30 May 1972 Lod Airport Massacre and the attack on Israel's athletes at the 1972 Munich Olympics. To neutralise the threat, Elazar ordered pre-emptive strikes against Palestinian bases in Lebanon and Syria and the assassination of key Palestinian leaders in Beirut.

The constant state of tension with Israel's Arab neighbours was the backdrop to events of October 1973. Israel had first occupied the strategically important Sinai Peninsula during the Suez Crisis of 1956 only to be forced by Washington a year later to hand it back to Egypt. President Nasser's decision in 1967 to ban Israeli shipping from the Straits of Tiran, effectively blockading the Gulf of Aqaba had helped to trigger the Six Day War the same year.

During the war Israel had recaptured and occupied Sinai. This was therefore a huge potential flashpoint. In February 1971, the UN had tabled a peace plan involving Egypt reopening the Suez Canal in return for partial Israeli withdrawal from Sinai. This followed an offer the previous December by Egypt's President Sadat in an article in the New York Times to recognise the State of Israel as defined by the UN Security Council (i.e. on its pre 1967 boundaries) in exchange for full withdrawal from Sinai.

This was a hugely significant step since it marked the first time an Arab country had offered to recognise Israel. Israeli Prime Minister Golda Meir set up a Committee to examine the proposal, which, inconveniently for her, decided unanimously in favour of the Egyptian offer. Meir overruled the Committee and sent a formal Israeli response on 26 February 1971 offering a partial withdrawal but categorically rejecting any return to Israel's pre-1967 borders.

Having had his diplomatic overture rebuffed, Sadat (see Chapter 17) for domestic reasons, began to favour a limited military conflict to restore Egyptian national pride after the humiliation of 1967 and to strengthen Egypt's negotiating position. His ally, President Hafez al-Assad of Syria, had other plans and favoured retaking the Golan Heights by force without any negotiations.

Sadat's other allies were far less keen, notably King Hussein of Jordan who felt the end result might be a re-run of 1967 and further territorial losses. Iraq and Lebanon preferred to remain neutral. Sadat nevertheless persisted including by building an alliance with Yasser Arafat of the PLO.

Thus by mid-1972, Sadat was set on military action and began to strengthen his forces with Soviet help in the form of MiG 21 fighter jets, SA-2, 3, 6 and anti-aircraft missiles, T-55 and T-62 battle tanks and, as Israeli forces were to discover to their cost, RPG-7, RPG-43 and AT-3 Sagger anti-tank missiles. The Soviets also provided training and Sadat replaced his senior military commanders.

Despite this and as a result of the Oslo Accords, the Soviet Union was keen to avoid a military conflict in the region that could escalate into one with the US. With this in mind, they began leaking Egyptian military planning with the result that a furious Sadat expelled 20,000 Soviet Military Advisers in July 1972. Sadat for his part continued his careful preparations including regular military exercises close to the border.

However, the frequency and scale of these was a stroke of genius since it created the impression in Israeli minds that Egypt was more interested in military posturing than actually trying to retake the lost territory.

Sadat's plan was for a limited incursion to retake territory on the East Bank of the Suez Canal and then to rely on international pressure to force Tel Aviv to negotiate. Egypt's large-scale military exercises in May 1973 had resulted in Elazar launching a general mobilisation.

This false alarm coupled with a second large scale Egyptian exercise in August that year without any cross-border incursion had two results. The first was that Elazar's credibility had been weakened. The second was that it had bred a certain complacency, to the point that the general mobilisation of the Egyptian and Syrian armies on 1 October that year was dismissed as the prelude to yet another military exercise. As such, the Israeli Defence Force's response was limited with a few additional reserve units being deployed on the Peninsula.

The reason for this complacency was nothing to do with Elazar. Israeli Military Intelligence believed, correctly, that Egypt would not go to war without Syria but also, incorrectly, that Egypt would not go to war until it had taken both delivery of and was trained to use the MiG-23s and Scud missiles. The Israelis knew that the first of these had only arrived in late August 1972. Israeli Military Intelligence also knew the full details of the Egyptian battle plan to recapture part of Sinai.

However, the combination of the expulsion by Egypt of the 20,000 Soviet military advisers in July 1972 and, the late arrival of the new kit, led them to conclude that the threat of military action in the Autumn of 1973 was negligible. When Egypt began more exercises next to the Suez Canal at the end of September, Israeli Military Intelligence dismissed it as yet another act of posturing by Sadat.

Indeed, the Egyptians cleverly had called up 20,000 reservists for the "exercises" and publicly announced their demobilisation on 4 October. Elazar by contrast was growing increasingly concerned given that the scale of the troop movements was far greater than anything previously seen for an exercise. This, Elazar noted was coupled with major troop movements on the Syrian border.

Despite voicing these concerns, the Chief of Military Intelligence, Major General Eli Zeira and Israeli Defence Minister, Moshe Dayan, remained unconvinced, the latter explicitly blocking Elazar's request on 5 October for a full mobilisation of reserves.

At a meeting at 08:05 on the morning of 6 October, Elazar tried again to persuade Dayan and Prime Minister Golda Meir to agree to pre-emptive air strikes against Syrian airfields at noon, Syrian missiles at 15:00 and Syrian ground forces at 17:00. Dayan argued against and Meir, conscious of the need for Israel to avoid being seen in US eyes to have started a war, refused the request.

Unfortunately, Elazar's instincts were correct. At 02:00 pm on 6 October the Syrian and Egyptian armed forces launched a coordinated attack on Israel, crossing ceasefire lines to enter the Golan Heights and Sinai Peninsula respectively. Both advances were virtually unopposed initially such was the element of surprise.

In Sinai, casualties were heavy. The Egyptians had 100,000 soldiers, 1,350 tanks and 200 guns against 450 Israeli soldiers in 16 forts on the opposite bank. Early attempts to halt the advance by Israeli tanks failed because the Egyptians were armed with anti-tank missiles. Elazar and General Ariel Sharon took the strategic decision to allow the Egyptians to continue to advance to draw them further away from their fortified, dug in positions on the ceasefire line. The Egyptian surface to air defences were intact and any attempt to halt the advance within their range would have been disastrous.

Within three days of the initial attack, Israel had fully mobilised its forces in the South and was ready to halt the Egyptian advance. At the same point in the North, Israeli forces had pushed the Syrians back across the ceasefire line.

In the following four days, Israeli forces in the North drove deep into Syrian territory ending up in a position where they were able to shell the outskirts of Damascus. Progress in the South by contrast was much harder. President Sadat of Egypt had ordered his forces back on the offensive to try to capture two strategic passes deep within Sinai that he hoped might serve as the new ceasefire line.

The Israelis met the new Egyptian offensive head on and halted it. By rapidly counter attacking, Israel was able to drive a wedge between the Egyptian forces and to cross the Suez Canal into Egypt. Casualties were heavy on both sides. Given the wider Cold war implications of the conflict, the UN attempted to broker a ceasefire. This broke down on 22 October allowing Israel to further strengthen its positions before a new ceasefire was brokered and implemented with US and Soviet backing on 25 October.

Israeli had been unprepared and had suffered heavy casualties as a result. Thanks in part to Elazar's cool head—in contrast to Dayan—the tide was turned with Elazar taking control and even taking the step of recalling three retired Generals—Shmuel Gonen, Rehavam Zeevi and Aharon Yarivlt. Nevertheless, it took five days to repel the Syrian forces in the North and a full ten days before the Israelis forced the Egyptians back across the Suez Canal.

By the end of the war Israeli forces had driven deep inside Syrian territory, had occupied the Southern side of the Suez Canal and had encircled the Egyptian Third Army on the Sinai Peninsula. Militarily Elazar had managed to turn the tables. However, the cost in terms of casualties, aircraft and tanks had been high and the public mood was toxic.

The result was a public inquiry—the Agranat Commission—was set up to establish why Israel had been caught unprepared and unaware. This process dragged on for months. Its interim report of 1 April 1974 called for Elazar's dismissal, unfairly—not least given Dayan and Zeira's role-stating that: "Elazar bears personal responsibility for the assessment of the situation and the (lack of) preparedness of the IDF". As an honourable man, Elazar immediately tendered his resignation in writing.

However, he also took the opportunity to highlight the double standards between the way he had been treated in comparison to the Politicians who had been fully consulted and had opposed the full call up of reservists and the launching of pre-emptive airstrikes. The public largely viewed the Commission as a whitewash and Elazar as the unfortunate scapegoat.

The war's wider significance was perhaps that it opened the way to the subsequent peace process and Camp David Accords (see Chapter 17) in 1978. For the Arab States it provided some closure on the military humiliation of the Six Day War while at the same time signalling to Israel that it could no longer rely on military superiority to maintain its security in the region.

Chevrolet Chevelle

The Chevrolet Chevelle was a mid-sized (by American standards) car produced from 1964 to 1977 in three distinct generations and with a wide range of different body styles. The car was a big seller for Chevrolet who, imaginatively, dubbed it "America's most popular mid-sized car" in their sales literature.

The model was first launched in 1964 in a bid to gain some of the market share that AMC had monopolised with its Rambler and Ford had launched its mid-sized Fairlane in 1962 to capture. The Chevelle was an instant hit with first year sales of 338,286 units. The model was offered in a large range of body styles from a two door pick up, two door coupe, two door convertible, four door sedan and initially a two-door station wagon (subsequently replaced by a four-door model).

There was also a dizzying range of trim options—the station wagons for example initially came in "Greenbrier", "Concours" and "Concours Estate" variants with an equally bewildering range of engine options from a 3.2 Litre straight six petrol to a 6.5 litre big block V8. By the second generation (1968–

72) station wagon trim options ranged from the basic "Nomad" and "Nomad Custom" to the "Concours" (of which there were two different variants).

The Israeli Defence Force used base model, khaki—painted, Chevelle station wagons as staff cars in the late 1960s and early 1970s. The car used by Lieutenant General Elazar is a second generation 1972 Chevelle four door "Nomad" station wagon featuring the revised frontal styling with single large headlights and a twin bar plastic front grille.

The engine was the basic 3.8 litre in-line six cylinder. The vehicle featured a dual action tailgate that could be opened in the traditional way or as a door hinged on one side. The cars overall length was 5.3 metres. Chevrolet produced 54,355 station wagons in 1972 for a range of domestic and international buyers. The IDF would have been classed as a "fleet buyer"—like US Police Departments—and as such would not only have benefitted from a discount but also the possibility to change levels of equipment in the vehicle.

The Chevelle model underwent a major restyling exercise for 1973 and continued in that form until it was axed in 1977.

Chevrolet

The Chevrolet Motor Company was founded in Detroit on 3 November 1911 by a Swiss racing driver and engineer named Louis Chevrolet with former Buick boss William Durant (see Chapter 6). Having been sacked in 1910 by General Motors, Buick founder Durant went into partnership with Chevrolet, William Little and R S McLaughlin the CEO of General Motors in Canada to form the new company to take market share from his former employers.

Despite having a design ready for production—the "Series C Classic Six"— Chevrolet did not start production until 1913. The famous Chevrolet logo was first used in 1914 after Chevrolet had spotted the design in a local newspaper advert for a coal company. Chevrolet sold his share of the company the same year to Durant following a disagreement between the two over design.

In a wonderful story of corporate revenge, Chevrolet became profitable enough by 1916 to allow Durant to buy General Motors who had sacked him six years previously. The deal in 1917 merged Chevrolet with General Motors albeit with Chevrolet surviving as a separate division.

From 1919 on all General Motors trucks were rebranded as Chevrolets. Throughout the 1920s, 30s and 40s Chevrolet was in direct competition with Ford and Chrysler's Plymouth sub brand. Chevrolet differentiated itself from its competitors by being the first to introduce a budget six-cylinder engine in the mid-1930s allowing it to retain a dominant position in the mid-sized car market using the strapline "a six for the price of a four".

During the Second World War Chevrolet shifted to military production making nearly half a million trucks, 2,500 staff cars, nearly 4000 Medium Armoured Cars and over 60,000 R-2800 and R-1830 Pratt and Whitney Radial Aircraft Engines as well as shells and anti-aircraft gun barrels. The 1950s were a golden era for the brand with the introduction of the glass-fibre bodied, two-seater Corvette in 1953 and the iconic 1957 Chevrolet saloon which featured Chevrolet's small block V8 engine.

This success continued into the 1960s when the Chevrolet Impala became one of the biggest selling models in US history. Chevrolet still holds the record for the longest production run of any mass-produced engine—its 1955 small block V8 is still in production 65 years later.

Chapter 17
1978 Cadillac Fleetwood

The date is 8 March 1979. The location is Cairo, Egypt. The motorcade is impressive with over a dozen motorcycle outriders. The two massive Cadillac Fleetwood limousines at the front of the motorcade are specially equipped with running boards and grab handles to allow armed secret service bodyguards to ride on the outside of the vehicle.

In the first car, waving towards the crowd is US President Jimmy Carter. Next to him is Egyptian President Anwar Sadat. Carter has just arrived in Cairo for talks with Sadat about the Middle East Peace Process as part of a trip to the region that would see him travel on to Tel Aviv on 10 March before returning to Cairo on 13 March en route back to the US. This shuttle diplomacy was part of Carter's commitment to capitalise on the previous year's Camp David Accords and to crystalise them into what would become the 1979 Egypt-Israel Peace Treaty signed in Washington later that month on 26 March 1979.

Sadat by this stage had already won a shared Nobel Peace Prize with his Israeli Counterpart Menachem Begin in 1978. Carter would have to wait another 33 years until 2002 for his. Within three years of the photo being taken Carter would be out of office—defeated by Ronald Reagan in the 1980 US Presidential Elections and Sadat would be dead—assassinated by Islamic militants at a military parade on 6 October 1981.

The Cadillac Fleetwood Limousine is rumoured to have been a gift from the Carter Administration and was one of several used by Sadat who followed in the tradition of his predecessor, Gamal Abdel Nasser who used a black Cadillac after seizing power in the 1952 Egyptian Revolution which overthrew King Farouk. After Sadat's assassination the vehicle was used by his successor Hosni Mubarak until it was finally sold off in 2002 in a palace auction. The car next resurfaced in May 2015 when it was put on sale for $108,000 online in the UAE on Dubizzle by an Egyptian named Hisham Refaat.

Although Anwar Sadat would become the third President of Egypt, he had been born into a poor family of Egyptian and Sudanese parents on Christmas Day 1918 in Monufia, Egypt. With few other options, he had joined the army and graduated aged 20 from the Royal Military Academy. His rise to power was linked to his first posting with the army to Sudan where he met and became friends with Gamal Abdel Nasser.

During the Second World War Sadat had been jailed having been caught trying to enlist the help of the Axis Powers in expelling the British from Egypt. Being of no fixed ideology Sadat had been a member of the Muslim Brotherhood, the pro monarchist Iron Guard of Egypt and the fascist Young Egypt group. Along with Nasser he was also a senior member of the Free Officers group and were instrumental in orchestrating the 1952 Egyptian Revolution removing King Farouk. Following the coup, the head of the Free Officers, General Mohammed Naguib, became President.

However, a year later he had been elbowed out by Nasser who ruled until his death in 1970. Sadat had twice served as Vice President to Nasser, making him the natural successor in October 1970.

It is a reflection of Sadat's ideological shape-shifting abilities that although his eleven-year period in office had begun with Egypt operating as a centrally planned economy allied with the Soviet Union, it ended with the country as a market economy allied to the US. Sadat was a pragmatic moderniser rather than an ideologue. He introduced the democratic elections and the multiparty political system his predecessor had long resisted.

Yet, astonishingly given his subsequent Nobel Peace Prize he had also been the prime mover in the 1973 Yom Kippur War (see Chapter 16) where he had attempted to retake the Sinai Peninsula, which Israel had occupied during the 1967 Six Day War. His popularity in Egypt and the Arab World had risen as a result. It was an irony therefore that his assassination took place at the annual 6 October national military parade designed to commemorate the war.

The reason was that despite regaining the Sinai Peninsula, the means by which he had achieved this feat—making peace with Israel—outraged the Muslim Brotherhood Islamic militants in Egypt and alienated the country from the Arab World. By the time of his death Egypt had been suspended from the Arab League.

Some have argued that although Sadat ultimately lost the Yom Kippur War that he and Hafez al-Assad of Syria had started on 6 October 1973, the campaign revived Egyptian national pride and boosted his standing in the Arab World and indeed with Israel. These factors were important in giving him both the political room for manoeuvre and gravitas that he subsequently used in the peace process. Ever the pragmatist, it seems clear that following the failure to re-take the Sinai Peninsula by force, Sadat adopted a strategy of negotiation.

Prior to this, he moved to create the conditions for rapprochement firstly by bilateral agreements with Israel on the disengagement of forces following the 1973 war. These were signed in January 1974 and September 1975. At the same time Sadat visited the US in October and November 1975 and the Vatican on 8 April 1976. He used both visits to discuss and to build Western support for, peace with Israel.

In doing this, he was sufficiently astute to avoid falling into the trap of an international process that was a prisoner of the Cold War superpower trade-offs. Thus, while professing support for the initiative, he bypassed the Carter inspired Geneva Conference on the Middle East created by the United States and Russia on 1 October 1977. His lack of enthusiasm for the cumbersome process was not dissimilar from that of his Israeli opposite number with whom he opened a secret back channel.

The result of that was he became, on 17 November 1977, the first Egyptian leader to visit Israel. He not only had talks with the Israeli Prime Minister— Menachim Begin—in Tel Aviv, but also was invited to address the Knesset in

Jerusalem where he set out his proposals for peace based on the implementation of UN Security Council Resolutions 242 and 238.

The US had been caught by surprise by Sadat's announcement on 9 November 1977 in the Egyptian Parliament of his intention to visit Israel and Begin's subsequent offer of an invitation. Although Washington suspected that Sadat's key objective might be the return of Sinai rather than lasting peace, they nevertheless were compelled to go along with the initiative.

In fact, the truth behind the timing of Sadat's announcement was even more prosaic: following the reintroduction of price controls on food after a failed attempt to remove them, he needed financial help from the West. From an Israeli perspective, Sadat's initiative offered the opportunity to negotiate with a single Arab negotiating partner rather than with the entire Arab League. Added to this, if a deal could be struck then Israel would have protected one flank and also driven a wedge into Arab unity.

Nevertheless, Carter was pragmatic enough to realise that this track was more likely to bear fruit in the short term than the broader Geneva process he had launched and accordingly offered US assistance. However, a Sadat idea to create a back channel via an undercover Israeli official posted to the US Embassy in Cairo was turned down flat by Carter who instead invited the two parties to Camp David for negotiations from 5–17 September 1978.

Carter was determined that the two would reach agreement and signalled that he would not allow them to leave in the absence of this. His tenacity, charm and determination played a crucial role in achieving this. Carter and his chief of staff Joe Biden, had to play a facilitating role between Begin and Sadat who fundamentally disliked and mistrusted each other. The log cabin layout of Camp David meant that Carter had to physically shuttle from one cabin to the other to pass messages and try out formulations following bilateral meetings with each party.

Carter proved himself to be a skilful mediator, on top of the detail and able to propose creative solutions and wordings on some of the most intractable issues. As the days rolled by Sadat and Begin began to wonder if they would ever be allowed to leave. After more than a week progress ground to a halt over the key impasse of Israeli withdrawal from Sinai and the West Bank.

The issue threatened to de-rail the process, but Carter ploughed on, sure in his mind that the high-level negotiating teams on each side had the capacity to find a way through. The isolation of Camp David and absence of any media meant that neither side was able to play to or be influenced by, their domestic audience.

By keeping both sides locked down for a full 13 days, Carter also made the price of failure far higher than that of reaching agreement. His strategy was vindicated and the two parties signed up to what have become known as the Camp David Accords comprising two distinct agreement: (i) a "Framework for Peace in the Middle East" and (ii) a "Framework for the Conclusion of a Peace Treaty between Egypt and Israel".

The first framework—for Peace in the Middle East—was based on UN Security Council Resolution 242, accepted the legitimate rights of the Palestinian people and foresaw the establishment of a fully autonomous Palestinian Authority in the West Bank and Gaza Strip within five years. This careful wording stopped short of statehood—an Israeli red line.

The framework envisaged further discussions between Israel, Egypt, the Palestinians and Jordan. Israeli troops would be withdrawn once a new self-governing authority had been elected. There was no mention of the Golan Heights or of Lebanon in the Framework, nor was Jerusalem mentioned. As such the framework had a number of flaws and was subsequently rejected by the UN General Assembly on the grounds that neither the UN nor the Palestinians had been involved and it did not comply the Palestinian rights of self-determination, return or national independence foreseen in UNSCR 242.

The second framework fared much better given that it formed the basis of the peace treaty that was signed in March 1979. The framework provided for Israel's withdrawal from the Sinai Peninsula including the 4,500 Israeli civilians who had settled in the area and for safe passage for Egyptians travelling through Israel en route to Jordan.

In return, Egypt agreed to re-establish diplomatic relations, to allow Israeli shipping safe passage through the Suez Canal and Straits of Tiran and to place strict limits on the military forces it could station on the peninsula.

Although implementation took three years, making peace provided significant economic benefits for Egypt both in terms of the return of its oil fields in western Sinai but also in terms of annual grants and aid packages worth of billions of dollars from the US. The US also provided training and equipment to modernise Egypt's armed forces worth more than US$1 billion annually. Israel also benefitted from annual grants and aid as well as annual military support of US$3 billion.

Egypt's reward in the Arab world for making peace was to be suspended from the Arab League for a decade. Jordan felt particularly aggrieved by what it saw as Egypt unilaterally negotiating away its rights over the occupied West Bank. This put King Hussein in an impossible position with his Arab neighbours.

The fracturing of Arab unity was an unintended bonus for Israel. However, the removal of the Egypt—Israel conflict also brought the plight of the Palestinians into sharper focus—something which the Camp David Accords had fudged and remains unresolved to this day. Nevertheless, for Carter the Accords were a major diplomatic triumph: for Begin and Sadat they were broadly popular domestically but also ignited significant opposition—something that was to prove fatal in Sadat's case.

For Begin this principally took the form of the Settler movement who were furious at being expelled from Sinai. For Sadat, his actions made him the key target of the Egyptian Islamic Jihad. Indeed, on 6 October 1981 at the annual military parade to mark the start of the Yom Kippur War (see Chapter 16) four members of the group who had infiltrated the President's close protection team opened fire from a truck as it passed the President and threw three grenades.

Sadat was fatally wounded, being hit by a total of 37 automatic rifle rounds, along with 10 others including the Cuban Ambassador and Omani General and an Orthodox Bishop. Hosni Mubarak, Sadat's Vice President, was also injured. Succeeding Sadat, he would go on to wage an internal war against the insurgents for the next 30 years as President, before being toppled from power during the 2011 Arab Spring.

1978 Cadillac Fleetwood Limousine

Sadat's car was the top of the range from America's premier motor manufacturer—Cadillac. Aimed squarely at the Royalty and Head of State market the Fleetwood was a production-built limousine engineered for professional use and incorporating heavy-duty components.

Its 144.5" wheelbase was long enough to allow for an extra row of folding seats in the rear to accommodate two extra passengers. Automatic climate control, electronic level control suspension which automatically adjusted to different loads was complimented by a massive seven litre (425 cubic inch) 16-valve OHV V8 engine fuelled by a Rochester 4-bbl Quadrajet carburettor and mechanical fuel pump. The engine produced 180 bhp @ 4,000 rpm and was capable—despite the vast bodywork—of 0–60 mph in 11.7 seconds, 0–100 mph in 38.8 seconds with a top speed of 112 mph.

The engine featured a High Energy Ignition System and was mated to GM's Turbo Hydra-Matic automatic transmission. All round disc brakes made sure that it stopped. The car was built to last, featuring extensive rust proofing "Zinc-o-metal" panels and bi-metal mouldings. Even the screws were microencapsulated in an epoxy compound to stop them working loose.

The 1978 Fleetwood marked a new generation of the luxury car with Cadillac reducing the size of the vehicle (albeit not appreciably to the untrained eye) partly to save weight and thereby improve fuel consumption but partly also to standardise a common platform across all Cadillac model ranges. This process had begun the previous year when General Motors downsized their cars in response to United States Federal CAFE standard legislation.

The result was the most space and fuel—efficient Cadillac Fleetwood in the model's history. The car was completely re-engineered and offered considerably more legroom and headroom than its predecessor. The 1978 Fleetwood had clean, crisp lines, a new front grille and rear tail-light assemblies blended in with the bodywork. It was more manoeuvrable. The lightweight (again comparatively) V8 engine gave the car a surprisingly lively performance.

However, the bodywork was no longer coach-built like its predecessors. Nevertheless, the options list was endless with a choice of no fewer than eleven leather and seven Florentine velour choices were available for the interior upholstery.

Cadillac

Cadillac is the second oldest US car brand (Buick—see Chapter 6—being the oldest) and was formed in 1902 from the remains of the Henry Ford Company (see Chapter 3) after Henry Ford had been forced to sell the company by investors. Henry Leland, who had been brought in to value the bankrupt company's assets persuaded Ford's former investors to keep the company intact and to re-found it as the Cadillac Automobile Company—named after the French explorer who had founded Detroit—Antoine Laumet de la Mothe, sieur de Cadillac.

Cadillac's first models were heavily based on the 1903 Ford Model A and were two seaters with, single-cylinder 10hp engines. The order books began to fill up after Cadillac displayed the model at the January 1903 New York Auto show. Cadillac's early success was based on the high quality of its engineering which made the cars more reliable than their rivals.

By 1909, Cadillac had been acquired by General Motors as the manufacturer's luxury brand ahead of Buick, Oldsmobile and Chevrolet. Production centred on large luxury vehicles and variants. A change of engine in 1915 to a 70hp flathead v8 gave the marque the performance to match its prestige meaning that Cadillacs were capable of reaching speeds of 65 mph.

In 1928, Cadillac was the first manufacturer to pioneer Synchro-Mesh transmission: way ahead of its rivals which still used crash gearboxes and required double de-clutching to make smooth gear changes.

Faced with competition from the likes of Lincoln, Cadillac hired designer Harvey Earl in 1926 to re-style their range. Capone's car is an example of the designer style bodywork that replaced the functional treatment given to earlier models. The steel roof—something which must have appealed to the security conscious Capone—was another Cadillac innovation. Known as the "turret" top it replaced the wood and fabric roofs traditionally fitted to saloon cars for the period.

The Great Depression following the 1929 Wall Street Crash hit Cadillac sales hard requiring it to adapt its model range to include mid-priced vehicles such as the 1936 Series 60; to streamline its production and to standardise engines and transmissions across the range. As a result, Cadillac was profitable by 1941 when America's entry into the Second World War switched production over to military production. Cadillac produced both tank engines, tanks such as the M5 Stuart Honey and the M24 Chafee, staff cars and also aircraft engines for fighter planes.

The 1950s and 60s were a golden era for Cadillac with yearly model changes and ever greater amounts of chrome and styling excess. The first Cadillac to feature tailfins was launched in 1948. By 1950 they were de rigueur for any self-respecting US car, growing in size and complexity—the 1959 Cadillac being a particularly fine example of the genre. By the mid-1960s they were far more restrained as bodywork became wider and boxier.

Yet, vestigial tail fins were still a feature of Cadillacs throughout the 1970s and were only finally dispensed with in 1979. By 1968 Cadillac were building 200,000 cars a year. Innovations in the decade included hydramatic automatic transmission, air-conditioning, front wheel drive, self-tuning radios. The list of options was endless as the cars got progressively larger and thirstier. Even the

1973 oil crisis (see Chapter 14) failed to burst the bubble with the firm reporting record sales in 1973.

Cadillac Fleetwood

The "Fleetwood" was manufactured by Cadillac—part of General Motors from 1976 until 1996. The use of the Fleetwood name on Cadillacs can be traced back as early as 1935 and was used on long wheelbase four door models available between 1935 and 1941 which could be ordered from General Motors' Fleetwood plant in Pennsylvania rather than the standard production Fisher Body.

The history of the name derives from the early years of the company when the Fisher Body Corporation—a company founded in 1908 by Lawrence Fisher and two of his six brothers—which produced bodywork for Cadillac—through the purchase of a controlling stake—became part of General Motors in 1919.

As a result, Fisher became Cadillac's General manager in May 1925 and bought the Fleetwood Metal Body Company in September of that year, making it part of the Fisher Body Corporation. The purchase was designed to increase the range of custom bodywork options available to Cadillac.

Interestingly, "The Fleetwood Body Company" of Fleetwood, Pennsylvania, had been founded by Harry Urich in the late 1900s by expanding a small-scale artisanal coach-building company of craftsmen, founded by Henry Fleetwood in Lancaster in England in the seventeenth century. Thus, the Fleetwood Body Company was able to claim over 300 years of coach-building experience.

The rapidly expanding automotive industry provided eager customers for Fleetwood's work and the company was a popular choice of coachwork on a number of different marques during the 1920s. Once effectively part of General Motors, Fleetwood worked exclusively for Cadillac and when the Fisher Body Corporation was fully absorbed into General Motors in 1929, Fleetwood also became fully part of the company and Fleetwood bodywork became a standard option across the Cadillac range.

Realising that ubiquity is the enemy of exclusivity, Cadillac adopted a new strategy for Fleetwood in the mid—1930s, restricting the option to only its most expensive models—the Series 75, 90 and Sixty Special. This approach was successful, essentially creating a niche sub-brand and from the late 1940s Cadillac began adding the Fleetwood name and logo on the back of its top tier models.

By the late 1950s, Cadillac added the Series 70 Eldorado Brougham to the list of those vehicles carrying the Fleetwood name. This was the first car with a Fleetwood body to carry the "Brougham" name. When the model was dropped in 1961, a Fleetwood body option was offered on the Eldorado Biarritz. In the same year, Sadat's predecessor—Abdel Nasser—bought a Series 75 Fleetwood Limousine as his official car.

Competition from smaller European and Japanese cars led to a re-think towards the end of the 1970s and in the 1980s with bodywork dimensions getting slightly smaller and fuel economy better. The DeVille, Fleetwood and Eldorado all became smaller, lighter and taller. Nevertheless, Cadillacs remained big, unwieldy cars by European standards.

Fleetwood became part of a Cadillac series names in 1977 when the Cadillac Fleetwood Brougham and the Cadillac Fleetwood Limousine—like the one used by President Sadat—were introduced to replace the ageing Fleetwood Sixty Special Brougham and the Fleetwood 75. The sub-brand continued on through the 1980s until finally being retired in 1996 when Cadillac ceased production of rear-wheel-drive cars.

Chapter 18
1980 Fiat Nuova Campagnola Popemobile

It is 17:15 pm on the afternoon of Wednesday 13 May 1981, a sunny day in St Mark's Square in Rome. There is a crowd of 20,000. Pope John Paul II is travelling in the back of a specially adapted, open topped, Fiat Campagnola. He is smiling kindly at the crowd. Those at the front, nearest to him are stretching out their hands to receive the Holy Father's blessing.

Further back in the crowd people are holding up cameras in the hope of getting a decent shot. They are not the only ones, to the left of the photo is a man pointing a Browning Hi-Power semi-automatic pistol at the Pontiff. Those around him in the crowd are oblivious as is the Pope and the two people travelling in the front of the vehicle. Seconds later shots ring out.

This was the fateful moment when Pope John Paul II was shot four times and critically wounded by Mehmet Ali Agca, a Turk from Sofia Bulgaria. In the ensuing chaos, Agca was able to leave the scene, throwing the pistol under a truck. But he was caught by Camillo Cibin, a Papal bodyguard, with the help of a nun and members of the public.

The Pope was wounded in his lower intestine, his right arm and his left index finger. Two of the crowd were also injured. The Pope fortunately would recover: Agca, a career criminal and murderer would serve a total 29 years in prison, despite being pardoned by Italian President Ciampi at the Pope's request in June 2000.

That the Pope survived is something of a miracle given that Agca was not acting alone. Preparations for the assassination had begun over a year earlier. Indeed, Agca, travelling under the alias of Vilperi, had travelled extensively in Southern Europe on different passports.

The Pope hovered between life and death in the ambulance on his way to hospital. On arrival surgeons operated for five and a half hours to remove the bullets and repair the damage. One bullet had penetrated the Pope's abdomen, severely damaging his intestines and narrowly missing his aorta and pancreas. Meanwhile, Roman Catholics everywhere prayed for his survival and recovery.

The details surrounding the assassination attempt remain shrouded in mystery to this day with both Bugaria and Russia cited as the originators of the plot. What is clear is that Mehmet Ali Agca was not acting alone. Details of Agca's early life are equally mysterious. He was born in 1958 in Malatya province of central Turkey, 200 miles from the Syrian border. The press at the time of the assassination attempt portrayed him as a life-long career criminal and drug smuggler who was responsible for the murder of a newspaper editor in Istanbul in 1979.

However, others suggest that he was in some way radicalised or recruited by the Grey Wolves—a Turkish neo-fascist organisation linked to the Turkish mafia—while studying at the University of Ankhara and before this had no criminal record. Agca confessed while in custody to having attended a terrorist training camp in Lebanon in 1977 supporting this theory.

That he subsequently became a hit man for the Grey Wolves is also borne out by his involvement in the February 1979 murder of Abdi Ipekci the left-wing editor of the Turkish newspaper Milliyet. Ipekci had used his editorials to expose and criticise Turkey's far right groups and their links with the government.

Incensed, Abdullah Çatli had ordered his execution. Agca was arrested and imprisoned for the murder but escaped a few months later after retracting his confession and threatening to name those responsible. Prison guards and officials were bribed to aid the escape, suggesting he had wealthy and influential sponsors.

Following his escape, Agca seems to have been able to travel around Europe and more widely around the Mediterranean using false documentation under the name of Vilperi. He allegedly carried out other missions for the Grey Wolves and somehow evaded capture despite being on an Interpol most wanted list and his photograph having been widely circulated.

He travelled to Sofia on 11 July 1980 to collect a forged Turkish passport from Omer Merran a drug dealer. Agca claimed that the mission to assassinate the Pope came from a Turkish gangster and member of the Grey Wolves, Bekir Celenk, while he was in Sofia.

However, following his prison escape the Turkish newspaper Millyet had published a letter Acga had reportedly sent them accusing the Pope of being an agent of "Russian and US imperialism" who should be "killed". After his trip to Sofia, Agfa went dark for eight months before arriving by train in Rome from Milan on 10 May 1981. Here he met with accomplices—a Turk and two Bulgarians.

According to Agca's testimony the operation was commanded by the military attaché at the Bulgarian Embassy in Rome, Zilo Vassilev. The plan was for Agca and his fellow Turk, Oral Çelik, to act as gunman and back up respectively. The Bulgarians would then create a diversion by setting off a bomb allowing the two to escape in the ensuing chaos. During Agca's trial he initially named Bulgarian and Russian agents as having helped prepare and execute the attack. However, midway through he changed his testimony to claim sole responsibility.

In an amazing act of forgiveness, the Pope made a public statement four days after the shooting asking people to pray for his would-be assassin, Agca, whom he had "sincerely forgiven". The Pope visited Agca in prison in 1983 and met his mother and brother in 1987.

On 14 June 2000, President Ciampi finally acceded to the Pope's request for clemency. Agca was released and deported to Turkey. On arrival he was immediately arrested and returned to prison to serve the remainder of his sentence for the murder of Abdi Ipekci. He was finally released on parole in 2006.

Who exactly ordered the assassination attempt remains a mystery not least because Agca repeatedly changed his story, even at times declaring himself to be the "messiah" and "Jesus reincarnated". His trial began in Rome on 20 July 1981 and lasted over two months. At various points he claimed to be acting alone or alternatively working with the Bulgarian and Russian secret services. He even said he had wanted to kill the "King of England" before realising that England had a Queen and deciding against it on religious grounds.

The American media attributed the assassination attempt to Moscow. The theory ran that the KGB Director, Yuri Andropov, had instructed the Bulgarian and East German secret services to carry out the hit because they feared the Pope's support for the Trade Union "Solidarity" in his home country of Poland (the Pope being Karol Józef Wojtyla) risked destabilising the Soviet puppet regime of General Jaruzelski.

It is true that the Pope's announcement of a pilgrimage to Warsaw had seriously rattled Andropov, who described the threat in a memorandum to Soviet schoolteachers as stemming from the Pope's "uncommon skills and great sense of humour" which made him "dangerous because he charms everyone, especially journalists". It is also true that the Pope was no fan of Communism and his first visit to his home country in June 1979 was designed to help undermine Communism.

However, Agca claimed to have had contact with a Bulgarian agent in Rome—something which the subsequent trial of the individual found to be false. Indeed, Agca initially made no claims of Bulgarian involvement until he had been kept in solitary confinement and visited by the Italian Secret Service.

The subsequent revelation to the US Senate Intelligence Committee in 1991 by a former CIA analyst involved in the case, Melvin A Goodman, that there was no evidence to substantiate the link and that evidence had been falsified, casts significant doubt on this explanation.

The Bulgarian Secret Service claimed that Agca's attribution of responsibility to them was in fact part of an anti-Communist smear operation conducted by the Italian Secret Service and the CIA with the assistance of the Grey Wolves—all of whom were cooperating in NATO's "Gladio" network designed to create tension and to destabilise the Eastern Bloc.

Abdullah Çatli, a senior leader in the Grey Wolves told a judge in court in Rome in 1985 that he had been contacted by the German BND intelligence agency who had offered him three Million Deutsch Marks if he "implicated the Russian and Bulgarian services in the assassination attempt".

More recently in 2006, the Mitrokhin Commission set up by Italian Prime Minister Silvio Berlusconi revived the original "Bulgarian Connection"/Moscow theory. However, the Commission's findings and sources were of questionable reliability—for example alleging that former Italian Prime Minister Romano Prodi was the "KGB's" man in Italy and have been widely discredited.

Fiat Campagnola Popemobile

The Popemobile that Pope Jean-Paul II was travelling in on the fateful afternoon of 13 May 1981 was a lightly modified white Fiat Campagnola. Production of this heavy-duty off-road vehicle started in 1951 and, like the British Land Rover (see Chapter 10) was based on the World War II US Army Jeep (see Chapter 9) The model was redesigned in 1974 but by 1981 remained virtually unchanged from those first produced thirty years earlier in 1951. Production ended in 1987.

The idea of a Popemobile was first developed for Pope John Paul I based on a Toyota Landcruiser but the Pope disliked it, preferring the traditional sedan chair. By contrast, his successor embraced the Popemobile concept and banished the sedan chair (*sedia gestatoria*) to the Vatican museum.

Although there had been specially built vehicles for papal visits such as a custom-built 1964 Lehmann-Peterson used by Pope Paul VI for his 1965 New York City visit and again in Bogota in 1970, the term "Popemobile" was not used until the pontificate of Pope John Paul II. Fiat presented a brand new, white, Fiat Campagnola—subsequently registered on Vatican City number plates SCV 1 (*Status Civitatis Vaticanae 1*)-to Pope John Paul II in 1980 during a visit to Turin, Italy.

The Pope used it until the assassination attempt when it too was consigned to the Vatican museum and replaced with a new armoured version of the Popemobile as the level of security and personal protection for the Holy Father was increased. The replacement Popemobiles were based on the Land Rover Santana (1983) and the Mercedes-Benz 230 GE (1990) which remained in service until 2002.

The vehicle was available in hard or soft top form and with a standard or short wheelbase. The popemobile was the standard wheelbase soft-top version. The vehicle is 3.775 metres (148.6 in) long, 1.580 metres (62.2 in) wide and 1.945 metres (76.6 in) high. The wheelbase is 2.300 metres (90.6 in). The vehicle is designed for off-road use with a minimum ground clearance is 0.27 metres

(10.6 in). This high ride height made it an ideal choice as a Popemobile since the occupant would be high above the heads of the crowd if standing in the back. The Popemobile was fitted with a handrail for precisely this purpose.

The engine is a four cylinder petrol from the Fiat 132 with a longer stroke increasing the cylinder capacity to 1995cc and developing a solid but uninspiring 59 kW (79 bhp) at 4600 rpm and a top speed of 75mph. The engine featured a light alloy cylinder head instead of the twin overhead camshafts of the 132, with a single side-mounted camshaft driven by a toothed belt and the valves driven by pushrods and rockers. An optional 2.5 litre diesel engine was available but the Popemobile had the petrol version.

The transmission is four wheel drive and the suspension system is independent using torsion bars to suspend all four wheels, with two shock absorbers for each of the rear wheels and a single shock absorber for each of the front wheels. All six shocks used were of identical and interchangeable.

The large square engine compartment gave easy access to the engine bay which was designed to permit "wading" up to 70 cm deep—admittedly not much called for in St Mark's Square.

The interior was sparse and utilitarian with the 57 litre fuel tank positioned under the twin passenger seat beside the driver to protect it when travelling over rough ground.

Fiat

Founded on 11 July 1899, by Giovanni Agnelli and his associates the Fabbrica Italiana di Automobili Torino—or FIAT for short—is Italy's largest car manufacturer. Now part of Fiat Chrysler Automobiles, the current configuration of Fiat Automobiles was formed in 2007. At its height in 1970, Fiat Automobiles produced 1.4 million cars in Italy. Today it has factories not only in Italy but also Brazil, Argentina, Poland and Mexico.

The fist Fiat factory opened in 1900 and by 1903 was turning a modest profit and making 135 cars a year. By 1906, the year the company was floated on the Milan stock exchange, production had risen to 1149 cars. Fiat's first model—the 4hp featured a 697cc twin boxer engine and a total production run of 25.

Fiat diversified into aero engines and during the First World War switched production exclusively to these, trucks and machine guns. Its first plant in the US opened in 1910 in Ploughkeepsie New York and its products were pitched to the luxury market being more than four times as expensive as a Ford Model T which cost $825 at the time.

The 1922 Fiat began construction of its Lingotto factory in Turin with its famous roof top test track. The new state of the art factory opened in 1923 allowing Fiat to have captured almost 90% of the domestic car market two years later. During the Second World War Fiat switched back to military production making biplanes and tanks all of which were woefully outdated compared to those produced by the Germans.

The fall of Mussolini saw the Agnelli family removed from the board of Fiat because of their close lies with the fascist government. The ban lasted almost 20 years until 1963 when Gianni Agnelli became chairman. Fiat holds the record for the most awards of European Car of the Year, having won the title no fewer than 12 times between 1967 (the Fiat 124) and 2008 (the Fiat 500).

Fiat was merged with a new company—Fiat Chrysler Automobiles on 12 October 2014.

Chapter 19
1988 Daimler Sovereign

The woman in the backseat of the car is staring at the camera while biting back tears. By contrast, the man next to her wearing large square glasses looks almost philosophical.

The car is black with stone-coloured upholstery—it is a 3.6 Litre Daimler Sovereign registered F496 PYT. The driver, out of shot, is Denis Oliver a Government Car Service driver. The date is Wednesday 28 November 1990 and Britain's first female Prime Minister Margaret Thatcher is leaving 10 Downing Street for the last time en route to Buckingham Palace to tender her resignation, having withdrawn from the second round of the second Conservative Party leadership contest in twelve months.

Thatcher was succeeded by John Major as Prime Minister who not only inherited the keys to No10 but also the armoured Daimler which he found cramped and uncomfortable but which he would continue using until it was replaced with a British Racing Green, longer wheelbase, Jaguar XJ40 in December of the following year.

F496PYT was the last in a series of specially modified Prime ministerial cars ordered for Margaret Thatcher during her eleven-year premiership. On winning the election in 1979, Thatcher inherited departing Labour Prime Minister James Callaghan's 1972 Rover P5B saloon which he in turn had inherited from his predecessor Harold Wilson. She very much liked the Rover with its solid quality, unpretentious styling, smooth V8 engine and standard Government car West of England cloth interior.

However, by 1979 it was already seven years old and the model had been dropped from Rover's range in 1973. After much deliberation, its replacement was a Daimler Sovereign—a high quality car that was judged to be less showy than its body double the Jaguar XJ6. Daimlers with leather interiors as standard became the vehicle of choice for the Prime Minister until her successor replaced F496PYT with an armoured long wheelbase Jaguar XJ12 having been seduced by the extra legroom in which to accommodate his six-foot frame.

F496PYT was armour-plated with bullet-proof glass and perhaps as a result of this or for greater rearward visibility, had its door mirrors fitted as wing mirrors. The car also featured the legendary Thatcher headrests. Although Margaret Thatcher was famous for only sleeping for four hours a night, she liked to powernap in the car. Such was the concern of her Special Branch Close Protection officer, Bob Kingston, that she might suffer a neck injury if the car were forced to brake hard or to take evasive action, he minuted her Private Secretary in September 1987:

I am concerned that, when the PM dozes in the official car, the design of the headrests is such that, far from supporting her head and neck, they cause her head to drop forward.

He went on to explain:

—this is in itself hazardous, but when the car is braked or turned or there is some other disturbance, she lifts her head very quickly and this I am sure will one day cause at least minor injury.

As a result, larger, more supportive, custom-built headrests were fitted.

The events leading up to the photograph are now largely forgotten. Having won a historic third General Election by a landslide in 1987—making her the first Conservative Prime Minister since the Earl of Liverpool in 1820 to record three consecutive wins—against Neil Kinnock's Labour Party, her third mandate was characterised by the introduction of the hugely unpopular Poll Tax and by her increasing hostility to the European Community. The latter was to sow the seeds of her political demise.

Thatcher had never been particularly popular during her premiership having the second worst personal approval rating of any of her predecessors since the war but equally had never been motivated by this viewing herself as a "conviction politician".

Born on 13 October 1925 in Grantham, Lincolnshire the daughter of Alfred Roberts a tobacconist and grocer, Margaret had won a scholarship to Kesteven and Grantham Girl's School where she had been Head Girl before going on to study Chemistry at Somerville College Oxford. Having worked as a research chemist after graduating she was rejected for a job at ICI on the grounds of being judged to be "headstrong, obstinate and dangerously self-opiniated".

These qualities were no bar to her rise within the Conservative Party and by 24 she had secured the nomination as Conservative candidate for Dartford. It was during the selection process that she met Denis Thatcher—a wealthy businessman, divorcee and her future husband—the second occupant in the back of F496PYT in the photograph.

Despite being unsuccessful in both the 1950 and 1951 General Elections, she was spotted by the media. She married Denis in December 1951, qualified as a barrister in 1953 and had twins the same year. Having failed to secure the Conservative nomination for the 1954 Orpington by-election, she was selected as the candidate for the safe seat of Finchley in 1958 and became an MP at the 1959 General Election. By 1961 she was on the frontbench as Parliamentary Undersecretary at the Ministry of Pensions and National Insurance in the MacMillan government.

Her voting record in opposition, where she narrowly missed appointment to the shadow cabinet thanks to Ted Heath's dislike of her, is interesting. She was one of a handful of Tories to vote in favour of decriminalising male homosexuality as well as in favour of legalising abortion while at the same time voting in favour of capital punishment.

By 1967, the US State Department had singled her out as a potential future Prime Minster by selecting her for the International Visitor Leadership Programme and to spend six weeks in the US. On her return Heath duly appointed her to the shadow cabinet. The subsequent Conservative victory in the 1970 General Election saw Thatcher in the Cabinet for the first time as Secretary of State for Education and Science.

After Heath's loss of the 1974 General Election triggered a leadership election in which she defeated both Heath on the first ballot and Whitelaw on the second making her Leader of the Opposition on 11 February 1975. The subsequent collapse of the Labour government following the series of strikes of the winter of 1978–79—the "winter of discontent"—triggered a General Election with Thatcher becoming Britain's first female Prime Minister on 4 May 1979 by a 44-seat majority.

Following the 1982 Falklands War, Thatcher won a second term by a landslide in the 1983 General Election against Michael Foot's Labour Party. A further landslide in 1987 cemented her reputation as a formidable electoral asset for the Conservative party. Yet, two years later she faced an internal Conservative Party leadership election when a virtually unknown back bench MP, Sir Anthony Meyer took on the role of stalking horse. Meyer was defeated, securing only 33 votes to Thatcher's 314, but the seeds of her demise had been well and truly sown.

The problem for Thatcher by 1989 was that after 10 years in power, 14 as leader of the Conservative Party and, with a Parliamentary majority of 102, she had arguably began to lose touch with not only public opinion, but more importantly with opinion in her own party. 1989 was a tumultuous year in the world, with the fall of the Berlin wall and the collapse of Communism.

Things were equally tumultuous within the Tory party. The unrest had been brewing for some time. The European Parliament elections in June of that year had seen Labour overtake the Conservatives for the first time since 1974. Added to this, Thatcher had pressed ahead with the Community Charge or "Poll Tax" the previous year in April 1988, despite opposition from senior members of her cabinet and widespread hostility amongst voters who saw the move as shifting the taxation burden from the wealthier, property—owning, classes to ordinary people.

This had been a long running desire of the Prime Minister—indeed she had first proposed it when she was Shadow Environment Secretary in 1974 and it had featured in the Conservative manifesto for the General Election that year. However, the policy had been shelved in favour of giving central government the power to cap rates set by local authorities—a policy designed to clip the wings of Labour run Councils in large urban areas. The "Poll Tax" was not however dead and re-emerged in the 1987 Tory manifesto.

In the autumn of 1988 she had delivered a deeply euro-sceptical speech at the College of Europe in Bruges in which she had famously stated:

We have not successfully rolled back the frontiers of the state in Britain, only to see them re-imposed at a European level with a European super-state exercising a new dominance from Brussels.

This coupled with her open hostility to German Reunification and opposition to joining the EC Exchange Rate Mechanism (ERM) resulted in the resignation of the Chancellor of the Exchequer, Nigel Lawson, in October 1989. Although Lawson's enthusiasm for British membership of the ERM was widely shared in Thatcher's Cabinet, it was diametrically opposed to the advice she was getting from her economic mentor Sir Alan Walters—a member of her so-called "kitchen cabinet".

Lawson had long seen his position as increasingly untenable and the departure after six years of such a highly respected figure triggered an internal party leadership contest. The campaign exposed further bitterness towards the Prime Minister with her predecessor, "Edward Heath" referring to her as:

A narrow little nationalist, unable to move with the whole movement of history in creating the greater Europe.

As discussed previously, Thatcher won the 1989 leadership contest by a thumping majority of 281. But her opponents within the Party smelled blood.

Rather than tack back towards the centre-ground Thatcher's response to having been challenged was to dig in. The decision to press ahead with the "Poll Tax" led to the formation of the All-Britain Anti Poll Tax Federation under the slogan "can't pay won't pay" and to civil unrest with rioting in central London on 31 March 1990 when a peaceful march of 200,000 protesters was hijacked by anarchists.

At this point, Thatcher's popularity amongst the electorate was heading for an all-time low. Her hostility towards the European Community had hardened. The previous summer she had removed Geoffrey Howe from the Foreign Office in retaliation for his part, along with Nigel Lawson, in forcing her to agree to the

"Madrid Conditions" whereby Britain would eventually join the ERM at the appropriate time. The unhappy Howe had been given the non-job of Deputy Prime Minister.

By the autumn of 1990, European Heads of State and Governments were actively discussing the creation of a Single Currency. British attempts to propose an alternative "hard ECU" while still retaining national currencies had not found support with European Partners. Nigel Lawson's successor as Chancellor of the Exchequer, John Major, had joined forces with Geoffrey Howe's successor as Foreign Secretary, Douglas Hurd to persuade Thatcher finally to join the ERM on 1 October 1990.

However, Thatcher deeply resented having been bounced and gave her most Eurosceptic speech to date to the Commons on 31 October. In the speech she derided the vision of Commission President Jacques Delors as the slippery slope towards a federal Europe, famously saying that her response was "No! No! No!" This was too much for Geoffrey Howe who tendered his resignation the following day. Howe's resignation on top of the opinion polls in September 1990 which had showed Labour as having a 14% lead over the Conservatives, triggered a second leadership challenge to Thatcher.

This time the challenger was more serious—Michael Heseltine—a former Cabinet Minister and fierce critic of Thatcher's leadership who had long courted the press and party as the heir apparent. Thatcher however decided to seize the initiative by getting her Press Secretary Bernard Ingham to brief the press that Heseltine had "lit the blue touch paper" before backing off and the moment had come to "put up or shut up". Thatcher sought to downplay Howe's resignation in a speech to the Lord Mayor's Banquet on 12 November.

This, in turn, triggered Howe's resignation speech delivered from the backbenches in the Commons the next day in which he dissected her leadership failings, particularly on Europe.

Under the Conservative Leadership election rules, Thatcher needed to win both a majority and also a lead of 15% of the electorate (56 votes given there were 372 Conservative MPs at the time) over her nearest rival to avoid a second round. If she failed to do this then other candidates could enter the race in the second round, which would take place a week after the first round.

The failure of any candidate to secure a majority and 15% in the second round would trigger a third round which would require only a simple majority. Heseltine—like Meyer before him—was effectively a stalking horse and few expected him to secure the leadership himself. Nevertheless, Thatcher took the threat he posed seriously enough to savage him in an interview with the Times.

The first ballot was held on Tuesday 20 November. Thatcher got 204 votes to Heseltine's 152—a majority but not the required 56 vote majority needed to avoid a second round. Her reaction was to carry on to the second round. However, on the advice of her campaign manage and Parliamentary Private Secretary, Peter Morrison, she decided to consult her Cabinet colleagues which she did on the afternoon and evening of 21 November.

The consensus of opinion among them was that she would lose. Some shaded this by saying they would of course support her but thought she would lose. Others—notably Kenneth Clarke and Malcolm Rifkind—preferred a more unvarnished approach. On this basis, Thatcher decided at 07:30 on 22 November to withdraw her candidature. She informed the Queen of her intention to resign and told the Cabinet at 09:00. Foreign Secretary Douglas Hurd and Chancellor John Major entered the race with her blessing following Cabinet.

Given that a Heseltine victory risked dividing the party, the Cabinet decided that Thatcher's successor should come from within its ranks. Major was not only seen as untainted but also, having grown up in Brixton in a poor household, as having wider electoral appeal.

This was borne out by the views of local Conservative Associations around the country who favoured Major over Heseltine by a margin of seven to one. The second round on Tuesday 27 November saw Major win 185 votes to Heseltine's 131—a majority of 54. A third round was avoided following the decision by Heseltine and Hurd to withdraw in favour of Major who was therefore elected unopposed.

Thatcher announced her resignation as Prime Minister to the Cabinet and the following morning, 28 November 1990 left Downing Street for the last time in her official car F496 PYT en route to Buckingham Palace to resign formally. As her Government Car Service Driver Denis Oliver recalled:

That was the only time a word wasn't spoken in that car from the time we left Downing Street until she came out of Buckingham Palace. Nobody spoke a word, not even Denis Thatcher. It was silence in the car all the way up. It was quite an emotional drive.

1988 3.6 Daimler Sovereign

F496 PYT was a 1988, armoured, automatic transmission, 3.6 litre Daimler Sovereign four dour saloon. The car featured leather upholstery and a walnut dashboard and door trims as standard. Power was provided by the tried and tested 3.6 Litre six-cylinder fuel-injected Jaguar engine producing 221 bhp and capable in non-armoured form of 0–6 in 7.4 seconds and a top speed of 135 mph.

However, the fact that F496PYT was armoured would most certainly have had a profound impact on performance not to mention fuel consumption which for the standard car was an eye watering 18.7 mpg. The car was finely balanced with independent twin wishbones at the front and coil springs and independent suspension at the rear. All round disc braking coupled with 15" "roulette" style alloy wheels and a ZR 4 speed automatic transmission ensured that the Prime Minister was both able to work—but also to catnap in the car.

As mentioned previously, F496PYT was fitted with special "Thatcher" headrests in the rear and also featured its door mirrors fitted to the front wings. The whereabouts of the car are not known—it does not appear on a search of the DVLA database yet is listed on other online motor trade sites. Footage of the car appeared in an episode of the TV drama "Spooks" in 2002.

Daimler

The early history of the Daimler Motor Company is covered in Chapter 1. Having lost the Royal Warrant in the 1950s as a result of the Palace's desire to distance itself from the extravagant excesses of Lady Docker the wife of Lord Docker the chairman of BSA and of Rolls Royce's determination to corner the Royal car market, Daimler was sold by the British Small Arms (BSA) Company to Jaguar Cars in 1960.

Initially, the marque continued to produce separate models such as the SP250 'Dart' and Majestic featuring the excellent Edward Turner designed 2.5 litre and 4.5 litre V8 engines as well as a badge engineered version of the Mk2 Jaguar—the Daimler V8 250—and the Jaguar 420—the Daimler 'Sovereign'. Equally, the Daimler bus business continued and was the second largest—next to Leyland—in the UK.

However, when Jaguar was swallowed by the British Leyland Motor Corporation (Chapter 13) in 1968, the badge engineering became standard practice. The Daimler DS420 limousine introduced in 1968 was basically a stretched Jaguar MK X. The Daimler Sovereign and Double Six were slightly more upmarket versions of the Jaguar XJ6 and the Jaguar XJ12 with leather seats as standard and a fluted grille and boot handle. The Daimler name was dropped all together in Europe in 1980 (having already become extinct in the US in 1967) and Jaguar adopted the Sovereign model name.

However, this gave rise to a market demand for "Daimler conversion kits" to convert Jaguars into Daimlers leading to the brand being revived in 1985. In the US Jaguars were marketed with Daimler specification under the brand Vanden Plas. F496 PYT was built in the Jaguar renaissance period of 1984–1989 when, in response to the need for massive capital investment it was decided to sell off Jaguar having first listed the company on the London Stock Exchange. The company found a willing buyer with deep pockets in the shape of Ford (see Chapter 3). The result was the new XJ40 model of which F496 PYT is an example.

Ford owned the company outright from 1989 until its sale to Tata in 2007. The last badge engineered variant of a Jaguar model—the "Super Eight" ceased production in 2007. The Daimler Motor Company Limited remains an active—albeit dormant—company filing annual accounts.

Chapter 20
1989 BMW 750i L

It is a sunny spring day in Bardejov in North-eastern Czechoslovakia in May 1990. It is six months since the Velvet Revolution that led to the fall of Communism in the country. A crowd of all ages has gathered in the medieval town hall square to welcome the arrival of a motorcade. The sense of joy, freedom and enthusiasm is palpable. A visitor wearing sunglasses, a white shirt with the sleeves rolled up and an undone top button is waving languidly from the passenger seat of a white BMW 750i L registered ADP 00-02.

Behind the first car an identical red one is just visible. It is clearly an official vehicle given the small Czechoslovakian flags fluttering on its front wings. The passenger has a careworn face, scruffy hair, a huge moustache. He is Vaclev Havel, former political dissident, writer and President of Czechoslovakia from 1989 until the country's peaceful dissolution in 1992.

The 750i L was one of 24 ordered by Havel to replace the former Communist regime's black Tatra 613 fleet. The Tatras reminded Havel of past repression and, by choosing BMWs in white, red and blue, he was able to make up motorcades in the colours of the Czech flag to boost national pride.

Some of the fleet were armoured—BMW being one of very few manufacturers at the time to offer this as a factory built option—this added greatly to their weight although the 12 cylinder 220kw engine coupled to an automatic transmission made the car no slouch with a top speed of 260km/h. Fuel consumption was a pitiful 20 litres/100km—14 miles to the gallon.

Havel preferred the less conspicuous (and faster) un-armoured version—preferably with cloth rather than leather seats—and would travel in different cars in the motorcade on different journeys. He also disliked sitting in the back seat—something which smacked too much of privilege and the hated old regime—preferring the front and often choosing to drive himself.

By his own admission, he habitually broke the speed limit: the immense power of the 750i was just too tempting. A chain-smoker, the ashtrays of the cars had a particularly hard life. The fleet was eventually replaced with Mercedes and many of the cars were scrapped, however a number survive to this day in the hands of collectors.

Being driven in a brand-new top specification BMW was an impossible dream for much of Havel's life. Having been born on 5 October 1936 into a wealthy middle-class family of property developers, his bourgeois background destined him for harsh treatment in the Post Second World War Czechoslovakian Communist system. This meant that he was obliged to pursue a technical rather than a humanities based secondary school education.

Thus, he worked during the day for four years as an apprentice laboratory technician in a chemicals plant. However, in the evening he took classes at a grammar school (gymnasium) in his free time. Nevertheless, despite having completed his secondary education he was barred by the authorities from studying anything other than a technical subject at university.

His attempt to get around this by studying economics was only partially successful: he had little interest in, let alone enthusiasm for, the subject and dropped out at the end of his second year. He was then obliged to complete his two-year military service between 1957 and 1959. It was therefore 1960 before he began looking for a career. With severe restrictions placed on his options as a result of his Middle-Class heritage, he found a job as a stagehand in the ABC Theatre in Prague.

At the same time, he began a correspondence course in drama wat the Prague Academy of Performing Arts. All the while he had been writing plays and the first of these—The Garden party—was performed in 1963. His second play—The memorandum—was also performed in New York in 1968, leading the regime to ban his work in Czechoslovakia and to subject him to movement restrictions including a ban on foreign travel.

Following the appointment of the reformist Alexander Dubcek as First Secretary of the Czechoslovakian Communist Party on 5 January 1968, the subsequent wave of reforms and relaxation of censorship of writers and the press greatly enhanced Havel's standing and profile. The increasingly openness alarmed Moscow and other members of the Warsaw Pact leading to the subsequent invasion of Czechoslovakia by half a million Soviet, Hungarian, Polish and Bulgarian troops and tanks, on the night of 20–21 August.

For Havel, this was a defining moment and one from where he moved from passive resistance to becoming an active political dissident. During the invasion itself, Havel broadcast a running commentary on Radio Free Czechoslovakia.

As a result, the new government banned him from theatre and he was forced to take a job at a brewery to earn enough to eat. Ironically, by trying to punish him, the authorities had provided Havel with new experiences which he fed directly into his writing—something which he now did and disseminated as "samizdat" (self-published texts) via underground networks. His time at the Krakonos brewery provided the inspiration for his Ferdinand Vanek character.

Havel was also involved in the drafting of and illegal dissemination of the Charter 77 document which criticised the government for failing to respect the commitments on human rights it had signed up to in the 1960 Czechoslovakian Constitution, the 1975 Helsinki Final Act and the 1966 UN covenants on political, civil, economic and cultural rights. Despite the seizure by the authorities of the original document, it was widely circulated and appeared in the press in Western Europe and the US.

The government took reprisals against the 1065 signatories of the document including dismissal from work, denial of education for their children, forced exile, loss of citizenship and imprisonment. In response, Havel helped to co-found the Committee for the Defence of the Unjustly Persecuted, an act for which he and five others were tried for subversion and sent to prison. Havel was jailed from May 1979 until February 1983.

However, despite the small number of signatories, the importance of the Charter was that it formed the nucleus of the future government who would negotiate the transfer of power from the one-party Communist system to a fully-fledged democracy in the Velvet Revolution of 1989.

It was that event as much as any other that cemented Havel's reputation as a great statesman. The revolution began on 16 November—the day before International Student's Day—with a peaceful Slovak student demonstration in Bratislava. This was followed by a larger student demonstration in Prague the following day to mark the 50th anniversary of the Nazi's storming of Prague University in 1939.

The authorities were jumpy—1989 had not been a good year for Central and Eastern European totalitarian Communist dictatorships. Soviet Union President Gorbachev's announcement on 7 July 1989 that the USSR would no longer use force against its Eastern Bloc allies marked a complete reversal of the Brezhnev doctrine that had crushed the 1956 Hungarian uprising and the 1968 Prague Spring.

The new policy was rapidly put to the test in Poland, who on 24 August elected its first non-Communist government since the Second World War and then in Hungary before the fall of the Berlin Wall in East Germany on 9 November 1989. The domino effect was therefore well and truly in motion by 17 November 1989. Despite the armed forces having been on standby in Bratislava, the demonstration had been so peaceful that there had been no need to deploy them. Prague was an altogether different matter however, being the seat of the Communist government.

Havel's Charter 77-inspired movement for a united society played a central role in organising the demonstration. By four in the afternoon 15,000 students had converged in a procession to visit the grave of Karel Hynek Macha—the Czech romantic poet. That this should have been the destination is a reflection of the central importance of writers, artists and intellectuals like Havel to the Revolution.

After visiting the grave, the students headed for central Prague where they were met by Riot Police blocking all exits. On instructions from the government the Riot Police attacked and dispersed the students. Rumours began to spread that a student had been killed.

Again, reflecting Havel's influence, the response was a strike of students and theatre actors, initially in Prague. In the absence of any productions, theatres were used as debating halls. However, the media remained firmly under the control of the Communist regime. Protestors therefore had to resort to using homemade banners and posters. Actors appeared on stage only to call for a General Strike on 27 November.

The US-funded Radio Free Europe played a crucial role in the wider dissemination of these messages. In the meantime, the theatre and student strike spread nationwide. Havel meanwhile established the Civic Forum of members of Charter 77, actors and members of the audience of Prague theatres. In Slovakia, scientists and artists formed a similar body—the Public Against Violence.

Both bodies called for the sacking of those responsible for the deployment of the riot police against the students and the release of all political detainees. In response, the government appealed, in vain, for calm. Representatives of the Civic Forum—minus Havel—met members of the government on 20 November but despite the Prime Minister's inclination to compromise, his cabinet refused to move.

As a result, the Civic Forum started calling for the end of the one-party State. 100,000 protestors gathered in Prague. On 21 November, the government was forced to concede a formal meeting with the Civic Forum. The government agreed not to use violence.

But it also continued to resist any democratic reforms. Mass protests began in Wenceslas Square in Prague and Hviezdoslav Square in Bratislava. The head of the Roman Catholic Church in Czechoslovakia publicly declared his support for the protesters. By contrast, the Chairman of the Communist Party, Milos Jakes appeared on State television to denounce them.

The next day the Civic Forum announced that the general Strike would go ahead as planned on 27 November. The government's stranglehold on media reporting began to crumble in both Prague and Bratislava. On 24 November the government resigned only to be immediately replaced by a new, more moderate, Communist government. State television started reporting what was happening and broadcasting Havel's speeches. The first free televised political discussions were also given airtime. The demonstrations in Prague had swelled to close to a million people.

There then followed the two-hour General Strike on 27 November. Faced with civil unrest on an unprecedented scale and with no prospect of Moscow coming to their aid to supress the uprising, the Communist Party finally announced on 28 November its intention to hand over power and to hold democratic elections. The Constitution was amended to remove references to the Communist Party and the border fences with Austria and West Germany were removed.

By 10 December a new non-communist government had been sworn in, former General Secretary of the Communist Party Alexander Dubcek became Speaker of the Parliament, and, on 29 December 1989, Havel became the President of Czechoslovakia. In June 1990, Czechoslovakia held its first democratic elections since the Second World war. However, with the old regime banished the historical ethnic rivalry within Czechoslovakia between the Czech and Slovak communities was thrown into starker relief.

On 1 January 1993 Czechoslovakia split peacefully into two separate countries: Slovakia and the Czech Republic—now Czechia.

BMW 750i L

Havel's choice of official transport was a conscious and symbolic break with the past. By choosing BMW he sent a clear signal of modernity, renewal and aspiration. His love of fast driving and powerful cars was doubtless also a significant factor. The BMW 7 Series had been around since 1977 and was the company's flagship luxury car. The first generation E23 cars featured six-cylinder engines which from 1983 received the added boost of a turbocharger.

Designed by Ercole Spada and Hans Kerschbaum, this trailblazing model was the first to feature such techno-wizardry as an on-board computer, dual-zone climate control, electronically adjustable suspension, anti-lock brakes, a driver's airbag and even a Dictaphone! Havel's fleet of 7 Series long wheelbase cars were from the second E32 generation of the model (1986–1994) At the time, Havel ordered the cars there was a choice of 3.4 litre straight six (for the 735i) or five litre, 295hp, V12 cylinder engines (750i).

Havel opted for the latter. This was the first time that BMW had offered a V12 engine on any model. Although capable of more, the engine was limited to 155 mph (250 kph)—a speed that the President regularly liked to achieve during his periodic bouts behind the wheel. The 0–60 time was an impressive 7.4 seconds. The car also featured projector lens headlamps, L-shaped taillights (where the indicator was above the main rear light cluster) and—importantly given BMW's rear wheel drive layout—traction control.

The transmission was a five-speed automatic. The long wheelbase 750i's overall length was 502.9 cm giving an extra 11.4cm of legroom to the rear passengers. The curb weight—unarmoured—was a hefty 1930kg. Traditional BMW styling cues included the "Hoffmeister kink" where the rear C pillar met the rear side window and the BMW kidney shaped grille albeit widened on the V12 750i.

The 750i L was available in "Highline" trim—something which the car Havel is travelling in in the photo does not feature. This included a long list of options such as full leather, electrically heated and adjustable seats, walnut veneer, a cool box in the rear with two crystal glasses and dual radio controls. However, at an additional 20,000DM and requiring a second alternator and battery to be fitted to the car, this was not something that the new Czechoslovakian government was tempted by.

BMW

The Bayerische Motoren Werke (BMW) was the name adopted in 1922 by the Bayerische Flugzeugwerke—a company founded six years earlier. However, the name had been in use since 1913 by the Rapp Motorenwerke and was associated with aircraft engines. On acquiring Rapp, Bayerische Flugzeugwerke adopted the BMW brand and the distinctive logo based on the flag of Munich. The post First World War restrictions on Germany's military capabilities forced BMW to switch production to motorcycle engines, brakes for railway locomotives as well as agricultural machinery.

In 1928, BMW began building cars having acquired Fahrzeugfabrik Eisenach which assembled Austin Sevens under licence. Thus, the first BMW car was in fact therefore a badge-engineered Austin Seven (see Chapter 13): the BMW 3/15. However, from these humble beginnings, BMW soon brought its formidable engineering and production capacities into play to produce a range of luxury and sports cars in the pre-Second World war period in addition to aircraft engines and motorcycles.

BMW rose to prominence in the 1930s thanks to its success on the racetrack and in rallies. The 1933, BMW 303, was the first to adopt the kidney-shaped grille and to feature a straight six-cylinder engine. The following year, Frazer Nash (AFN Ltd) in the UK became importers and assemblers of BMW cars branded as "Frazer Nash BMW". The 303 model was replaced in 1936 by the iconic 328, an aluminium bodied car capable of over 90mph which became the styling inspiration for William Lyons's post-war Jaguar XK120.

The debut of the 328 was at the Eifelrennen race at the Nürburgring in 1936, where Ernst Henne won the 2.0-litre class. It went on to dominate the following year achieving no fewer than 100 class wins. It won its class in the RAC Tourist Trophy in 1937 and 1938c—the year in which it won the Alpine Rally and the Mille Miglia. Before the outbreak of war in 1939, it had won the RAC Rally and its class at Le Mans.

With the outbreak of the Second World War production was switched exclusively to aircraft engines and motorcycles—against the wishes of the company's General director Franz Josef Popp who argued strongly to maintain car production. Between 1939–45 BMW built over 30,000 aircraft engines including the 801, a 1,500-plus horsepower engine used in the Focke-Wulf Fw 190A. In common with other German manufacturers of the period the company used forced labour on its production lines.

As a key part of Nazi industrial production capacity, BMW's factories were bombed by the Allies and largely destroyed. Immediately after the war, BMW was prohibited from returning to its pre-war car production. The company's Eisenach factory was in the Soviet sector and was requisitioned to build "EMW" cars based on the company's pre-war models.

Interestingly, one of the pre-war Mille Miglia winning 328s (disguised as a Frazer Nash) as well as BMW's technical plans for the car were rescued from the bombed BMW factory by representatives from the Bristol Aeroplane Company and Frazer Nash (AFN) Fritz Fiedler, the car's designer, was also recruited by AFN who then loaned him to the newly formed Bristol Cars Ltd where he designed the Bristol 400 which was heavily based on the 328. Bristol also supplied Fiedler-designed engines to Frazer Nash.

Meanwhile, in West Germany, BMW clung onto life by making motorcycles and kitchenware. It was not until the 1950, when the decision was taken to re-start car production that BMW's reputation began to revive. Despite the launch of the innovative and beautiful 507 roaster, the company was almost bankrupt by 1959 having sold only 252 of the model given its huge $12,000 price tag. Again, somehow BMW managed to hang on—this time by building Isetta bubble cars under licence.

The renaissance began in 1960 when Herbert and Harold Quandt took a controlling stake in the company and launched a new range of "Neue Klasse" small, modern, sporty cars: the 2002 series. The success of this model allowed the company to expand its production capabilities and to re-enter motorsport in the following decade by forming its Motorsport division. The achingly beautiful 3.0 CSL racer was to dominate competition for the remainder of the 1970s.

At the same time, the BMW 3 Series and 5 series executive saloon car ranges were launched along with the slogan "The Ultimate Driving Machine". This positioned BMW perfectly for the aspirant 1980s. The addition of the 7 Series provided the company with a foothold in the lucrative Chief Executive/Head of State and government market. It is therefore not surprising that Havel should have been attracted to the brand.

By the following decade the company was the global powerhouse it remains. In 1996, it bought the Rover Group, taking over Mini, Land Rover (see Chapter 10), Rover and MG. It subsequently sold Land Rover to Ford (see Chapter 3) and spun off the Mini as a sub-brand in 2000. In 1998, it even bought Rolls-Royce (see Chapter 4).

Bibliography

Chapter 1

Bentley-Cranch, D. (1992) *Edward VII: Image of an Era 1841–1910*. London: HMSO.

Culshaw, D. and Horrobin, P. (2013) *Daimler. The Complete Catalogue of British Cars 1895–1975*. Poundbury: Veloce Publishing.

Douglas-Scott-Montagu, E. and Burgess-Wise, D. (1995) *Daimler Century: The full history of Britain's oldest car maker*. Sparkford: Patrick Stephens.

Hough, R. (1992) *Edward and Alexandra: Their Private and Public Lives*. London: Hodder and Stoughton.

Magnus, P. (1964) *King Edward The Seventh*. London: John Murray.

Nixon, St J. (1946) *Daimler 1896 to 1946: 50 years of the Daimler Company*. GT Foulis and Co.

Pigott, P. (2005) *Royal Transport: an inside look at the history of Royal travel*. Dundum Press.

Richardson, K. (1977) *The British Motor Industry 1896–1939*. London: Archon Books.

Ridley, J. (2012) *Bertie: A life of Edward VII*. London: Chatto and Windus.

Weir, A. (1996) *Britain's Royal Families: The Complete Genealogy*. London: Random House.

Chapter 2

Albertini, L. (2005) *Origins of the war of 1914*. New York: Enigma Books.

Banac, I. (1984) *The National Question in Yugoslavia: Origins, History, Politics*. Cornell University Press.

Bushell, C. and Stonham, P. (1988) *Jane's Urban Transport Systems*. Coulsden, UK: Jane's Information Group.

Butcher, T. (2014) *The Trigger: Hunting the Assassin Who Brought the World to War*. New York: Grove Press.

Culshaw, D. and Horrobin, P. (2013) *Daimler. The Complete Catalogue of British Cars 1895–1975*. Poundbury: Veloce Publishing.

Dedijer, V. (1966) *The Road to Sarajevo*. New York: Simon and Schuster.

Haajanen, LW. (2017) *Illustrated Dictionary of Automobile*.

King, G. and Woolmans, S. (2013) *The Assassination of the Archduke*. London: Macmillan.

Murray, A. (2000) *World Trolleybus Encyclopedia*. Yateley, UK: Trolleybooks.

Preston, B. (2014) 'The Car that Witnessed the Spark of World War I'. New York Times, 10 July 2014.

Remak, J. (1971) *The First World War: Causes, Conduct, Consequences*. Wiley.

Roberts, P. (1974) *Carriage to Car. Veteren and Vintage Cars*. London: Octopus Books.

Schindler, JR. (2002) *Disaster on the Drina: The Austro-Hungarian Army in Serbia 1914. War in History*. (9 92): pp. 159–195.

Strachan, H. (2001) *The First World War*. Oxford: Oxford University Press.

Taylor, AJP. (1963) *The First World War: An Illustrated History*. Hamish Hamilton.

Wanner, C. (2011) 'Der "gute Bär". Zur Biographie des Esslinger Rennfahrers und Nürburgringsiegers Otto Merz (1889–1933)' In: *Esslinger Studien*, ed. by Stadtarchiv Esslingen a.N. vol. 48, 2011/12, pp. 179–215.

Chapter 3

Bak, R. (2003) *Henry and Edsel: The Creation of the Ford Empire*.

Batchelor, R. (1994) *Henry Ford: Mass Production, Modernism and Design*. Manchester, UK: Manchester University Press.

Brinkley, D. G. (2003) *Wheels for the World: Henry Ford, His Company and a Century of Progress*.

Carnarvon, F. (2007) *Carnarvon and Carter—The story of the two Englishmen who discovered the tomb of Tutankhamun*. UK: Highclere Enterprises.

Carnarvon, F. (2009) *Egypt at Highclere—The discovery of Tutankhamun*. Highclere Enterprises.

Carter, H. and Mace, A. (1923) *The tomb of Tut Ankh Amen, volume 1*. London.

Carter, H. 'Journal and diary Jan–May 1923'. http://griffith.ox.ac.uk/gri/4sea1no2.html.

Carter, H. 'Journal and diary 1922'. http://griffith.ox.ac.uk/gri/4sea1not.html.

Carter, H and Mace, A. C. (1977) *The Discovery of the Tomb of Tutankhamun*. Courier Dover Publications.

Clymer, F. (1955) *Henry's wonderful Model T, 1908–1927*. New York: McGraw-Hill.

Cross, W. (2016) *Carnarvon, Carter and Tutankhamun Revisited: The hidden truths and doomed relationships*. UK: Book Midden Publishing.

Desroches-Noblecourt, C. and Okasha, S. (1963) *Tutankhamun: Life and Death of a Pharaoh*. New York: New York Graphic Society.

Ford, B. (1995) *Howard Carter, Searching for King Tut*. New York, USA: Freeman and Company.

Foster, M S. (1975) 'The Model T, The Hard Sell and Los Angeles Urban Growth: The Decentralisation of Los Angeles During the 1920s'. Pacific Historical Review 44.4 (November 1975): 459–484.

Georgano, G. N. (1985) *Cars: Early and Vintage, 1886–1930*. London: Grange-Universal.

Haag, M. (2005) *The Rough Guide to Tutankhamun: The King: The Treasure: The Dynasty*. London

Haruhito, S and Wada, K. (1995) *Fordism Transformed: The Development of Production Methods in the Automobile Industry*. Oxford, UK: Oxford University Press.

Hoving, T. (1978) *The Search for Tutankhamun: The Untold Story of Adventure and Intrigue Surrounding the Greatest Modern Archaeological Find*. New York: Simon and Schuster.

James, T. G. H. (2012) *Howard Carter: The Path to Tutankhamun*. London: Tauris Parke Paperbacks.

Lacey, R. (1986) *Ford: The Men and the Machine*. Boston, USA: Little, Brown.

Lewis, D. (1976) *The Public Image of Henry Ford: An American Folk Hero and His Company*. Detroit, USA: Wayne State University Press.

McCalley, B W. (1994) *Model T Ford: The Car That Changed the World*. Iola, WI, USA: Krause Publications.

Neubert, O. (1972) *Tutankhamun and the Valley of the Kings*. London: Granada Publishing Limited.

Reeves, N and Taylor, J. H. (1992) *Howard Carter before Tutankhamun*. British Museum. London, UK.

Rubenstein, J. M. (1992) *The Changing U.S. Auto Industry: A Geographical Analysis*. London: Routledge.

Studer-Noguez and Isabel. (2002) *Ford and the Global Strategies of Multinationals: The North American Auto Industry*. Routledge.

Watts, S. (2005) *The People's Tycoon: Henry Ford and the American Century*.

Wik, R M. (1972) *Henry Ford and Grass-Roots America*. USA: University of Michigan Press.

Winstone, H.V.F. (2006) *Howard Carter and the discovery of the tomb of Tutankhamun* (Revised edition). Barzan, Manchester.

Chapter 4

Bird, A. and Hallows, I. (2002) *The Rolls-Royce Motor Car*. Batsford Books.

Evans, M. (2004) *In the Beginning: the Manchester Origins of Rolls-Royce*. Derby, UK: Rolls-Royce Heritage Trust.

Fischer, L. (1964) *The Life of Lenin*. London: Weidenfeld and Nicolson.

Lee, S. J. (2003) *Lenin and Revolutionary Russia*. London: Routledge.

Goldstein, E. (2013) *The First World War Peace Settlements, 1919–1925*. London: Routledge.

Merridale, C. (2017) *Lenin on the Train*. London: Penguin Books.

Lih, L. T. (2011) *Lenin. Critical Lives*. London: Reaktion Books.

Payne, R. (1967) *The Life and Death of Lenin*. New York: Simon and Schuster.

Pipes, R. (1996) *The Unknown Lenin: From the Secret Archive*. New Haven, Connecticut: Yale University Press.

Pugh, P. (2001) *The Magic of a Name—The Rolls-Royce Story: The First 40 Years*. Icon Books.

Read, C. (2005) *Lenin: A Revolutionary Life*. London: Routledge Historical Biographies.

Schmermund, E and Edwards, J. (2016) *Vladimir Lenin and the Russian Revolution*. Enslow Publishing.

Shub, D. (1966) *Lenin: A Biography*. London: Pelican.

Yakovlev, Y. (1988) *The Story about the Ulyanov Family, Lenin's Childhood and Youth*. Progress Publishers.

Chapter 5

Hyde, C K. (2005) *The Dodge Brothers: The Men, the Motor Cars and the Legacy*. Detroit: Wayne State University Press.

Arnold, O. (1979) *The Mexican Centaur: An Intimate Biography of Pancho Villa*. Tuscaloosa, AL, USA: Portals Press.

Braddy, H. (1955) *The Cock of the Walk: Qui-qui-ri-qui! The Legend of Pancho Villa.* University of New Mexico Press.

Brenner, A. (1984) *The Wind that Swept Mexico.* University of Texas Press.

Brinkley, Douglas (2004) *Wheels for the World: Henry Ford, his Company and a Century of Progress, 1903–2003.*

Caballero, R. (2017) *Orozco: Life and Death of a Mexican Revolutionary.* University of Oklahoma Press.

Clendennin, C. C. (1972) *The United States and Pancho Villa: A Study in Unconventional Diplomacy.* New York, USA: Kennikat Press.

Curcio, V. (2000) *Chrysler: The Life and Times of an Automotive Genius.* Oxford University Press.

De Quesada, A. (2012) *The Hunt for Pancho Villa: The Columbus Raid and Pershing's Punitive Expedition 1916–17.* London: Bloomsbury.

Gonzales, M. J. (2002) *The Mexican Revolution: 1910–1940.* University of New Mexico Press.

Katz, F. (1981) *The Secret War in Mexico: Europe, the United States and the Mexican Revolution.* University of Chicago Press.

Katz, F. (1998) *The Life and Times of Pancho Villa.* Stanford University Press.

Krauze, E. (1997) *Mexico: Biography of Power.* New York: HarperCollins. Translated from Spanish.

O'Brien, S. (1991) *Pancho Villa.* New York, USA: Chelsea House.

Quirk, R E. (1981) *The Mexican Revolution, 1914-1915: The Convention of Aguascalientes.* New York: The Citadel Press.

Reed, J. (1969) *Insurgent Mexico (1914).* New York, USA: Simon and Schuster.

Vlasic, B. and Stertz, B. A. (2000) *Taken for a Ride: How Daimler-Benz Drove Off with Chrysler.*

Wasserman, M. (2012) *The Mexican Revolution: A Brief History with Documents.* Bedford Cultural Editions Series.

Womack, J. Jr. (1986) *The Mexican Revolution in The Cambridge History of Latin America*, vol. 5. Cambridge University Press.

Chapter 6

Beaverbrook, Lord (1966) Taylor A. J. P. (ed.). *The Abdication of King Edward VIII.* London: Hamish Hamilton.

Bradford, S. (1989) *King George VI.* London: Weidenfeld and Nicolson.

Broad, L. (1961) *The Abdication.* London: Frederick Mulle.

Bloch, M. (1996) *The Duchess of Windsor*. London: Weidenfeld and Nicolson.

Bloch, M. (1988) *The Secret File of the Duke of Windsor*. London: Bantam Books.

Bloch, M. (ed) (1986) *Wallis and Edward: Letters 1931–1937*. Summit Books.

Bush, O A. (1983) 'The McLaughlin Carriage Company'. *The Carriage Journal*: Vol 21 No 1 Summer 1983. The Carriage Association of America Inc., Salem, New Jersey

Davies, C. (2001) 'Car that took King into exile goes on sale'. *The Daily Telegraph*. London.

Dunham, T. B. (1987) 'The Buick: A Complete History'. *Automobile Quarterly*. pp. 394—395.

Donaldson, F. (1974) *Edward VIII*. London: Weidenfeld and Nicolson.

Godfrey, R. (editor) (1998) *Letters From a Prince: Edward to Mrs Freda Dudley Ward 1918–1921*. Little, Brown and Co.

Gustin, L. R. (2008) *Billy Durant Creator of General Motors*. Ann Arbor: University of Michigan Press

Higham, C. (2005) *Mrs Simpson*. London: Pan Books.

King, G. (1999) *The Duchess of Windsor*. New York: Citadel Press.

McIntyre Hood, M. (1967) *Oshawa: "The Crossing Between the Waters": A History of "Canada's Motor City"*. Published as a Canadian Centennial project by McLaughlin Public Library Board.

Parker, J. (1988) *King of Fools*. New York: St. Martin's Press.

Pigott, P. (2005) *Royal Transport: An Inside Look at The History of British Royal Travel*. Dundurn.

Roberts, A.; edited by Fraser, A. (2000) *The House of Windsor*. London: Cassell and Co.

Robertson, H. (1995) *Driving Force, The McLaughlin Family and the Age of the Car, McClelland and Stewart*.

Sebba, A. (2011) *That Woman: The Life of Wallis Simpson, Duchess of Windsor*. London: Weidenfeld and Nicolson.

Weir, A. (1995) *Britain's Royal Families: The Complete Genealogy,* Revised edition. London: Random House.

Wheeler-Bennett, Sir J. (1958) *King George VI*. London: Macmillan.

Williams, S. (2003) *The People's King: The True Story of the Abdication*. London: Allen Lane.

The Duke of Windsor (1951) *A King's Story*. London: Cassell and Co.

The Duchess of Windsor (1956) *The Heart has its Reasons: The Memoirs of the Duchess of Windsor*. London: Michael Joseph.

Ziegler, P. (1991) *King Edward VIII: The official biography*. New York: Alfred A. Knopf.

https://www.bonhams.com/auctions/15348/lot/706/

Chapter 7

Badsey, S. (1990) *Normandy 1944 Allied Landings and Breakout*. London.

Barnett, C. (1960) *The Desert Generals*. London: Cassell.

Baxter, C. (1999) *Field Marshal Bernard Law Montgomery, 1887–1976: A Selected Bibliography*. Greenwood Press.

Beevor, A. (2009) *D-Day: The Battle for Normandy*. London: Penguin Viking.

Bierman, J. and Smith, C. (2002) *The Battle of Alamein: Turning Point, World War II*.

Bierman, J. and Smith, C. (2002) *Alamein: War Without Hate*. Penguin Group.

Brighton, T. (2009) *Masters of Battle: Monty, Patton and Rommel at War*. Penguin.

Bungay, S. (2002) *Alamein*. Auram.

Caddick-Adams, P. (2012) *Monty and Rommel: Parallel Lives*. London: Arrow Books.

Carafano, J. J. (2008) *After D-Day: Operation Cobra and the Normandy Breakout*. Stackpole.

Chambers, M. (2012) 'The Devil's General? German film seeks to debunk Rommel myth'. *Reuters*.

Churchill, W. (1986) 'The Second World War'. Volume 4: *The Hinge of Fate*.

Citino, R. (2007) *Death of the Wehrmacht: The German Campaigns of 1942*. University Press of Kansas.

De Lannoy, F. (2002) *Afrikakorps, 1941–1943: the Libya Egypt Campaign*. Bayeux: Heimdal.

Greene, J. and Massignani, A. (1994) *Rommel's North Africa Campaign: September 1940–November 1942*. Conshohocken, PA: Combined Books.

Hamilton, N. (1986) *Monty: The Field-Marshal 1944–1976*. London: Hamish Hamilton Ltd.

Hastings, M. (2004) *Armageddon: The Battle for Germany, 1944–1945*. Knopf.

Horch, A. (1937) *Ich baute Autos*. Schützen-Verlag, Berlin: Vom Schmiedelehrling zum Autoindustriellen.

Kelly, O. (2002) *Meeting the Fox: The Allied Invasion of Africa, from Operation Torch to Kasserine Pass to Victory in Tunisia*. New York: J. Wiley.

Kirchberg, P. and Pönisch, J. (2006) *Horch. Typen—Technik—Modelle*. Delius Klasing, Bielefeld.

Kriebel, R. and Gudmundsson, B. I. (1999) *Inside the Afrika Korps: The Crusader Battles, 1941–1942*. London: Greenhill.

Lang, W. (2007) "Wir Horch-Arbeiter bauen wieder Fahrzeuge". Geschichte des Horch-Werkes Zwickau 1945 bis 1958. Bergstraße Verlagsgesellschaft mbH.

Latimer, J. (2001) *Tobruk 1941: Rommel's Opening Move*. Oxford: Osprey Military.

Pönisch, J. (2000) *100 Jahre Horch-Automobile 1899–1999*. Aufstieg und Niedergang einer deutschen Luxusmarke. Zwickau.

Robinson, James R. (1997) 'The Rommel Myth'. *Military Review Journal*.

Shirer, W L. (2003) *The Rise and Fall of the Third Reich: A History of Nazi Germany*. Gallery Books.

Urban, M. (2005) *Generals Ten British Commanders Who Shaped The World*. London: Faber and Faber.

Williams, A. (2004) *D-Day to Berlin*. London: Hodder and Stoughton.

Windrow, M. (1976) *Rommel's Desert Army*. Osprey

Chapter 8

Alford, K. D. (2003) *Nazi Plunder: Great Treasure Stories of World War II*. Da Capo Press.

Beevor, A. (1998) *Stalingrad: The Fateful Siege, 1942–43*. Viking Press.

Reichhardt, H. J. (October 1988) Bei Kroll 1844 BIS 1957, Landesarchiv Berlin, KalekreuthstraBe 1-2, Berlin 30.

Dear, I. C. B. and Foot, M. R. D., eds. (2005) [1995]. *The Oxford Companion to World War II*. Oxford University Press.

Evans, R. J. (2008) *The Third Reich at War*. London: Penguin Group.

Hernström, S. (2003) *Mercedes-Benz: The Supercharged 8-Cylinder Cars of the 1930s*. Vol. 2. Sparreholm, Sweden: Gamla Bilsalongen.

Kesselring, A. (1970) *A Soldier's Record*. Greenwood Press.

Klara, R. (2017) *The Devil's Mercedes: The Bizarre and Disturbing Adventures of Hitler's Limousine in America*. New York: Thomas Dunne Books.

Kosche, L. (1982) 'The Story of a Car'. Article in *After the Battle*, number 35 (1982) pp. 0–13.

Mackenzie, S. P. (2014) *The Second World War in Europe*: Second Edition. Routledge Publishing.

Melin, J. (1985) *Mercedes-Benz: The Supercharged 8-Cylinder Cars of the 1930s*. Vol. 1. Gothenburg, Sweden: Nordbok International.

Melvin, M. (2010) *Manstein: Hitler's Greatest General*. Weidenfeld and Nicolson.

Moczarski, K. (1981) *Conversations With an Executioner*. Prentice-Hall.

Mitcham, S. Jr. (2009) *Defenders of Fortress Europe: The Untold Story of the German Officers During the Allied Invasion.* Potomac Books Inc.

Scott-Moncrieff, D., Nixon, St J. and Paget, C. (1955) *Three-Pointed Star*. London: Cassell.

Shirer, W. L. (1960) *The Rise and Fall of the Third Reich*. New York: Simon and Schuster.

Taylor, B. (1999) *Mercedes Benz Parade and Staff Cars of the Third Reich: An Illustrated History*. Conshohocken, PA, USA: Combined Publishing.

Weinberg, G. (1970) *The Foreign Policy of Hitler's Germany Diplomatic Revolution in Europe 1933–36*. University of Chicago

Williamson, G. (2006) *German Commanders of World War II*. Osprey Publishing.

Chapter 9

Ackerson, R C. (2006) *Jeep CJ 1945–1986*. UK: Veloce Publishing.

Allen, T. and Dickson, P. (2006) *The Bonus Army: An American Epic*. London: Walker and Company.

Ambrose, S. E. (1993) *Band of Brothers: E Company, 506th Regiment, 101st Airborne: From Normandy to Hitler's Eagle's Nest*. Touchstone Books.

Atkinson, R. (2007) *The Day of Battle: The War in Sicily and Italy, 1943—1944 (The Liberation Trilogy)*. New York: Henry Holt and Company.

Axelrod, A. (2006) *Patton: A Biography*. London: Palgrave Macmillan.

Beevor, A. (2015) *Ardennes 1944: Hitler's Last Gamble*. London: Viking Penguin Random House.

Blumenson, M. (1972) *The Patton Papers: 1885–1940*. Boston, MA: Houghton Mifflin.

Blumenson, M. (1974) *The Patton Papers: 1940–1945*. Boston, MA: Houghton Mifflin.

Blumenson, M. (1985) *Patton: The Man Behind the Legend*. New York: William Morrow and Company.

Brighton, T. (2009) *Patton, Montgomery, Rommel: Masters of War*. New York: Crown Publishing Group.

Brown, A. (1994) *Jeep: The Unstoppable Legend*. Lincolnwood, IL: Publications International.

Collins, M. and King, M. (2013) *The Tigers of Bastogne: Voices of the 10th Armored Division in the Battle of the Bulge*. Casemate.

D'Este, C. (1995) *Patton: A Genius for War*. New York: Harper Collins.

English, J. (2009) P*atton's Peers: The Forgotten Allied Field Army Commanders of the Western Front, 1944–45*. Stackpole Books.

Essame, H. (1974) *Patton: A Study in Command*. New York: Scribner and Sons.

Evans, Major G. F. (22 June 1972) *The 501st Parachute Infantry at Bastogne, Belgium December 1944*. United States Army Centre of Military History Historical Manuscripts Collection 8-3.1 BB 2.

Farago, L. (1981) *The Last Days of Patton*. Yardley, PA: Westholme Publishing LLC.

Hirshson, S. (2003) *General Patton: A Soldier's Life*. New York: Harper Perennial.

Hunt, D. (1990) [1966] *A Don at War* (revised ed.). UK: Frank Cass.

Jowett, P. and de Quesada, A. (2006) *The Mexican Revolution 1910–20*. London: Osprey Publishing.

Naldrett, A. (2016) *Lost Car Companies of Detroit*. UK: The History Press.

Parker, D. S. (1999) *Battle of the Bulge: Hitler's Ardennes Offensive, 1944–1945*. London: Greenhill Books.

Patton, G. S. (1947) *War as I Knew It*. New York: Houghton Mifflin Co.

Showalter, D. E. (2006) *Patton And Rommel: Men of War in the Twentieth Century*. New York: Berkley Books.

Wallace, B. G. (1946) *Patton and His Third Army*. Harrisburg, PA: Military Service Publishing Co.

Zaloga, S. (2010) *George S. Patton: Leadership, Strategy, Conflict*. Oxford, UK: Osprey Publishing.

Zaloga, S J. (2011) [2005]. *Jeeps 1941–45. New Vanguard 117*. Bloomsbury Publishing (Osprey).

https://www.sfchronicle.com/bayarea/article/Francis-Jeep-Sanza

Chapter 10

Best, G. (2001) *Churchill: A Study in Greatness*. London & New York: Hambledon and Continuum.

Blake, R. and Louis, W. R., eds. (1993) *Churchill: A Major New Reassessment of His Life in Peace and War*. Oxford: Oxford University Press.

Chapman, G. (2009) *Illustrated Encyclopedia of Extraordinary Automobiles*. DK Publishing.

Charmley, J. (1993) *Churchill, The End of Glory: A Political Biography*. London: Hodder & Stoughton Ltd.

Charmley, J. (1995) *Churchill's Grand Alliance, 1940–1957*. London: Hodder and Stoughton Ltd.

Churchill, W. (1966b) [first published 1952]. *Teheran to Rome: 13 November 1943–5 June 1944. Closing the Ring. The Second World War*. Vol. X (4th ed.) London: Cassell and Co. Ltd.

Churchill, W. (1954a) [first published April 1954]. *The Tide of Victory: June 1944–December 1944. Triumph and Tragedy. The Second World War*. Vol. XI (2nd ed.) London: Cassell and Co. Ltd.

Churchill, W. (1954b) [first published April 1954]. *The Iron Curtain: January 1945–July 1945. Triumph and Tragedy. The Second World War*. Vol. XII (2nd ed.) London: Cassell and Co. Ltd.

Colville, J. (1987) *The Fringes of Power, Volume Two: September 1941–April 1955*. Sevenoaks, UK: Hodder and Stoughton Ltd.

Gilbert, M. and Churchill, R. (1966) *Winston S. Churchill, The Official Biography*. London: Heinemann.

Gilbert, M. (1991) *Churchill: A Life*. London: Heinemann.

Hackett, K. (28 March 2008) 'Land Rover: The sands of time'. *The Telegraph*.

Hastings, M. (2009) *Finest Years. Churchill as Warlord, 1940–45*. London: Harper Collins.

Hitchens, C. (2002) 'The Medals of His Defeats'. *The Atlantic*. Washington DC: The Atlantic Monthly Group.

Jenkins, R. (2001) *Churchill*. London: Macmillan Press.

Johnson, B. (2014) *The Churchill Factor: How One Man Made History*. London: Hodder and Stoughton.

Johnson, P. (2010) *Churchill*. New York: Penguin.

Langworth, R. (2008) *Churchill in His Own Words*. London: Ebury Press.

Morrison, B. (1993) *Land Rovers in military service*. Brooklands Books.

Rhodes, J. R., ed. (1974) *Winston S. Churchill: His Complete Speeches, 1897–1963*. London: Chelsea Publishing.

Robbins, K. (2014) [1992]. *Churchill: Profiles in Power*. London: Routledge.

Roberts, A. (2018) *Churchill: Walking with Destiny*. London: Allen Lane.

Robson, G. (1981) *The Rover Story*. Patrick Stephens.

Robson, G. (1986) *The Range Rover/Land-Rover*. David and Charles.

Seldon, A. (2010) *Churchill's Indian Summer: The Conservative Government, 1951–1955*. London: Faber and Faber.

Smith, G. S. (2021) *Duty and Destiny: The Life and Faith of Winston Churchill*. USA: Eerdmans.

Soames, M. (1998) *Speaking for Themselves: The Personal Letters of Winston and Clementine Churchill*. London: Doubleday.

Taylor, J. (2013) *Land Rover: 65 Years of the 4 × 4 Workhorse*. UK: Crowood Press.

Toye, R. (2010) *Churchill's Empire: The World that made him and the World he made*. London: Macmillan.

Land Rover Series One Club website.

Land Rover Club website.

https://www.bbc.com/news/uk-england-20017339

Chapter 11

Bloom, H. (2009) *Albert Camus*. Infobase Publishing.

Brisville, J. C. (1959) *Camus*. Gallimard.

Bronner, S E. (2009) *Camus: Portrait of a Moralist*. University of Chicago Press.

Carroll, D. (2007) *Albert Camus the Algerian: Colonialism, Terrorism, Justice*. Columbia University Press.

Catelli, G. (2019) *La mort de Camus*. Balland.

Cohn, R G. (1986) 'The True Camus'. *The French Review*. 60 (1): 30–38. JSTOR 393607.

Curtis, J L. (1972) 'The absurdity of rebellion'. *Man and World*. 5 (3): 335–348. doi:10.1007/bf01248640.

Flood, A. (5 December 2019) 'New book claims Albert Camus was murdered by the KGB'. *The Guardian*.

Foley, J. (2008) *Albert Camus: From the Absurd to Revolt*. McGill-Queen's University Press.

Hawes, E. (2009) *Camus, a Romance*. Grove Press.

Horton, C. *The Encyclopedia of the Car*.

Hughes, E J. (2007) *The Cambridge Companion to Camus*. Cambridge University Press.

King, A. (1964) *Albert Camus*. Grove Press.

King, A. (1992) *Camus's L'Etranger: Fifty Years on*. UK: Palgrave Macmillan.

Lawrence, M. (1991) *A to Z of Sports Cars*. UK: Bay View Books.

Lottman, H. (1979) *Albert Camus: A Biography*. Axis.

McCarthy, P. (1982) *Camus: A Critical Study of His Life and Work*. Hamish Hamilton.

Rey, P. L. (2006) *Camus: l'homme révolté*. Gallimard.

Schaffner, A. (2006) Agnès Spiquel (ed.) *Albert Camus: l'exigence morale: hommage à Jacqueline Lévi-Valensi (L'esprit des lettres) Editions Le Manuscrit*.

Sedgwick, M. *The Facel Vega 1954–1964*.

Sharpe, M. (2015) *Camus, Philosophe: To Return to our Beginnings*. BRILL.

Sherman, D. (2009) *Camus*. John Wiley and Sons.

Smith, Patrick. *Lost Star Cars: The Albert Camus Facel Vega*.

Sprintzen, D. (1991) *Camus: A Critical Examination*. Temple University Press.

Tegler, E. (2007) '1959 Facel Vega HK500: For the Few Who Own the Finest'. *Autoweek*. March 2007.

Thody, P. M. W. (1957) *Albert Camus: A Study of His Work*. Hamish Hamilton.

Todd, O. (2000) *Albert Camus: A Life*. Carroll and Graf.

Willsher, K. (2011) 'Albert Camus might have been killed by the KGB for criticising the Soviet Union, claims newspaper'. *The Guardian*. 7 August 2011.

Wood, J. (2002) *The Ultimate History of Fast Cars*. Paragon Books.

https://www.theguardian.com/books/2019/dec/05/albert-camus-murdered-by-the-kgb-giovanni-catelli

https://ms-my.facebook.com/tracalbi/posts/2768597693197808

https://www.francebleu.fr/infos/faits-divers-justice/il-y-a-60-ans-le-prix-nobel-de-litterature-albert-camus-trouvait-la-mort-dans-l-yonne-1577961262

https://viaretro.com/2018/12/the-unattainable-dream-facel-vega-and-albert-camus/

Chapter 12

Banham, R. (2002) *The Ford Century: Ford Motor Company and the Innovations that Shaped the World*. Artisan Books.

Bonsall, T. E. (1992) *The Lincoln Motorcar: The Complete History of an American Classic*. Baltimore, USA: Stony Run Press.

Brauer, C. J. (1977) *John F. Kennedy and the Second Reconstruction*. Columbia University Press.

Bugliosi, V. (2007) *Reclaiming History: The Assassination of President John F. Kennedy*. New York: Norton.

Burgess-White, D. (1974) Ward, I. (ed.) *The World of Automobiles: An Illustrated Encyclopedia of the Motor Car*. Vol. 10. Orbis Publishing.

Burner, D. (1988) *John F. Kennedy and a New Generation*. Pearson Longman.

Dammann, G. H. and Wagner, J. K. (1987) *The Cars of Lincoln-Mercury*. Florida, USA: Crestline Publishing Co.

Davis, M. W. R. (2002) *Ford Dynasty: A Photographic History*. Arcadia Publishing.

Douglass, J. W. (2008) *JFK and the Unspeakable: Why He Died and Why It Matters*. New York: Orbis Books.

Flammang, J. (1999) *Standard Catalog of American Cars 1976–1999*, 3rd Edition. Iola, WI, USA: Krause Publications.

Giglio, J. (1991) *The Presidency of John F. Kennedy*. University Press of Kansas.

Gunnell, J. (2002) *Standard Catalog of American Cars 1946–1975* (4th ed.). Iola, WI, USA: Krause Publications.

Harper, P. and Krieg, J. P. eds. (1998) *John F. Kennedy: The Promise Revisited*. Greenwood Press.

Hersh, S. (1997) *The Dark Side of Camelot*. Chicago IL USA: Turabian.

Huffman, J P. (2009) 'The Top Presidential Limousines of All Time'. *Popular Mechanics*. January 2009.

Johnson, L. (1971) *The Vantage Point: Perspectives of the Presidency, 1963–1969*. New York: Holt, Rinehart and Winston.

Kelin, J. (2007) *Praise from a Future Generation: The Assassination of John F. Kennedy and the First Generation Critics of the Warren Report*. San Antonio, TX USA: Wings Press.

Kimes, B. (1996) *Standard catalog of American Cars 1805–1942* (third ed.) Iola WI USA: Krause publications.

Manchester, W. (1967) *The Death of a President: 20 November–25 November 1963*. New York: Harper and Row.

Niedermeyer, P. (2013) *Curbside Classic: 1965 Lincoln Continental—The Last Great American Luxury Car*. April 2013.

Poe, N. *Lincoln Motor Plant*. U.S. National Park Service.

Rabe, S. G. (2010) *John F. Kennedy: World Leader*. Washington D.C: Potomac Books.

Stokes, L. (1979) *Report of the Select Committee on Assassinations of the U.S. House of Representatives*. Washington, D.C: United States Government Printing Office.

Sturdivan, L. M. (2005) *The JFK Myths: A Scientific Investigation of the Kennedy Assassination*. USA: Paragon House.

Thompson, J. (1967) *Six Seconds in Dallas: A Micro-Study of the Kennedy Assassination*. New York: Bernard Geis Associates.

Trost, C. and Bennett, S. (2003) *President Kennedy Has Been Shot*. USA: Sourcebooks.

Warren, E. (1964) *Report of the President's Commission on the Assassination of President Kennedy*. Washington, D.C: United States Government Printing Office.

Whalen, T. J. (2014) *JFK and His Enemies: A Portrait of Power*. Rowman and Littlefield Publishers.

White, T. H. (1965) *The Making of the President, 1964*. New York: Atheneum Publishers.

'Would a bubble-top have saved Kennedy? More answers from the strange story of JFK's Lincoln limo'. *Dallas News*. 22 November 2019. https://boundarystones.weta.org/2013/11/22/strange-saga-jfk-assassination-car

Chapter 13

Barthes, R. (1957) *Mythologies—"La Nouvelle Citroen"*. Paris: Editions du Seuil.

Bell, D. S. and Gaffney J., eds. (2013) *The Presidents of the French Fifth Republic*. Palgrave Macmillan.

Bell, D., et al. (1990) *A Biographical Dictionary of French Political Leaders since 1870*. New York: Simon and Schuster.

Bellu, R. (2005) '"Automobilia". Toutes les voitures françaises 1975 (Salon Paris Oct 1974)'. *Paris: Histoire and collections*.

Bobbitt, M. (2016) *Citroën DS: Revised and updated edition*. Veloce Publishing.

Broustail, J. and Greggio, R. (2000) *Citroën: Essai sur 80 ans d'antistratégie*. Paris: Vuibert.

Cogan, C. (1995) *Charles de Gaulle: A Brief Biography with Documents*. New York: St martin's Press.

Fenby, J. (2010) *The General: Charles de Gaulle and the France He Saved.* Skyhorse.

Fenby, J. (2016) *France: A Modern History from the Revolution to the War with Terror.* New York: St martin's Press.

Gaffney, J. (2010) *Political Leadership in France. From Charles de Gaulle to Nicolas Sarkozy.* Palgrave Macmillan.

Gallard, P. (2004) *A l'assaut du monde: L'aventure Peugeot-Citroën.* Paris: Bourin.

Georgano, N. (2000) *The Beaulieu Encyclopedia of the Automobile.* London: Stationery Office.

Heilig, R. A. and Heilig, P. (2008) *Citroen DS and ID All Models (except SM) 1966 to 1975: The Essential Buyer's Guide.* Veloce Publishing.

Jackson, J. (2018) *De Gaulle.* Harvard University Press.

Jackson, J. (2018) *A Certain Idea of France: The Life of Charles de Gaulle.* London: Penguin.

Kulski, W. W. (1966) *De Gaulle and the World: The Foreign Policy of the Fifth French Republic.* Syracuse University Press.

Lacouture, J. (1990) *De Gaulle: The Ruler 1945–1970.* New York: WW Norton.

Ledwidge, B. (1982) *De Gaulle.* London: Weidenfeld and Nicolson.

Lewis-Beck, M. S., et al. eds. (2012) *French Presidential Elections.* London: Palgrave Macmillan.

Nahum, A. for The Design Museum. (2009) *Fifty Cars That Changed the World.* London: Conran Octopus.

Nester, W. R. (2014) *De Gaulle's Legacy: The Art of Power in France's Fifth Republic.* London: Palgrave Macmillan.

Plume, C. and Demaret P. (1973) *Target De Gaulle: The Thirty-One Attempts to Assassinate the General.* Richard Barry (trans.) Corgi.

Reynolds, J. (1996) *Original Citroën DS.* Bay View Books.

Shennan, A. (1993) *De Gaulle.* London: Longman.

Soustelle, J. (1962) *L'Espérance Trahie.* Paris: Editions de l'Alma.

Thody, P. (1998) *The Fifth French Republic: Presidents, Politics and Personalities: A Study of French Political Culture.* London: Routledge.

Venner, D. (2004) *De Gaulle: La Grandeur et le Néant.* Paris: Editions du Rocher.

Williams, C. (1997) *The Last Great Frenchman: A Life of General De Gaulle.* London: Wiley.

Willson, Q. (1995) *The Ultimate Classic Car Book*. DK Publishing.

http://parisisinvisible.blogspot.com/2015/03/tracking-charles-de-gaulle-in-petit.html

https://www.midilibre.fr/2012/08/22/il-y-a-50-ans-charles-de-gaulle-echappe-a-l-attentat-du-petit-clamart,551439.php

http://www.politique.net/2014012501-fause-ds-19-de-gaulle-attentat-petit-clamart.htm

Chapter 14

Alvandi, R. (2016) *Nixon, Kissinger and the Shah: The United States and Iran in the Cold War*. Oxford University Press.

Amini, P. (2002) 'A Single Party State in Iran, 1975-78: The Rastakhiz Party-the Final Attempt by the Shah to Consolidate his Political Base.' *Middle Eastern Studies* 38.1 (2002): 131–168.

Ansari, A. M. (2003) *Modern Iran since 1921: The Pahlavis and After*. London: Longman.

Cooper, A. S. (2011) *The Oil Kings: How the U.S., Iran and Saudi Arabia Changed the Balance of Power in the Middle East*. New York: Simon and Schuster.

Cooper, A. S. (2016) *The Fall of Heaven: The Pahlavis and the Final Days of Imperial Iran*. Henry Holt and Co.

Devos, B. and Werner, C. (eds) (2013) *Culture and cultural politics under Reza Shah: the Pahlavi State, new bourgeoisie and the creation of a modern society in Iran*. Routledge (2013).

Ghazvinian, J. (2021) *America and Iran: A History, 1720 to the Present*. Knopf.

Harris, D. (2004) *The Crisis: The President, the Prophet and the Shah—1979 and the Coming of Militant Islam*. New York: Little, Brown and Co.

Kinzer, S. (2003) *All the Shah's Men: An American Coup and the Roots of Middle East Terror*. John Wiley and Sons.

Kurzman, C. (2005) *The Unthinkable Revolution in Iran*. Harvard University Press.

Lyons, P. (1988) *The Complete Book of Lamborghini*. Publications International Ltd.

Milani, A. (2011) *The Shah*. Palgrave Macmillan.

Offiler, B. (2015) *US Foreign Policy and the Modernisation of Iran: Kennedy, Johnson, Nixon and the Shah*. Springer.

Reza, M. (1980) *The Shah's Story*. M. Joseph.

Saikal, A. (1980) *The Rise and Fall of the Shah 1941–1979*. Princeton University Press.

Sackey, J. (2008) *The Lamborghini Miura Bible*. Veloce.

Takeyh, R. (2014) 'What really Happened in Iran: The CIA, the Ouster of Mosaddeq and the Restoration of the Shah.' *Foreign Affairs* 93.4 (2014): 2–12.

Farmanfarmaian, M and Farmanfarmaian, R. (2007) *Blood and Oil: A Prince's Memoir of Iran, from the Shah to the Ayatollah*. Random House.

Pahlavi, F. (2004) *An Enduring Love: My Life with the Shah*. A Memoir. Miramax Books.

Pasini, S. (ed) (1984) 'Lamborghini: Catalogue Raisonné 1963–1984'. *Automobilia*.

Miura Jota—'The STORY'. www.lambocars.com

http://www.themiuraregister.com

https://kidston.com/motorcars/1317-1968-Lamborghini-Miura-P400/

https://www.lambocars.com/miura-svj-and-customised-miura/

https://www.telegraph.co.uk/news/worldnews/middleeast/iran/1473603/Shahs-car-collection-is-still-waiting-for-the-green-light.html

https://www.deseret.com/1997/3/16/19300521/cage-pays-a-hefty-450-000-for-shah-s-red-lamborghini

Chapter 15

Atkins, S E. (2004) *Encyclopedia of Modern Worldwide Extremists and Extremist Groups*. Connecticut, US: Greenwood Publishing Group.

Aust, S. (1987) *The Baader-Meinhof Group: The Inside Story of a Phenomenon*. Oxford, UK: The Bodley Head.

Aust, S. (2009) *Baader-Meinhof: The Inside Story of the R.A.F.* Oxford, UK: Oxford University Press.

Baumann, B. I. (1981) *How It All Began: Personal Account of a West German Urban Guerilla*. Arsenal Pulp Press.

Becker, J. (1998) *Hitler's Children: The Story of the Baader-Meinhof Terrorist Gang*. Diane Publishing Company.

Bielby, C. (2012) *Violent Women in Print: Representations in the West German Print Media of the 1960s and 1970s*. New York: Camden House.

Boyn, O. (2011) *The Divided Berlin, 1945-1990: The Historical Guidebook*. Berlin: Amber Books Limited.

Chalk, P. (2013) *Encyclopedia of Terrorism. ABC-CLIO*. California, US: Santa Barbara.

Ciment, J. (2015) *World Terrorism: An Encyclopedia of Political Violence from Ancient Times to the Post-9/11 Era*. New York: Taylor and Francis.

Demaris, O. (1977) *Brothers in blood: the international terrorist network*. New York: Scribner.

Dornberg, J. (1976) *The New Germans: Thirty Years After*. New York: Macmillan.

Eager, P. W. (2016) *From Freedom Fighters to Terrorists: Women and Political Violence*. Aldershot, UK: Ashgate.

Von. Frankenberg, R. (1973) [1961]. *Porsche: the Man and his Cars. G.T. Foulis and Co*. Oxfordshire, UK: Henley-on-Thames.

Frère, P. (2006) *Porsche 911 Story*. London: J H Haynes.

Gerhardt, C. (2018) *Screening the Red Army Faction: Historical and Cultural Memory*. UK: Bloomsbury.

Leffingwell, R. (1993) *Porsche Legends: Inside History of the Epic Cars*. Osceola, WI, US: Motorbooks International.

Leffingwell, R., Ingram, C. and Furman, M. (2014) *Porsche Unexpected: Discoveries in Collecting*. Philadelphia, PA, US: Coachbuilt Press.

Ludvigsen, K. (2019) *Porsche: Excellence Was Expected. Vol. Book 1: Surpassing Expectations (1948–1971)*. Cambridge, MA, US: Bentley Publishers.

Martin, G. (2011) *The SAGE Encyclopedia of Terrorism*. Thousand Oaks, California, US: SAGE Publications.

Meredith, L. (2000) *Porsche 911*. UK: Sutton Publishing.

Morgan, P. (1995) *Original Porsche 911*. UK: MBI Publishing.

Paternie, P. C. (2001) *Porsche 911*. MotorBooks/MBI Publishing.

Paternie, P. C. (2004) *Porsche 911 Red Book 1965–2005*. MotorBooks/MBI Publishing.

Raby, P. (2005) *Porsche 911 Identification Guide*. Beaworthy, UK: Herridge and Son.

Moncourt, A. (2008) *Daring To Struggle, Failing To Win: The Red Army Factions 1977 Campaign Of Desperation*. Oakland, California, US: PM Press.

Scharloth, J. and Klimke, M. (2008) *1968 in Europe: a history of protest and activism, 1956–1977*. New York: Palgrave Macmillan.

Schmeidel, J. C. (2008) *Stasi: Shield and Sword of the Party*. London, UK: Routledge.

Seiff, I. (1989) *Porsche: Portrait of a Legend*. London: Macdonald Orbis.

Smith, J. and Moncourt, A., eds. (2013) *The Red Army Faction, A Documentary History. Vol. 2: Dancing with Imperialism*. Oakland, California, US: PM Press.

Townshend, C. (2002) *Terrorism: A Very Short Introduction. Very Short Introductions*. Oxford, UK: Oxford University Press.

Trahair, R. C. S. and Miller, R. (2009) *Encyclopedia of Cold War Espionage, Spies and Secret Operations*. New York: Enigma Books.

Vague, T. (1994) *Televisionaries: The Red Army Faction Story*. Oakland, California, US: AK Press.

Varon, J. (2004) *Bringing the War Home: The Weather Underground, the Red Army Faction and Revolutionary Violence in the Sixties and Seventies*. Berkeley, US: University of California Press.

Weber, J. and Parsons, N. (2004) *Germany, 1945–1990: A Parallel History*. Budapest: Central European University Press.

Winkler, H. A. (2007) *Germany: the Long Road West*. Oxford, UK: Oxford University Press.

Wisowaty, D. L. (1975) *The Baader-Meinhof group, 1968–1972: an account of its activities and an analysis of its ideology*.

Wood, J. (1997) *Porsche: The Legend*. Bath, UK: Parragon Books.

Wood, J., ed. (1985) *Great Marques of Germany*. London: Octopus Books.

Wright-Neville, D. (2010) *Dictionary of Terrorism. Polity*. Cambridge, UK.

Wie die Baader-Meinhoff-Bande den Porsche von Rainer Schlegelmilch entführte | Classic Driver Magazine

Chapter 16

Asher, J. and Hammel, E. (1987) *Duel for the Golan: the 100-hour battle that saved Israel*. New York: William Morrow and Company, Inc.

el Badri, H. (1979) *The Ramadan War, 1973*. Fairfax, VA, US: T. N. Dupuy Associates Books.

Bar-Joseph, U. (2012) *The Watchman Fell Asleep: The Surprise of Yom Kippur and Its Sources*. New York: SUNY Press.

Bregman, A. (2002) *Israel's Wars: A History Since 1947*. London: Routledge.

Brook, I. (2011) *In the Sands of Sinai: a Physician's Account of the Yom Kippur War*. Charleston, US: CreateSpace.

Dupuy, T. N. (1978) *Elusive Victory: The Arab—Israeli Wars, 1947–1974*. San Francisco, S: Harper and Row.

Garrett, J. (21 October 2011) 'A Century of Chevy, From Cheap Date to America's Sweetheart'. *The New York Times*. 9 January 2012.

Gawrych, G. (2000) *The Albatross of Decisive Victory: War and Policy Between Egypt and Israel in the 1967 and 1973 Arab-Israeli Wars*. Greenwood Publishing Group.

Genat, R. (2000) *Chevrolet SS*. MotorBooks International.

Gunnell, J. (2011) *Standard Catalog of Chevrolet, 1912–2003: 90 Years of History, Photos, Technical Data and Pricing*. Cincinnati, US: F+W Media.

Gunnell, J. (2005) *American Cars of the 1960s: A Decade of Diversity*. Krause Publications.

Gunnell, J. (2003) *Standard Catalog of Chevelle 1964–1987*. Krause Publications.

Gunnell, J., ed. (1987) *The Standard Catalog of American Cars 1946–1975*. Kraus Publications.

Gustin, L. R. (2008) *Billy Durant: Creator of General Motors*. University of Michigan Press.

Heikal, M. (1975) *The Road to Ramadan*. London: Collins.

Herzog, C. (2003) *The War of Atonement: The Inside Story of the Yom Kippur War*. London: Greenhill Books.

Herzog, C. (1982) *The Arab-Israeli Wars*. New York: Random House.

Herzog, C. (1989) *Heroes of Israel*. Boston, MA, US: Little, Brown.

Israeli, R. (1985) *Man of Defiance: A Political Biography of Anwar Sadat*. London: Weidenfeld and Nicolson.

Israelyan, V. (2003) [1995]. *Inside the Kremlin During the Yom Kippur War*. Pennsylvania State University Press.

Karsh, E. (2002) *The Iran-Iraq War, 1980–1988*. Oxford: Osprey Publishing.

Kimes, B. R. (1996) Clark, H A. (ed.) *The Standard Catalog of American Cars 1805–1945*. Kraus Publications.

Morris, B. (2001) *Righteous Victims*. New York: Vintage Books.

Ma'Oz, M. (1995) *Syria and Israel: From War to Peace making*. Oxford: Clarendon Press.

Ma'Oz, Z. (2006) *Defending the Holy Land*. University of Michigan Press.

O'Balance, E. (1979) *No Victor, No Vanquished: The Yom Kippur War* (1979 ed.). Barrie and Jenkins.

Quandt, W. B. (2005) *Peace Process: American diplomacy and the Arab—Israeli conflict since 1967*. Washington, DC: Brookings Institution/University of California Press.

Quandt, W. B. (1976) 'Soviet Policy in the October 1973 War'. *Rand Corp*.

Rabinovich, A. (2017) *The Yom Kippur War: The Epic Encounter That Transformed the Middle East*—Revised Edition. New York: Schocken Books.

Rodman, D. (2016) *Israel in the 1973 Yom Kippur War: Diplomacy, Battle and Lessons*. Sussex Academic Press.

al Sadat, M. A. (1978) *In Search of Identity: An Autobiography*. London: Collins.

Shlaim, A. (2001) *The Iron Wall: Israel and the Arab World*. W.W. Norton and Company.

Rubenstein, J. M. (2002) *The Changing U.S. Auto Industry: A Geographical Analysis*. London: Routledge.

Steffe, J. (2004) *Chevelle SS, 1964–1972: A Muscle Car Source Book*. JC Publications.

Chapter 17

Avner, Y. (2010) *The Prime Ministers: An Intimate Narrative of Israeli Leadership*. The Toby Press.

Bentley, J. (1952) *The Old Car Book*. Fawcett Books.

Berenji, S. (2020) 'Sadat and the Road to Jerusalem: Bold Gestures and Risk Acceptance in the Search for Peace'. *International Security* 45.1 (2020): 127–163.

Bonsall, T. E. (2003) *The Cadillac Story*. CA, US: Stanford University Press.

Bonsall, T. E. (2004) *The Cadillac Story: The Postwar Years*. CA, US: Stanford University Press.

Brands, H. W. (1994) *Into the Labyrinth: The United States and the Middle East, 1945–1993*. McGraw Hill.

Bregman, A. (2005) *Elusive Peace: How the Holy Land Defeated America*. Gardners Books.

Eidelberg, P. (1979) *Sadat's Strategy*. Dollard des Ormeaux, Quebec, Canada: Dawn Books.

Finklestone, J. (2013) *Anwar Sadat: visionary who dared*. Routledge.

Flammang, J M. (1999) *Standard Catalog of American Cars 1976–1999*. Iola, WI, US: Krause publications.

Flammang, J. M. (1999) *Standard catalog of American cars, 1976–1999*. Iola, WI, US: Krause Publications.

Flory, Jr. J. K. (2008) *American Cars 1946–1959*. Jefferson, NC, US: McFarland and Coy.

Flory, Jr. J. K. (2004) *American Cars 1960–1972*. Jefferson, NC, US: McFarland and Coy.

Gold, D. (2007) *The Fight for Jerusalem: Radical Islam, the West and the Future of the Holy City*. Washington, DC: Regnery Publishing, Inc.

Gunnell, J. (2005) *Standard Catalog of Cadillac 1903–2005*. Iola, WI, US: Krause Publications.

Haykal, M. H. (1982) *Autumn of Fury: The Assassination of Sadat*. WM Collins & Sons & Co.

Hinton, C. A. (2004) *Camp David Accords*. Heritage Books inc.

Hurwitz, H Y. (2010) *Peace in the Making*. Jerusalem: Gefen Publishing House.

Israeli, R. (2019) *"Sadat: The Calculus of War and Peace." The Diplomats, 1939-1979*. Princeton University Press.

Kimes, B. (1996) *Standard Catalog of American Cars 1805–1942*. Iola, WI, US: Krause publications.

Kowalke, R. (1997) *Standard Catalog of American Cars 1946–1975*. Iola, WI, US: Krause publications.

McCall, W. (1982) *80 Years of Cadillac La Salle*. Sarasota, FL, US: Crestline Publishing.

McCall, W. M. P. (1992) *80 Years of Cadillac LaSalle*. Osceola WI, US: Motorbooks International.

Meital, Y. (1997) *Egypt's Struggle for Peace: Continuity and Change, 1967–1977*. US: University Press of Florida.

Quandt, W. B. (1988) *The Middle East: Ten Years After Camp David*. Washington D.C.: Brookings Institution Press.

Quandt, W. B. (1986) *Camp David: Peacemaking and Politics*. Washington D.C.: Brookings Institution Press.

Sela, A., ed. (2002) *The Continuum Political Encyclopedia of the Middle East*. New York: Continuum.

Stein, K. (1999) *Heroic Diplomacy: Sadat, Kissinger, Carter, Begin and the Quest for Arab—Israeli Peace*. Oxford: Taylor and Francis.

Telhami, S. (1990) *Power and leadership in international bargaining: the path to the Camp David accords*. US: Columbia University Press.

Waterbury, J. (1983) *The Egypt of Nasser and Sadat: The Political Economy of Two Regimes*. Princeton University Press.

Wagner, R. L. (2002) *Cadillac: A Century of Excellence*. Metro Books.

Chapter 18

Agca, A. (2013) *Mi avevano promesso il paradiso: La mia vita e la verità sull'attentato al papa*. Publisher GeMS.

Beare, D. (2019) *Fiat: The First Fifty Years, Vol 1*. Treddol, UK: Stinkwheel Publishing.

Berry, J. and Renner, G. (2004) *Vows of Silence: The Abuse of Power in the Papacy of John Paul II*. New York, London, Toronto, Sydney: Free Press.

Davies, N. (2004) *Rising '44: The Battle for Warsaw*. London: Viking Penguin.

Duffy, E. (2006) *Saints and Sinners, a History of the Popes* (Third ed.) Yale University Press.

Gaddis, J. L. (2006) *The Cold War: A New History*. Penguin Books.

Garruzzo, G. (2014) *Fiat: The Secrets of an Epoch*. Springer.

Goktas, H. (20 January 2006) *Man who shot pope must return to jail: Turkish court*. Reuters.

Hebblethwaite, P. (1995) *Pope John Paul II and the Church*. London: Rowman and Littlefield.

Kent, P. C. (2002) *The Lonely Cold War of Pope Pius XII: The Roman Catholic Church and the Division of Europe*. McGill-Queen's University Press.

Kostin, S. and Raynaud, É. (2011) *Farewell*. Amazonencore.

Koehler, J. O. (2011) *Spies in the Vatican: The Soviet Union's Cold War Against the Catholic Church*. Pegasus Books

Kwitny, J. (March 1997) *Man of the Century: The Life and Times of Pope John Paul II*. New York: Henry Holt and Company.

Lee, M. A. (3 March 1997) 'Les liaisons dangereuses de la police turque'. *Le Monde diplomatique* (in French).

Mannion, G, ed. (2008) *The Vision of John Paul II: Assessing His Thought and Influence*. Collegeville, Mn: Liturgical Press.

Maxwell-Stuart, P. G. (2006) *Chronicle of the Popes: Trying to Come Full Circle*. London: Thames and Hudson.

Newton, P. (12 January 2006) *Man who shot pope freed*. CNN Associated Press.

Noonan, P. (2005) *John Paul the Great: Remembering a Spiritual Father*. New York: Penguin Group.

O'Connor, G. (2006) *Universal Father: A Life of Pope John Paul II*. London: Bloomsbury Publishing.

Pope John Paul II. (2004) *Rise, Let Us Be On Our Way*. Warner Books.

Pope John Paul II (2005) *Memory and Identity—Personal Reflections*. London: Weidenfeld and Nicolson.

Quinnell, A. J. (1987) *In the name of the father*. New American Library.

Reese, T. J. (1998) *Inside the Vatican: The Politics and Organisation of the Catholic Church*. Harvard University Press

Renehan, E. and Schlesinger, A. M. (2006) *Pope John Paul II*. Chelsea House. London.

Sandok, O. S. M. *Peter Lang*. New York.

Stanley, G. E. (2007) *Pope John Paul II: Young Man of the Church*. Fitzgerald Books.

Stourton, E. (2006) *John Paul II: Man of History*. London: Hodder and Stoughton.

Szulc, T. (2007) *Pope John Paul II: The Biography*. London: Simon and Schuster Publishing Group.

Trigilio Jr., Rev J., Brighenti, Rev K. and Toborowsky, Rev J. (2011) *John Paul II for Dummies*. John Wiley and Sons.

Walsh, M. (1994) *John Paul II: A Biography*. London: HarperCollins.

Weigel, G. (1999) *Witness to Hope: The Biography of Pope John Paul II*. New York: HarperCollins.

Wojtyla, K. (1993) *"Thomistic Personalism." In Person and Community*. Translated by Theresa.

Wojtyła, K. (1981) *Love and Responsibility*. London: William Collins Sons and Co. Ltd.

'Security Chief for the Vatican Was 'Guardian Angel' to Pope'. *The Wall Street Journal*. 6 November 2009.

Chapter 19

Aitken, J. (2013) *Margaret Thatcher: Power and Personality*. A and C Black.

Barr, D. (2013) *Maggie and Me*. A and C Black.

Beckett, A. (2010) *When the Lights Went Out: Britain in the Seventies*. Faber and Faber.

Beckett, C. (2006) *The 20 British Prime Ministers of the 20th Century: Thatcher*. Haus.

Blundell, J. (2008) *Margaret Thatcher: A Portrait of the Iron Lady*. Algora.

Blundell, J. (2013) *Remembering Margaret Thatcher: Commemorations, Tributes and Assessments*. Algora.

Burgess-Wise, D. (1974) 'Daimler: Limousines Fit for Kings and Nobility'. In Northey, T (ed.) *World of Automobiles*. Vol. 5. Orbis. London, UK.

Butler, D., et al. (1980) *The British General Election of 1979*. Palgrave Macmillan.

Butler, D. (1994) *British Political Facts 1900–1994*. Macmillan.

Byrd, P., ed. (1988) *British Foreign Policy under Thatcher*. St. Martin's Press.

Campbell, J. (2000) *Margaret Thatcher: The Grocer's Daughter. Vol. 1*. Pimlico.

Campbell, J. (2003) *Margaret Thatcher: The Iron Lady. Vol. 2*. Pimlico.

Campbell, J. (2011) Freeman, D (ed.) *The Iron Lady: Margaret Thatcher, from Grocer's Daughter to Prime Minister*. Penguin Books.

Cowley, P. and Bailey, M. (2000) 'Peasants' Uprising or Religious War? Re-examining the 1975 Conservative Leadership Contest'. *British Journal of Political Science*. 30 (4): 599–630.

Culshaw, D. and Horrobin, P. (2013) *"Daimler". The Complete Catalogue of British Cars 1895*. Poundbury, Dorchester, UK: Veloce Publishing.

Davenport-Hines, R. P. T. (2004) *Dudley Docker: The Life and Times of a Trade Warrior*. Cambridge, UK: Cambridge University Press.

Douglas-Scott-Montagu, E. J. B. and Burgess-Wise, D. (1995) *Daimler Century: The full history of Britain's oldest car maker*. Sparkford, Somerset, UK: Patrick Stephens.

Evans, E. J. (2004) *Thatcher and Thatcherism*. Routledge.

Floud, R. and Johnson, P., eds. (2004) *The Cambridge Economic History of Modern Britain: Structural Change and Growth, 1939–2000*. Vol. 3. Cambridge University Press.

Hastings, M. and Jenkins, S. (1983) *The Battle for the Falklands*. Macmillan.

Howe, G. (1994) *Conflict of Loyalty*. Macmillan.

Lanoue, D. J. and Headrick, B. (1998) 'Short-Term political Events and British Government Popularity: Direct and Indirect Effects'. *Polity*. 30 (3): 417–433.

Lawson, N. (1992) *The View from No. 11: Memoirs of a Tory Radical*. Bantam Books.

Marr, A. (2007) *A History of Modern Britain*. Pan Books.

Moore, C. (2013) *Margaret Thatcher: From Grantham to the Falklands*. Vol. 1. Knopf Group.

Moore, C. (2015) *Margaret Thatcher: Everything She Wants*. Vol. 2. Penguin Books.

Moore, C. (2019) *Margaret Thatcher: Herself Alone*. Vol. 3. Penguin Books.

Nixon, St. J. C. (1946) *Daimler 1896 to 1946: 50 Years of the Daimler Company, G.T.* Foulis and Co.

Purvis, J. (2013) 'What Was Margaret Thatcher's Legacy for Women?'. *Women's History Review*. 22 (6): 1014–1018.

Reitan, E. A. (2003) *The Thatcher Revolution: Margaret Thatcher, John Major, Tony Blair and the Transformation of Modern Britain, 1979–2001*. Rowman and Littlefield.

Seldon, A., et al. (2000) *Britain under Thatcher*. Taylor and Francis.

Seldon, A. (2007) *Blair's Britain, 1997–2007*. Cambridge University Press.

Sked, A. and Cook, C. (1993) *Post-War Britain: A Political History, 1945–1992* (Fourth ed.) Penguin.

Smith, B. E. (1980) *The Daimler Tradition* (2nd rev. ed.). Isleworth, UK: Transport Bookman.

Stewart, G. (2013) *Bang!: A History of Britain in the 1980s*. Atlantic Books.

Taylor, J. (2016) *"Jaguar Mk1, Mk2, S Type and 420—The Complete Story" by James Taylor, Crowood.*

Thatcher, M. (1993) *The Downing Street Years*. HarperCollins.

Thatcher, M. (1995) *The Path to Power*. HarperCollins.

Thatcher, M. (2003) *Statecraft: Strategies for a Changing World*. Harper Perennial.

Thorley, N. (2000) *Daimler. Suttons Photographic History of Transport series*. Stroud, UK: Sutton Publishing.

Vinen, R. (2009) *Thatcher's Britain: The Politics and Social Upheaval of the Thatcher Era*. Simon and Schuster.

Wapshott, N. (2007) *Ronald Reagan and Margaret Thatcher: A Political Marriage*. Sentinel.

Margaret Thatcher remembered by her chauffeur Denis Oliver | Margaret Thatcher | The Guardian.

Custom-made headrest was built to protect Thatcher during naps in Daimler | The Scotsman.

Ministerial drivers: The silent front-seat witnesses—BBC News.

PMs' cars: Thatcher liked to doze and Major wanted more leg room | Margaret Thatcher | The Guardian.

Chapter 20

Garton-Ash, T. (1990) *We the People: The Revolution of '89, Witnessed in Warsaw, Budapest, Berlin and Prague*. Cambridge University Press.

Glenn, J. K. (1999) 'Competing Challengers and Contested Outcomes to State Breakdown: The Velvet Revolution in Czechoslovakia'. *Social Forces*. September 1999. 78:187–211.

Grunert, M. and Triebe, F. (2006) *Das Unternehmen BMW seit 1916 [The BMW Company since 1916] (in German)*. Königswinter, Germany: Heel Verlag.

Hodges, D. (2000) *BMW. Suttons Photographic History of Transport series*. Stroud, UK: Sutton Publishing.

Holy, L. (1996) *The Little Czech and The Great Czech Nation: National identity and the post-communist transformation of society*. Cambridge University Press.

Keane, J. (2000) *Václav Havel: A Political Tragedy in Six Acts*. New York: Basic Books.

Kiley, D. (2004) *Driven: Inside BMW, the Most Admired Car Company in the World*. John Wiley and Sons.

Kittler, E. (2001) *Deutsche Autos seit 1990, Band 5* (1. ed.—in German). Stuttgart, Germany: Motorbuch Verlag.

Kriseová, E. (1993) *Václav Havel. Trans. Caleb Crain*. New York: St. Martin's Press.

Kukral, M. A. (1997) *Prague 1989: Theater of Revolution*. New York: Columbia University Press.

Lewandowski, J. (2006) *BMW: Typen und Geschichte [BMW: Types and History] (in German) (3rd ed.)*. Bielefeld, Germany: Delius Klasing.

Lewin, T. (2022) *BMW Century (2nd ed.)*. Beverly, MA, US: Motorbooks.

Noakes, A. (2010) *The Ultimate History of BMW: From the innovative 328 sports car and the Isetta bubble car to the 5 Series Gran Turismo*. Bath, UK: Parragon Books.

Oswald, W. (2001) *Deutsche Autos 1945–1990, Band 4* (1. ed.). Stuttgart, Germany: Motorbuch Verlag.

Pontuso, J. F. (2004) *Václav Havel: Civic Responsibility in the Postmodern Age*. New York: Rowman and Littlefield.

Rocamora, C. (2004) *Acts of Courage*. New York: Smith and Kraus.

Schrader, H. (2011) *BMW: Passion—Power—Perfektion [BMW: Passion—Power—Perfection] (in German).* Stuttgart, Germany: Motorbuch Verlag.

Schrader, H. (2016) *BMW: Von 1981 bis heute [BMW: From 1981 to today]. Typenkompass series (in German).* Stuttgart, Germany: Motorbuch Verlag.

Shepherd, R. H. E. (2000) *"Czechoslovakia" The Velvet Revolution and Beyond.* New York: St. Martin's Press, Inc.

Symynkywicz, J. (1995) *Václav Havel and the Velvet Revolution.* Parsippany, New Jersey, US: Dillon Press.

Werner, C. (2006) *Kriegswirtschaft und Zwangsarbeit bei BMW [War Economy and Forced Labour at BMW] (in German).* Munich, Germany: Oldenbourg.

Williams, K. (2009) 'Civil Resistance in Czechoslovakia: From Soviet Invasion to "Velvet Revolution", 1968–89,' in Roberts, A and Garton Ash, T (eds.) *Civil Resistance and Power Politics: The Experience of Non-violent Action from Gandhi to the Present.* Oxford University Press.

Williams, K. (2016) *Václav Havel.* London: Reaktion Books.

Wolchik, S L. (1990) 'Czechoslovakia's 'Velvet Revolution'.' *Current History.* 89:413–16, 435–37.

Zantovsky, M. (2014) *Havel: A Life.* New York: Grove Press.

Picture Credits

COVER
Copyright owner: SWNS
Chapter 1
Copyright owner: Agefotostock
Chapter 2
Copyright owner: Alamy
Chapter 3
Copyright owner: Heritage Images
Chapter 4
Copyright owner: Alamy
Chapter 5
Copyright owner: London Scala Archives
Chapter 6
Copyright owner: Alamy
Chapter 7
Public domain from 1944 (Nazi) German magazine
Chapter 8
Copyright owner: Getty Images
Chapter 9
Copyright owner: Alamy
Chapter 10
Copyright owner: SWNS
Chapter 11
Copyright owner: Collection Bernard Dudoignon
Chapter 12
Copyright owner: Alamy
Chapter 13
Copyright owner: Shutterstock

WHERE ARE THEY NOW?

Chapter 1: 1899 12hp registered AA 16

National Motor Museum, Beaulieu, New Forest, Hampshire, United Kingdom, SO42 7ZN. Tel: +44 1590 612345. Email: info@beaulieu.co.uk

Chapter 2: 1910 Graf & Stift 28/32 PS Double Phaeton registered A11 1118

Museum of Military History, Vienna, Austria. Arsenal, Objekt 1, Ghegastrasse 1030 Vienna. Tel: +43 (1) 79561-0. Email: contact@hgm.at

Chapter 3: 1922 Ford Model T Touring

No longer survives.

Chapter 4: 1922 Rolls Royce 40/50 Silver Ghost chassis number #79YG

Gorki Leninskiye Museum, Ulitsa Tsentral'naya, 1, Gorki Leninskiye, Moscow Oblast, Russia, 142712

Tel: +7 495 548-93-09. Email: info@mgorki.ru

Chapter 5: 1923 Dodge Touring Car

Museo Francisco Villa, 5 de Febrero, Zaragoza y, Zona Centro, 34000 Durango, Dgo., Mexico.

Tel: +52 618 835 0936.

Chapter 6: 1936 McLaughlin Buick 90 Limousine registered CUL 421

In private collection.

https://www.bonhams.com/auctions/15348/lot/706/

Chapter 7: 1939 Horch 830 BL

Destroyed by the Royal Air Force in 1944.

Chapter 8: 1940 Mercedes Benz 770K W150 type II Grosser Offener Tourenwagen registered IA V 148697

Canadian War Museum, 1 Vimy Place, Ottawa, Ontario, K1A 0M8.

Tel: Local: 819-776-7000. Toll free: 1-800-555-5621.

Email: vimy.biblio@warmuseum.ca

Chapter 9: 1943 MB Jeep

American Armory Museum, 4144 Abernathy Road, Fairfield Ca. 94534, USA

Tel: +1 707-389-6846

https://www.facebook.com/pages/category/Community-Museum/American-Armory-Museum-1762044990748879/

Chapter 10: 1954 Series 1 Land Rover registered UKE 80

Emil Frey Museum, Bahnhofpl. 2, 5745 Safenwil, Switzerland.

Tel: +41 62 788 79 45 (Simon Bundi)

Email: simon.bundi@emilfreyclassics.ch

Chapter 11: 1957 Facel Vega FV3B

Destroyed 1960.

Chapter 12: 1961 Lincoln Continental Convertible Limousine

The Henry Ford Museum, 20900 Oakwood Blvd.

Dearborn, MI 48124-5029

Tel: Call Center: +1 313-982-6001

Email: research.center@thehenryford.org

Chapter 13: 1962 Citroen DS 19 registered 5249 HU 75

Mémorial Charles de Gaulle—52330 Colombey-les-deux-églises—FRANCE

Tel: +33(0)3.25.30.90.80

Email: contact@memorial-charlesdegaulle.fr

Chapter 14: 1968 Lamborghini Miura P400 registration TEH 3986 (WGC 330F) chassis #3303

In private collection.

https://www.kidston.com/motorcars/1317-1968-Lamborghini-Miura-P400/

Chapter 15: 1971 Porsche 911 Targa

Lost, presumed scrapped.

Chapter 16: 1972 Chevrolet Chevelle Station Wagon

Unknown, presumed scrapped.

Chapter 17: 1978 Cadillac Fleetwood

In private collection.

https://www.timesofisrael.com/sadats-limo-goes-on-sale-for-108000/

Chapter 18: 1980 Fiat Campagnola Popemobile registered SCV 1.

Vatican Museum, Viale Vaticano, 00165 Rome, Italy

Tel: +39 06 69883332

Email: musei@scv.va

http://www.museivaticani.va/content/museivaticani/en/collezioni/musei/padiglione-delle-carozze/fiat-1107-nuova-campagnola.html

Chapter 19: 1988 Daimler Sovereign registered F496 PYT

Unknown—not on DVLA computer yet still on HPI check database.

Chapter 20: 1989 BMW 750i L

Unknown although a number of cars from the same Czechoslovakian government order survive in private collections.

http://www.aucars.cz/index.php?obj=330&dd=MjA3OA==

Indexes

Printed in Poland
by Amazon Fulfillment
Poland Sp. z o.o., Wrocław
15 February 2024

1f129760-7d96-4cd7-8bc1-cf34ef148c6aR01